Literary Criticism in Perspective
Benjamin Franklin V, Editor

James Hardin, General Editor

About *Literary Criticism in Perspective*

Books in the series *Literary Criticism in Perspective,* which appears in
the framework of the series *Studies in English and American Literature,
Linguistics, and Culture,* trace literary scholarship and criticism on
major and neglected writers alike, or on a single major work, a group of
writers, a literary school or movement. In so doing the authors —
authorities on the topics in question who are also well-versed in the
principles and history of literary criticism — address a readership con-
sisting of scholars, students of literature at the graduate and under-
graduate level, and the general reader. One of the primary purposes of
the series is to illuminate the nature of literary criticism itself, to gauge
the influence of social and historic currents on aesthetic judgments once
thought objective and normative.

M. Jimmie Killingsworth

The Growth of *Leaves of Grass*: The Organic Tradition in Whitman Studies

CAMDEN HOUSE

Library of Congress Cataloging-in-Publication Data

Killingsworth, M. Jimmie.
The growth of Leaves of grass : the organic tradition in Whitman
studies / M. Jimmie Killingsworth.
p.   cm. -- (Studies in English and American literature,
linguistics, and culture)
Includes bibliographical references and index.
ISBN 1-879751-44-5
1. Whitman, Walt, 1819-1892. Leaves of grass. 2. Whitman, Walt,
1819-1892--Criticism and interpretation--History.   I. Title.
II. Series.
PS3238.K43   1993
811'.3--dc20   92-46142
CIP

Contents

Preface   ix

1: The Organic Tradition   1

2: The Person   9

    Type and Token in Early Whitman Biography   11

    The Advent of Modern Critical Biography   18

    Psychoanalytical Criticism   37

3: The Poet   46

    Defending the Poet   50

    Analytical Criticism since the 1950s   58

    Literary-Historical Criticism since the 1950s   74

4: The Prophet of Democracy   85

    Spiritual Politics   87

    The Body Politic and the Political Body   101

5: The Language   125

    The Linguistic Turn   127

    Upon Closing: Two Reflections   139

Works Cited   142

Index   150

Acknowledgments

At one of the first scholarly gatherings I attended as a new professor, Harold Aspiz remarked to me that he had found no group of scholars as congenial and mutually supportive as the people in Whitman studies. I am not sure why this is so, but my subsequent experience has proved it again and again.

So many people have encouraged and helped me in my studies of Whitman that I could hardly name them all in this short space. I would be remiss, however, not to mention the man who got me started in the field, F. DeWolfe Miller, as well as three others who have buoyed me up with continuing advice and encouragement—Jerome Loving, Robert K. Martin, and Ed Folsom. In the preparation of this particular study, no one has helped more than Loving and my other very generous colleague at Texas A&M, Kenneth Price. James Perrin Warren also offered some key words at an important time during the project, for which I thank him.

In addition, I am pleased to acknowledge the contributions of my associates Dean Brown and Jacqueline Palmer. They both read the manuscript and made valuable suggestions on matters of style and substance. Finally, I am grateful to the series editors Benjamin Franklin V and James Hardin for their advice, encouragement, and patience.

mjk
November 1992

To DeWolfe Miller

Preface

This monograph, the Whitman volume in Camden House's series *Literary Criticism in Perspective*, does not pretend to be a complete critical guide to Whitman studies. For bibliographical purposes, Whitman scholars already have the annotated secondary bibliographies of Scott Giantvalley and Donald Kummings, as well as Joel Myerson's authoritative descriptive bibliography of primary sources and the continuing list of new works presented in the *Walt Whitman Quarterly Review*. For evaluative reviews of critical studies, we have a variety of sources, chief among them Gay Wilson Allen's handbooks, Roger Asselineau's essay in *Eight American Authors*, the regular overviews of recent scholarship offered by *American Literary Scholarship*, and some fine reviews of the critical literature given in the introductions of recent books, the best of which build upon the long critical tradition rather than trying quixotically to dismiss, neglect, or somehow replace it.

What I hope to add to this wealth is simply perspective. I examine several threads of inquiry in Whitman studies that form a common conceptual strand. My argument is that the theory of organicism informs not only Whitman's best work but also the sturdiest line of descent in the critical tradition. In the history of ideas, the organic tradition stands for growth, process, holism, and fluidity against the tradition of mechanical rationalism, with its analytical insistence that the whole is no more than the sum of its parts. All that is organic mimics the life of an individual organism in its passage from birth to maturity to death and on to decay, which Whitman called the "good compost" that sustains the lives of future organisms.

Scholars have found organic metaphors a particularly useful means of explaining the development of *Leaves of Grass*. They have been directed to this mode of explanation largely by the need to account for Whitman's continual nurturing of his book. With each edition, he would add new poems, tinker with others, and eliminate some altogether, so that, paralleling his own life stages, *Leaves of Grass* seemed to take on a life of its own—a rebellious youth, a vigorous middle age, and, sadly, a dotage. A criticism able to comprehend these changes in the terms of life processes and human experience has thus prevailed over a criticism that prefers the closed and completed structures of the committed formalist.

My argument is not terribly original, but only elaborates Whitman's own position and the commentary of his most influential critics. Agreeing with his friend, the great naturalist John Burroughs, Whitman saw his book as "a series of growths, or strata, rising or starting out from a settled foundation or centre and expanding in successive accumulations" (qtd. in Allen, *Handbook* 107). Picking up the thread in a 1902 essay, Oscar Triggs suggests that *Leaves of Grass* should be understood as "a growth" and should be "related to the author's own life process." "Succeeding editions," Triggs claims, "have the character of expansive growths, like the rings of a tree" (102). Gay Wilson Allen, surveying these passages in the widely read *Walt Whitman Handbook* of 1946, asks, "Why does the critic fall so easily into these biological metaphors in discussing the 'growth' of *Leaves of Grass*?" (105) Allen decides finally that this recourse is all but inevitable, given the "nature of the work, the manner of its publication, and the theory by which the poet composed and interpreted his poems" (105). He concludes, "[The] seminal conception of the first edition was a new sort of allegory . . . an attempt, extending over nearly half a century, to make a life into a poetic allegory. In a novel and daringly literal application of the 'organic' theory of literary composition, Walt Whitman began his first edition with the attempt to 'incarnate' in his own person the whole range of life, geography, and national consciousness of Nineteenth-Century America" (105-6).

Organic conceptions have endured in Whitman scholarship. In a pivotal study from the fruitful decade following the publication of Allen's *Handbook*, Roger Asselineau combines an examination of the poet's life with a study of the "life" of *Leaves of Grass* under the sign of an organic metaphor—the evolution of Walt Whitman. In the same generation, James E. Miller writes, "*Leaves of Grass* grew, much of its own accord, like a seed that contains within itself from the very beginning all its potential of size and shape. Whitman tended the seed, carefully cultivated it, and tried at times to abandon it; but he always returned to it, sometimes to prune, sometimes to graft, always to encourage fulfillment of its destined design" (*Walt Whitman* 38). Yet more recently, in a study that in many ways challenges the organic tradition of previous scholarship, Michael Moon still retains the narrative approach of a critic sensitive to changes produced in the revision of the *Leaves*. Ultimately, he finds himself unable to resist the attraction of Whitman's "model for the similar ways in which texts and selves are, ideally speaking, endlessly . . . composed and decomposed, divided from and reunited with others" (135). Nor can Moon finally deny the powerful tug of the connection between man and book. Discussing Whitman's abandonment of the "poetry of the body" after 1865, he concludes that "the *Leaves of Grass* project as he commenced it and partially carried it out in the first dozen years after 1855 was itself to prove, like the man who wrote it, both an uncanny survivor and a piteous casualty of the ravages of the Civil War" (220-21).

Within this critical heritage—which joins the earliest commentators on *Leaves of Grass* like John Burroughs and Oscar Triggs with modern biographers and literary historians like Allen and Asselineau, rhetorical critics like Richard Chase and James Miller, and even deconstructionist psycho-semiologists like Moon—the organic impulse has remained strong. It therefore offers a suitable place from which to launch an overview of Whitman criticism that, though brief, strives to give a sense of what has proved clearest and most durable among Whitman's readers in the last century and a half.

My goal is thus to suggest the range and the varieties of organicism in the critical tradition and thereby highlight the key narratives that have shaped our understanding of the growth of *Leaves of Grass* from a thin quarto of untitled poems published in 1855 to a chief monument in the canon of American literature. In addition, I explore alternatives to this tradition and look to the future of Whitman studies. For the sake of brevity in covering a field of scholarship that has averaged an annual production of over one hundred items since 1955 (Kummings ix), I cannot mention every study (not even all the good ones), and I must all too frequently sacrifice details and depth. I concentrate mainly on book-length works that are relatively accessible to English-speaking readers. I can only hope that the suggestiveness of what remains is not unduly damaged by such compromises, so that further studies will grow from the hints and directions I am finally able to offer.

1: The Organic Tradition

In one way at least, the critics of *Leaves of Grass* have followed the author. Like Whitman's own, their works exhibit a persistent commitment to mythic patterns based on analogies with the organic world. Over the century since Whitman's death, three strains of organicism have emerged in the critical tradition, each of which is a variation on the theme of growth. These three variations I call the genetic, the progressive, and the cyclic.

Genetic organicism implies that the work of the poet grows from an essential center of being (metaphorically speaking, a gene)—the poet's true self or reason for being. It further suggests that every poem in the work as a whole, or that every line and every word in each of the organically unified poems, like the single cell of an organism, radiates from an informing center and carries with it some identifying sign of its relation to that center. The genetic approach seeks a key—some event, formula, theme, or perspective—that will define the essential Whitman and thereby discover the leading means of interpreting his poems. From his earliest admirers down to critics of the present day, the search continues. We have seen the prophetic Whitman, the American Whitman, the international Whitman, the neurotic Whitman, the political Whitman, the gay Whitman, the omnisexual Whitman. But I doubt—and few of the authors of these genetic schemes would claim—that we have seen the final Whitman, the one that would, or could, exhaust the search for the essential meaning of the poems.

In contrast to the image of radial growth implicit in genetic organicism, the other two versions of organic criticism emphasize the kind of sequential growth implicit in concepts like progress and evolution. The progressive version shows how, from humble beginnings and out of the fragmented odds and ends of life and work, the poet's art emerges and ascends to some glorious completion or fulfillment. Whereas Whitman's earliest admirers may have preferred this hopeful and ascending narrative, modern critics have largely rejected it in favor of a cyclic version of organic growth. Based on an analogy to the life cycle of organisms, the modern approach follows the poet's work through stages of emergence, proliferation, maturation, and decline, admitting loss as well as gain as a consequence of organic growth.

In his own writings, Whitman uses all three versions of organicism as tropes, themes, and structural principles, moving toward a powerful synthesis in the best poems. In "Song of Myself," for example, the republican author names "myself" as the radial center, the representative of his nation and indeed the whole human race. His master trope, as Mutlu Konuk Blasing rightly notes, is synecdoche, the part standing for the whole. The synecdochal state of "Myself" depends, however, upon an extended process of becoming, a progressive development. Having evolved over centuries, the character is said to have surpassed the creatures and elements of the earth without entirely forgoing his close association with them: "I find I incorporate gneiss and coal and long-threaded moss," he declares in one celebrated passage, "and fruits and grains and esculent roots, / And am stucco'd with quadrupeds and birds all over" (*Leaves* 1855, 57). He has "distanced what is behind [him] for good reasons," but he claims the ability to "call any thing close again when I desire it" (*Leaves* 1855, 57).

In this portrait of the supreme democratic personality, therefore, the politics tend to be representative and republican; the cosmology, cumulative and evolutionary; the outlook, progressive, ascending toward an ultimate crowning achievement—"myself," the free and fully developed human being. By the end of the poem, though, the progressive organicism yields to the cyclic. Without denying the immortality of the self's mighty presence, that "likeness" becomes diffused, coaxed "to the vapor and the dusk": "I bequeath myself to the dirt to grow from the grass I love," declares the speaker; "If you want me again look for me under your bootsoles" (*Leaves* 1855, 87-88). In poems like the 1855 "Sleepers" and the 1860 "Calamus," the poet leavens yet more strongly the progressive version of human evolution with traces of doubt and tragic irony, stressing the cyclic passage from health to illness, from progress to stasis (or even regression), from mania to melancholy, from immersion in the human flood of existence to isolation and alienation, from life to death.

That Whitman's critics use these same tropes, patterns, and modes as ways of organizing their studies and as interpretive heuristics seems to bear out Jerome McGann's provocative claims that "the scholarship and criticism of Romanticism and its works are dominated by ... [an] absorption in Romanticism's own self-representations," that this romantic ideology "continues to be translated and promoted" and "works continue to be taught and valued for that ideology," and that "when forms of thought enter our consciousness as forms ... of feeling—which is what takes place through poetry and art—the forms threaten to reify as ideology in the secondary environment of criticism" (1, 3, 13). Of special interest to Whitman studies is McGann's critique of the "creative process" as it was described by the Romantics themselves and as it has been taken up by critics of English romantic poetry: "The critic will trace out a pattern of 'poetic development' which will show (say)

Keats's or Byron's progress from certain interesting but undeveloped ideas, through various intermediate stages, to conclude in some final wisdom or 'achievement'" (22, 135).

Such a master narrative—in this case, the progressive version of organicism—is ideological to the extent that it prevents other possible representations of the author's writing and biography from coming forward. A scholar with an interest in historical and social criticism, for example, may have to resist the master narrative to see how contingent factors in the biographical and historical record relate to the composition of the poet's work. Social and political insights could be blocked by an all too faithful adoption of the romantic conception of the unity of thought and poetic practice—"the grand illusion of every romantic poet," that "poetry, or even consciousness, can set one free of the ruins of history and culture" (McGann 137). McGann's assertion that, because of an absorption in romantic self-representations, criticism of the romantic poets has been ideologically motivated and hence "uncritical" challenges critics and literary historians to examine scholarly and interpretive trends over time and to ask whether we have been unjustly influenced or even blinded by the dazzling work of a Keats, Byron, or Whitman.

It is largely this challenge that motivates my work in this monograph. My purpose is to map critical trends that can be traced to the poet's own organic view of the world and to invite readers to consider their relation to these mythic patterns and ideologies. Unlike McGann in his critique of scholarship in English Romanticism, however, I am not inclined to dismiss the organicism of Whitman's critics as "ideological" in the pejorative sense—that is, as merely the product of "false consciousness" or bourgeois mystification. On the contrary, I admire the vitality of the organic perspective and respect its power to sustain important social movements in the present—above all, the environmental movement, which has its intellectual roots in the romantic period, as well as some versions of contemporary feminism and participatory politics. As such, it may be more of a strength than a weakness that Whitman's critics have extended his world view in their own work, have made their contribution to the growth of *Leaves of Grass*. I do not intend, therefore, to censure the trends I identify—neither from some "objective" perspective (assuming this is possible, which I doubt) nor from the perspective of a single alternative perspective (Marxism, for example). Rather I bring the trends and narrative patterns forward, consider possible alternatives, and take steps in the history of criticism that should ultimately keep the critical tradition in Whitman studies free from charges that it has been blindly ideological, hagiographical, or uncritical.

I focus particularly on the way the different forms of organicism merge or compete with each other. The sequential versions of organicism, for example, tend to undermine genetic versions, the center giving way to the chronological flow of biography and history. Yet the requirements of unity, which are applied to critical studies as well as poems by scholarly institutions (journals, university presses, and departments of English), lead critics to seek overarching themes by which to explain the relation of episodes in the life of Whitman (or the "life" of his book). The demand for a unity that accommodates change produces a criticism dominated by narratives with a thesis. Still under the sway of the romantic ideal of unity and the romantic representation of the creative process, critics establish their authority and originality by producing a unified concept that can be easily remembered, readily packaged, distributed among the academic institutions, and preserved in the critical tradition.

Certainly, then, institutional influences and the attractiveness of the organic features within the poems themselves help to account for the prevalence of organic models in the critical tradition. A yet more significant influence may have been Whitman's own compositional practices, in which some version of sequential organicism is implicit. With every edition of *Leaves of Grass*, Whitman added new poems and revised old ones. The composition of the book, begun in notebooks of the early 1850s, never ceased until his death in 1892. Thus, no single line of a poem, no single version of a poem, and no one edition of the *Leaves* can be said fully to represent the whole. By constant intrusions upon the book, the author bequeathed to his critics a near obsession with poetic evolution and a strong taste for narrative. By his own hand, moreover, he led critics who favored formal, linguistic, and semiological study toward an interaction with what McGann has identified as "those other traditional fields of inquiry so long alienated from the center of our discipline: textual criticism, bibliography, book production and distribution, [and] reception history" (81).

In its many editions, *Leaves of Grass* demands to be read as a story whose subject is the growth of the book as much as the growth of the poet. For this reason, the sequential versions of organicism have been reproduced again and again in the critical tradition, although over the years the preferred master narrative has undergone shifts and variations. Whitman's personal friends and admirers, true to the romantic ideology, preferred the pattern of genetic or progressive organicism. This first generation in the critical tradition explained the growth of the poet as a sequence of steps toward an ever clearer expression of an ever higher order of consciousness and poetic accomplishment. These early scholars would come to be debunked for their hero-worship and Victorian excesses by the next generation of critics, who profited both by increasing methodological rigor and by the simple historical distance of a changing literary and professional scene. Gradually Whitman's critics ceased, for example, to follow the author's friends and literary executors in accepting the "death-bed edition" of 1891-92 as the culmination of the poet's development, the crowning (therefore representative) achievement of a busy career. To modern critics, this simple solution to the textual and bibliographical problems of *Leaves of Grass* would come to seem arbitrary, since the poet was still revising in his last years and would likely have continued had he lived longer. Critics who had not known him personally eventually perceived the Whitman of the 1870s and 1880s as a very different poet from the one he had been in the 1850s and early 1860s. Almost without exception, these modern readers preferred the earlier Whitman. The poet of the 1850s was "protomodern" in both his experiments with free verse and his sexual candor, while the older poet became steadily more intrigued with spiritual matters and with traditional aesthetics. Growing in number with each new edition, the set pieces on nature and religion with their conventional poetic diction ("you" yielding to "thee" and "thou," for example) began to compete, however weakly, with the politically and sexually charged "poetry of the body" written in the antebellum years. Moreover, the aging poet altered many of the early poems and omitted others, leaving behind a litter of fragments and discarded texts that critics have cherished nearly as much as what remained in 1892 as the "official" or "authoritative" *Leaves of Grass*.

Out of concern that the "death-bed" edition obscures the accomplishments of the early editions, and out of admiration for (amounting to identification with) the protomodern Whitman, the critics of the twentieth century have struggled with the scholarly difficulties of reading and sorting poems in various stages of development over six editions. Though submitting to the needs imposed by the poet's continuous composition of his book, the master narrative that has emerged severely revises the plot that Whitman preferred, a glorious epic ending on a high note with the 1891-92 edition superseding all others. While accepting some elements of the progressive narrative—the sudden, indeed mysterious, flowering of the poet in his midlife decade— the modern story of the growth of *Leaves of Grass* rejects the idea of continuous and unbroken progress. Instead the story goes something like this: *Leaves of Grass* appeared first in 1855 as a strong combination of what had hitherto been thin lines of development in the author's life and career—politics, journalism, popular literary excursions, reading, working, and loafing in the vast milieu of New York at midcentury, a world of high stimulation, replete with prostitutes, homosexual encounters, intellectual and social ferment, fiery politics, and astonishing diversity among ethnic groups, classes, occupations, tastes, and opinions. Whitman filled notebooks full of thoughts and feelings—jottings that gradually evolved into overflowing sentences arranged experimentally in verses that emerged finally as poems in the first edition of *Leaves of Grass*. Following its appearance in 1855 came a rapid luxuriance—two more editions, each greatly expanded, in the next five years. With this proliferation, however, the poet—having already attained middle age, after a prolonged adolescence and literary apprenticeship—reached artistic maturity all too quickly with the third edition of 1860 or perhaps the fourth of 1867. Then came a long period of decline. The poems added in the 1870s and 1880s added weight without muscle. The revisions obscured rather than enhanced the accomplishment and radical energy of the earlier poems.

The "death-bed" edition finalized nothing. With the work of Whitman's followers, the book would continue to grow after the poet's death, evolving into editions of "complete" works and ultimately into a magisterial three-volume variorum *Leaves of Grass*. Though this work has saved much toil for Whitman scholars, it has not eliminated the need to look at the different editions. Because the editors of the variorum had to begin somewhere, they took the 1891-92 edition, the most nearly complete, as their base, and thereby reduced to footnotes the great early editions of 1855, 1856, and 1860—not to mention such events as the separate printing of *Drum-Taps* and the appearance of the centennial *Leaves* of 1876, two great steps of a writer striving to become America's national poet. The recent bibliographical work of Joel Myerson has forcefully reiterated the presence of multiple editions, each with its characteristic preservation of historically determined conditions of production.

In the cyclic version of the master narrative, the critical tradition has discovered a means of organizing the poet's life and work that remains plausible and rich in possibilities for interpretation. It has been adopted and transformed to accommodate at least four overlapping modes of critical inquiry, each of which may be traced to precedents established by Whitman's poetic practice and his own commentary on the poems. The oldest and deepest of these, which I treat in chapter 2, focuses on Walt Whitman the person. From the first books about the poet—those of William Douglas O'Connor, John Burroughs, and Richard Maurice Bucke—to many of the newest studies, the biographical impulse has largely driven the critical enterprise, giving rise not only to personal and critical biographies but also to a large body of psychoanalytical criticism and numerous volumes of letters, notebooks, and personal writings of all kinds. Whitman biography never yielded entirely to the rise of New Criticism at midcentury, but rather interacted with the new approach, producing the second mode of inquiry, which focuses on Walt Whitman the poet, the topic of chapter 3. Largely a product of the high modern formalism in works like Matthiessen's *American Renaissance* but, again, rooted in Whitman's own occasional comments, this approach often combines close reading and career studies or comparative literary history in an interpretive framework that reflects the growing concerns of twentieth-century professionalism and the increasing division of labor in modern times. No longer a person in the simple sense, Whitman becomes a figure in literary history, a persona in his work, a writer in a culture given to defining identity by the professional role a person takes (see Wilson).

The dominance of this approach has relented somewhat in the 1980s and 1990s, as Whitman's critics have become immersed in a new kind of culture, which, like that of Jacksonian democracy, values diversity and recognizes difference. The postmodern world of contemporary criticism has witnessed a revival of studies that consider Walt Whitman the prophet of democracy, the subject of chapter 4. Studies arising from this interest tend to go in two directions, depending on whether they emphasize the prophetic, or spiritual, dimension of Whitman's ethos, or the physical, economic, and sexual dimensions. Much as the biographical mode takes at his word the poet who claimed to write the song of himself, the first of these new approaches—beginning in Whitman's own lifetime with Bucke's writings and developed recently in studies of mysticism, shamanism, and prophesy in *Leaves of Grass*—understands Whitman less as an individual person, the subject of biography, than as a voice, a presence, a bringer of a word whose value stands apart from the accomplishments of the historical individual. Alongside (and often overlapping with) these studies, other recent criticism—bolstered by developments in feminism, critical theory, and gay studies—has focused on Whitman's treatment of politics not as merely the problem of government, but as the general flow of power among individuals and groups. The authors of these works—who often produce as well as explicate texts with aims in the realm of cultural politics—have taken seriously Whitman's romantic drive to align poetry with utopian politics and have charted anew the relationship of the poems to the social and historical contexts of *Leaves of Grass*. Finally, new alternatives to interpreting the poems have arisen from the field of language study, beginning in 1983 with C. Carroll Hollis's ground-breaking *Language and Style in Leaves of Grass*. Whitman himself referred to the *Leaves* as a "language experiment" and during the 1850s wrote a number of unpublished essays on American language. Chapter 5 discusses the study of the language of *Leaves of Grass* both as a current activity and as a significant field for future work.

The historian of this tradition faces a problem similar to that confronted by Whitman's earliest readers. It is tempting to take the present as the point of ultimate accomplishment, thus submitting to the production of a Whig history that makes a progressive narrative of its own, the story of how the critical tradition took root and grew to wondrous heights. The plot would proceed as follows: A cast of nineteenth-century disciples, with a crusty amateurism but an altogether appropriate energy, carried forth the seeds and grafts of interpretive reasoning taken from the Master himself, favoring the biographical and prophetic modes. They kept *Leaves of Grass* alive until the professional schools of American literary criticism could take hold in the 1930s and 1940s. Beginning slowly, finding sympathy among literary historians and socialist critics, then weathering the storm of conservative formalism,

Leaves of Grass reemerged in the post-War period of the 1950s as an intellectual force to be reckoned with. During the cold war, the McCarthy era, and the onset of the nuclear age—a time of political and social turmoil comparable to the 1850s and 1860s, when *Leaves of Grass* first appeared amid the growing violence of civil war—Whitman's reputation steadily improved. The number of books and articles on *Leaves of Grass* proliferated, expanding yet again with the social movements that have culminated modernity—the civil rights movement, the sexual revolution that accompanied the war in Vietnam, the peace movement, feminism, gay liberation, environmentalism, and finally multiculturalism.

Though there is an element of truth in this hopeful construction, the growth of the critical tradition in Whitman studies has hardly been as steady and even as such a narrative would indicate. By dealing with five different modes of critical practice, seen as separate lines of inquiry, each with its own chapter, I try to suggest a multilinear growth with periods of decline and revival keyed to historical and social contingencies. Of course, this approach requires me not only to depart from the straight chronology preferred in the series for which I write, but also occasionally to obscure connections among the different lines of development. To correct at least partially the latter deficiency, I attempt to map as many of the intersections as coherence allows. As for the departure from a stricter chronology of critical perspectives, I beg the reader's indulgence and hope that the complexity of my subject and the wish to avoid a Whiggish history free me from too much blame.

2: The Person

In *A Backward Glance O'er Travel'd Roads,* an 1888 prose memoir, Whitman insists that there is a close connection between his life experiences and his poems: "After continued personal ambition and effort, as a young fellow, to enter with the rest into competition for the usual rewards, business, political, literary, &c . . . , I found myself remaining possess'd, at the age of thirty-one to thirty-three, with a special desire and conviction . . . a feeling or ambition to articulate and faithfully express in literary or poetic form, and uncompromisingly, my own physical, emotional, moral, intellectual, and œsthetic Personality" (*Leaves of Grass: Norton* 563). *Leaves of Grass* arose, according to this genetic view, from a inability of the creative personality to find proper outlets in pursuit of the "usual rewards." In a move that by 1888 had become typical of his prose reflections on his earlier poetic accomplishments, Whitman projects his failures in business and politics onto the American culture at large while nevertheless claiming to speak for that culture in a way that only a centrally located and strong-voiced poet could. His book attempts, he says, "in the midst of, and tallying, the momentous spirit and facts of its immediate days, and of current America— . . . to exploit that Personality, identified with place and date, in a far more candid and comprehensive sense than any hitherto poem or book" (563). Thus, "Given the Nineteenth Century, with the United States, and what they furnish as area and points of view, 'Leaves of Grass' is, or seeks to be, simply a faithful and doubtless self-will'd record. In the midst of all, it gives one man's—the author's— identity, ardors, observations, faiths, and thoughts, color'd hardly at all with any decided coloring from other faiths or other identities" (563).

From Whitman's earliest friends who took up the pen on his behalf—William Douglas O'Connor, John Burroughs, and Richard Maurice Bucke—down to Harold Bloom with his vision of the strong poet heroically wresting poems from inherited language and poetic form, a number of Whitman's interpreters have followed the poet in seeking the origin of poems, the genetic center, in the personality of the poet. As a result, the sturdiest thread in Whitman scholarship is biographically oriented.

As the passage from *A Backward Glance* shows, however, Whitman's view entails a special understanding of the relation of biography to poetic production. Somewhat against the current of what we now consider to be Romantic poetics, more in line with Victorian spiritualism and American republicanism, he does not count himself a grand and alienated artist so much as a medium or a representative of a particular people, place, and time. As he explains the situation to Bucke, "I often have to be quite vehement with my friends to convince them that I am not (and don't want to be) singular, exceptional, or eminent. I am willing to think that I represent vast averages, and the generic American masses—that I am their voice; but not that I should be in any sense considered an exception to ordinary men" (Bucke, *Walt Whitman* 66-67). He insists on a "life and times" view of poetic biography. His book emerged, he says, "out of my life in Brooklyn and New York from 1838 to 1853" (qtd. in Bucke 67). Nevertheless, he views his accomplishment as something special. Though dependent upon the historical and social context of American life, the book is the result of his "absorbing a million people, for fifteen years, with an intimacy, an eagerness, an abandon, *probably never equalled*" (qtd. in Bucke 67; italics added).

The desire to encompass poetic originality coupled with the desire to preserve the ideology of American republicanism accounts for the tension in these reminiscences of the elderly Whitman. The historical context was one of increasing specialization—the process that Alan Trachtenberg calls the "incorporation" of America in the late nineteenth century, a process which "proceeded by contradiction and conflict" (7). It was a time when a poet increasingly had to be merely a poet and could hardly aspire, in the manner described in the 1855 preface to *Leaves of Grass*, to be a prophetic and shaping force in politics, religion, and the general life of the culture (see Wilson). In the emerging social order, the ideology of individualism was still energetically espoused in public discourse, but in reality it was increasingly at odds with the culture's advancing division of labor and rationalization of social relations (Trachtenberg 5). The individual became less of a person and more of a function. Whitman appears to have felt and expressed the typical self-conflicts of this age as an alternate desire to be, on the one had, original and different, and, on the other hand, representative and one with the common American self. Two concepts of poetic genius warred within him—the Romantic view of the genius alienated from the historical context and the older, bardic view of the genius who consummates and contains his culture and his age.

Beginning in the early twentieth century, critical studies of Whitman have tended to resolve the tension in favor of poetic specialization. This trend has two effects. First, biographers are increasingly inclined to write critical biographies, with an emphasis on Whitman's life as a literary figure. Second, there is a growing tendency to portray Whitman in the mold of the romantic ideology by stressing the poet's difference from his contemporaries. This difference may be presented as alienated protomodernism or (less flatteringly) as some form of neurosis. The earliest studies, especially those of Burroughs and Bucke, lay the groundwork for this move by elevating Whitman from the status of common citizen to that of literary genius. By so doing, they violate Whitman's stated views against an elitist conception of his democratic character, but, ironically, they do so often with Whitman's blessing.

Type and Token in Early Whitman Biography

In the case of Burroughs's first book, *Notes on Walt Whitman as Poet and Person*, published in 1867, Whitman not only approved of the project but actually contributed third-person accounts of his life and poetic activity, actively collaborating with the author in producing the first critical study of his life and work (Hier). William Douglas O'Connor's famous pamphlet *The Good Gray Poet* appeared the year before Burroughs's little book. But, though O'Connor's work is a monument of American literary history—most impressive as a fellow writer's defense of a friend against public attack and possible censorship (as both Loving and Freedman make clear in their books on the O'Connor-Whitman relation)—it is not a critical study. As Milton Hindus rightly notes, *The Good Gray Poet* comprises "an *ad hominem* defense" designed "to meet an *ad hominem* attack" (Hindus 115). O'Connor's book is a counterattack against negative reviews in the press, which O'Connor presents as gratuitous and slanderous. It is also an attempt to balance the record and preserve the poet's reputation in the wake of the notorious "Harlan Incident," the "summary dismissal" of Whitman from his government job, ostensibly for having written an immoral book (Loving 54-62). O'Connor argues that not only the poems but also the character of Walt Whitman stands above rather than below the moral and artistic standards of the day—that, in fact, the spiritual and moral depth of the poems have their source in the personality of their author, much as God's creation reflects His greatness.

While O'Connor does not pursue very far or very systematically the critical implications of this genetic approach to the relation of poet and poems, Burroughs does, thereby establishing this key point of departure in the critical tradition. In the preface to his *Notes*, Burroughs writes, "In History, at wide intervals, in different fields of action, there come . . . special developments of individuals, and of that something we suggest by the word Genius—individuals whom their own days little suspect, and never realize, but who, it turns out, mark and make new eras, plant the standard ahead again, and in one man personify vast races or sweeping revolutions. I consider Walt Whitman such an individual" (3). Alongside such admiring utterances, however, we feel the correcting hand of Whitman himself, urging Burroughs away from an elitist emphasis on individual accomplishment, stressing instead the republican theme that the poet preferred (in the tension-filled language that anyone familiar with Whitman's prose will recognize): "I consider that America is illustrated in him; and that Democracy, as now launched forth upon its many-vortexted experiments for good or evil, (and the end whereof no eye can foresee,) is embodied, and for the first time in Poetry grandly and fully uttered, in him" (3-4).

Yet Burroughs remains reluctant to give up his theme. He repeatedly suggests, for example, that the true audience of Whitman's poetry is not the mass of men and women that the poet loved, but rather a literary elite—perhaps the O'Connor circle in Washington or the group of English admirers developing among the Pre-Raphaelites. (About the time Burroughs was writing, William Michael Rossetti was preparing to bring out a collection, *Poems of Walt Whitman*, finally published in London in 1868.) With more prescience than the poet himself could manage, Burroughs understands the avant-garde appeal of *Leaves of Grass*. He describes Whitman as "the subject of peculiar interest to *choice circles* both in this country and in Europe"; but, urged by Whitman himself, he nourishes the hope for a broader and more personal response to the poems, which are, he says "destined to a general renown unlike any other—the renown of personal endearment" (4). As if to model the personal response that Whitman preferred, Burroughs gives an account of his first acquaintance with the poems, then the person, of Walt Whitman. The result of his meeting Whitman and his consequent admission into the "choice circle" of the O'Connor household led Burroughs to identify the man Whitman closely with the literary text that bore his name. "His book and himself now fused in my mind," he writes, "and, as it were, remained one" (13). The timing of Burroughs's publication in 1867 reveals the motive he shared with O'Connor—his desire to defend Whitman in the wake of the Harlan affair. His treatment of Whitman's service in the war hospitals in Washington addresses such purposes, for example, though it also fits quite well within the genetic scheme of relating poet and poems.

If Burroughs's admiration of Whitman is clear enough in *Notes*, it becomes almost worshipful in his *Whitman: A Study*, first published in 1896, soon after Whitman's death and well after Burroughs had established himself as one of the most respected naturalists in America. Freed from Whitman's personal insistence on the republican side of his project, *Whitman: A Study* expresses most fully Burroughs's conviction about the poet's uniqueness and exalted status among poets and people. He universalizes Whitman as a type and removes any hint that he was also a token of ordinary life or his historical moment. "Whitman will always be a strange and unwonted figure among his country's poets," says Burroughs, "a cropping out . . . of the old bardic strain," a strong exemplar of the rare breed of men and women "who are like an irruption of life from another world, who belong to another order, who bring other standards, . . . and whom their times for the most part decry and disown,—the primal, original, elemental men [and women]" (*Whitman* 16, 21).

Burroughs's polemic impulse in both books, however, does not overwhelm altogether his scholarly motives. *Notes on Walt Whitman as Poet and Person* establishes a number of problems and points of inquiry that have continued to absorb Whitman's critics. Above all, Burroughs was the first to discuss the growth of *Leaves of Grass* from edition to edition, beginning with the 1855 book and moving down through 1860, the edition that he had encountered in his first reading, and on through the poems of *Drum-Taps*, which had been published just before he issued the *Notes*. Settling into an extended treatment of the most recent edition—the 1867 *Leaves*, which included *Drum-Taps* for the first time—Burroughs also sets the precedent for taking as a critical standard the last published, most complete edition as the authoritative version on which to base his readings. Unlike later critics, though, Burroughs does not show a special fondness for any single edition. The problem of how one version of the *Leaves* relates to the next does not much interest him. The overriding genetic theory of organic development that absorbs him appears to have kept such questions from entering his mind. In his view, each edition emerged naturally from the preceding one (like the annual growth of a tree) and from the informing center of the great poetic personality.

If this approach creates some blind spots, however, it also has an enabling effect, allowing Burroughs to pose a key problem that has haunted the organic tradition in Whitman studies—the apparently sudden emergence of *Leaves of Grass* in 1855. An organic historiography prefers a relatively continuous pattern of development and casts doubt upon explanations that require miracles, special revelations, revolutions, or massive catastrophes. In Emerson's famous congratulatory letter, for example, the Concord sage greets the 1855 *Leaves* with a mixture of pleasant shock—"I rubbed my eyes a little, to see if this sunbeam were no illusion"—and organic sanity, evident in the suggestion that the seeming miracle "must have had a long foreground somewhere, for such a start" (qtd. in Hindus 21). The assumption of a continuous evolution and gradual outcropping has undergirded historicist scholars throughout the tradition, coming to its fullest fruition in Floyd Stovall's *The Foreground of Leaves of Grass* (1974). But the early critical studies relish the possibility of a miraculous outpouring of poetic vision and performance. Burroughs argues, "The student of Whitman's life and works will be early struck by three things,—his sudden burst into song, the maturity of his work from the first, and his self-knowledge and self-estimate" (*Whitman* 79). This statement suggests a crystallized development of Whitman's poetic impulse, centering on the 1855 *Leaves*, which, in Burroughs's reading, sprang from the author's head suddenly and in a state of completeness and maturation. He concedes the possibility of the "long foreground" supposed by

Emerson (80), but declines to develop the idea, insisting that "the fit of inspiration came upon him suddenly ... like the flowering of the orchards in spring" (79). Ignoring Whitman's reading and literary apprenticeship, Burroughs argues that, before 1855, Whitman "produced nothing above mediocrity": "A hack writer on newspapers and magazines, then a carpenter and house-builder in a small way, then that astounding revelation 'Leaves of Grass,' the very audacity of it a gospel in itself" (80). Burroughs's interpretation has certainly not lacked adherents, even among modern critics, notably Malcolm Cowley, who fully accepted the "miracle" thesis, though he added a modernist touch by claiming that editions after the 1855 *Leaves* progressively diminished in power and beauty, as if the flower of inspiration faded quickly (or the machine of poetic production rapidly lost energy).

Burroughs balances the organic metaphor of "flowering" (80) against the romantic or biblical concept of sudden revelation, a turning from old ways, a break in the continuity of preceding practice—"something analogous to Paul's conversion" (80). Again, he depends largely upon the genetic principle of the overall unity of the *Leaves of Grass* project. Having discovered his true nature, Burroughs suggests, Whitman would not depart from it. "I have divided my subject into many chapters," Burroughs says of the thematic section of *Whitman: A Study*, "yet I am aware that they are all but slight variations of a single theme,—viz., Whitman's reliance upon absolute nature": "the poet declared at the outset of his career [in 1855] that at every hazard he should let nature speak," and thereafter he "never flinched or wavered for a moment" (191). Burroughs argues that Whitman had pierced through the sediments of civilization to touch the deepest springs of human instinct. Thoreau seems to have thought something similar. "It is as if the beasts spoke," the author of *Walden* says in a letter to a friend, commenting at once on Whitman's somewhat disturbing "sensuality" and on the lack of purity in an audience shocked by such free expression: "Of course, Walt Whitman can communicate to us no new experience, and if we are shocked, whose experience is it we are reminded of?" Thus, despite his animality, Whitman suggested for Thoreau, in final analysis, "something a little more than human" (qtd. in Bucke *Walt Whitman* 142). Burroughs's reading thus relies upon a standard transcendentalist theme. What Whitman discovered beneath the trappings of civilization, he reasons, was human nature, the true self, so that *Leaves of Grass* "has, strictly speaking, but one theme,—personality, the personality of the poet himself" (*Whitman* 83). In the genetic organicism represented in such statements, Burroughs discovers an informal rationale, if not a full blown theory, for the extraordinary attention that the critical tradition gives to the details of the poet's personal life. In his own time, such an outlook justifies the work of Whitman disciples like R. M. Bucke and Horace Traubel, who recorded the old poet's conversations in nearly obsessive detail. In the tradition at large, the genetic theory inspires the phenomenal outpouring of biography and the collection and publication of most every scrap of paper to which the poet applied pen or pencil.

Along with Burroughs, the genetic tradition owes an especially large debt to R. M. Bucke, the Canadian alienist who established Whitman's reputation among mystics and students of alternative religious experiences—the theosophists of the early century, for example, and the "New Agers" of our own time. Like Burroughs's books, Bucke's *Walt Whitman* (1883) demonstrates a fascination with the sudden emergence of the *Leaves* in 1855. Also like Burroughs, Bucke attributes this development to something extraordinary in Whitman's character and experience. He suggests that Whitman achieved "cosmic consciousness" in a life-transforming revelation in the early 1850s, the result of which was the 1855 *Leaves of Grass*. (In chapter 4, I give a fuller account of Bucke's views on "cosmic consciousness.")

Despite Whitman's pleasure at having found such a disciple, internal evidence in Bucke's *Whitman* indicates that the poet and his friend may have disagreed on the supposed mysticism of the poems. Evidently, Whitman could not get comfortable with Bucke's attribution to him of "cosmic consciousness," and, as he did with Burroughs, Whitman kept pushing Bucke toward a recognition of the poet's need to identify with the common mass of men and women. Nevertheless, we now know that, as with Burroughs's *Notes*, Whitman both contributed to and approved final copy for Bucke's book. And, since the republican theme comes through only intermittently and is usually expressed in direct, first-person quotations from Whitman—"I have told you how I used to spend many half-nights with my friends the pilots on the Brooklyn ferry-boats" (qtd. in *Walt Whitman* 67)—we may conclude that the poet's resolve to remain a hero of the common people had, by the 1880s, relented somewhat. By that time, even Whitman had to face the reality that his most devoted audience came from an intellectual, if avant-garde, elite—men and women like John Burroughs, R. M. Bucke, William and Nellie O'Connor, Anne Gilchrist, Horace Traubel, and Edward Carpenter. Bucke's book thus continues to build upon the view expressed by both O'Connor and Burroughs that Whitman was an extraordinary figure. In this view, the poet's experience transcended that of the ordinary mass of men and women, and *Leaves of Grass* encapsulated his experience in a form that would continue to speak down through the generations to the most perceptive and sensitive audiences. The downside of the argument is that the message of the poet would likely be rejected by readers with a taste for common sense and conventional language—the everyday citizen, the pedestrian, the philistine. Bucke agrees with Burroughs that no ordinary writer could have accomplished what Whitman did: "If the man were merely an ordinary person, such a purpose, such a book, written with absolute sincerity, would possess the most extraordinary interest; but *Leaves of Grass* has an interest far greater, derived from the exceptional personality which is embodied in it" (*Walt Whitman* 137).

In addition to the focus on this transcendent personality—along with the idea that Whitman, "as far as such a thing is possible, embodied himself" in his book (175)—and the interest in the sudden appearance of *Leaves of Grass*, Bucke's *Walt Whitman* shares with Burroughs's books the emphasis on the cumulative development of the poems, which Bucke treats in a fairly detailed chapter on "The History of *Leaves of Grass*—(1855-82)." Also like Burroughs, Bucke argues for the absolute originality and uniqueness, even the anti-literary quality, of the poems: "The problem ... was to express not what he heard, or saw, or fancied, or had read, but one far deeper and more difficult to express, namely Himself.... This is something that, as I believe, was never before dared or done in literature" (136-37).

But Bucke's presentation differs from Burroughs's in a subtle way. Whereas Burroughs understands Whitman's great achievement as essentially a triumph of nature, the poet having allowed his truest and best instincts and insights to find expression in his poems, Bucke tends to present Whitman as a great artificer, an active presence that molds nature to his needs. In the history of the different editions, for example, Bucke follows the standard line of genetic organicism in suggesting that the different editions "are simply successive expansions or growths, strictly carrying out the one idea," but he also resorts to an architectonic metaphor. Recalling Whitman's work as a carpenter, he says that "upon the publication of the second edition the fundamental and important parts of the author's work were done, the foundations squarely and solidly laid, and the lines of the edifice drawn with a sure hand" (141). Extending the figure, he writes, "After the long period of [the book's] own and its author's growth, we have it at last in the 1882-83 edition, completed as conceived twenty-six years ago.... Now it appears before us, perfected, like some grand cathedral that through many years or intervals has grown and grown until the original conception and full design of the architect stand forth" (155).

Without directly taking issue with these comments of Bucke, Burroughs attempts to remove from his last book on Whitman (which followed Bucke's) any hint of the mechanical and artificial. In *Whitman: A Study*, he argues, *Leaves of Grass* "is not a temple: it is a wood, a field, a highway" (136). Extending the argument into cultural criticism in an effort to defend Whitman against charges of "artlessness," Burroughs claims, "The love of the precise, the exact, the methodical, is characteristic of an age of machinery, of a commercial and industrial age like ours. These things are indispensable in the mill and counting-house, but why should we insist upon them in poetry?" (149). He concludes: "Whitman did not have ... the architectonic power of the great constructive poets. He did not build the lofty rhyme.

He did not build anything, strictly speaking. He let himself go. He named his book after the grass, which makes a carpet over the earth, and which is a sign and a presence rather than a form" (169).

This last remark hints strongly at the aesthetic and even the political implications of the organic tradition. If the aesthetic looks toward the idea that form follows function, the political or ethical preference is for a nondomineering, though inviting, attitude toward the other, toward difference and diversity, both in nature and in society. We should recognize that, in Burroughs's adoption of this ideological position, there was more at stake than the correct interpretation and defense of Whitman's poems; the critic's summoning of this gentle ethos also reveals his participation—indeed, along with John Muir, his leadership—in the first generation of wilderness protection based on natural mysticism (see Nash). Burroughs's differences with Bucke on this matter are typical of the time, when the mechanical warred with the organic for cultural dominance in scientific as well as economic communities (see Nicolson; Merchant; Botkin).

As with so many controversies over *Leaves of Grass*, this one more or less divides a contradiction within Whitman's concepts as they evolved over the several editions. The early poems, especially the 1855 "Song of Myself," tend to bear out Burroughs's view of Whitman's relation to nature. Not so with others—beginning as early as the 1856 *Leaves*. In the second edition, new poems like "Poem of Procreation" (later "A Woman Waits for Me") draw frequently upon the mechanical metaphors implicit in Whitman's "spermatic economy" (Aspiz; Killingsworth, *Poetry of the Body*). Likewise, "Song of the Broad-Axe" foreshadows later, more explicit rationalizations of manifest destiny and the technological onslaught against nature, a thematic trend that reaches its zenith in poems like "Song of the Redwood-Tree" and "Song of the Exposition," both published in the 1870s. Such performances leave Whitman open to Michael Moon's exposé of the castration complex in the 1856 *Leaves*, as well as to the critique of recent environmentalists. Bruce Piasecki and Peter Asmus, for example, say of Whitman: "the glory he finds in the sound of saws once again reminds us what is wrong with America's estimate of nature" (89; see also Folsom; Byers). Even when the poet, in a deep awareness of his own inevitable death, identifies with the fallen redwood, his act of abdication, "clearing the ground for broad humanity, the true America, heir of the past so grand" (*Leaves: Norton* 210), could only inspire "a conservationist's horror," as Cecilia Tichi rightly notes (249). Therefore, only by careful selection and perhaps a few selective blindnesses could Burroughs's interpretation of the whole of *Leaves of Grass* serve the ideological as well as the critical ends of the organic tradition, fostering a nurturing and nature-loving ethos for the poet-hero and ignoring the more aggressive implications of Whitman's enthusiasm for the technological mastery of nature.

Their differences notwithstanding, the two men of science, Burroughs and Bucke—one favoring the organic, the other embracing the mechanical view of the artistic relation to nature—established Whitman's life and work as an unusual case worthy of scholarly, even scientific, attention. They set the stage for the subsequent fascination with Whitman's difference from his contemporaries and from other writers in the history of literature. After Burroughs and Bucke came other amateur scholars from among Whitman's friends and acquaintances—enthusiastic collectors and conversationalists like Horace Traubel, the Gilchrists, William Sloane Kennedy, and Thomas Donaldson. They would reproduce Whitman's talk, preserve and publish his letters, and offer anecdotes about the poet in memoirs and reminiscences. In addition to those who knew Whitman directly, distant admirers added informal studies and narratives of their personal response to the poet's call for reader-comrades. The South African statesman Jan Christian Smuts, for example, produced the eloquent *Walt Whitman: A Study in the Evolution of Personality*, whose title (anticipating the work of Roger Asselineau) suggests the connection between Whitman's own growth, that of his book, and the progress of organic development in general. In the old style of personalist and genetic discourse, Smuts argues that "the subject of *Leaves of Grass* . . . is the personality of Whitman; it is a self-analysis, a self-portraiture. The main figure in the painting is Walt Whitman himself; while America, American civilisation, and nineteenth-century progress furnish the setting, the environment, the background to that figure" (60). Lovingly offered, the memories and impressions of this generation became the subject matter, the data, of professional critical biographers in the next generation.

The Advent of Modern Critical Biography

The difference between the early biographers and the next generation is largely a matter of tone. By the turn of the century, scholars began to take more interest in their own professional status—and the "impartiality" or "objectivity" implied in the ethos of professionalism. Consequently, they tended to treat Whitman as a literary subject rather than, more broadly, as an extraordinary mortal. This movement would produce what we now call critical biography, the advent of which is first described in Gay Wilson Allen's essay on early Whitman biography. Originally published in the *Walt Whitman Handbook* of 1946 (then updated in Allen's *Walt Whitman As Man, Poet, and Legend* of 1961 and again in *The New Walt Whitman Handbook* of 1975), the essay is titled "The Growth of Whitman Biography" to conform to the (somewhat Whiggish) perceptions of the leading modern critic in the organic tradition. By the time he wrote his essay, Allen says, the biographical tradition "had flourished with astonishing luxuriance" (*Walt*

Whitman Handbook 89). The critical biographies that Allen holds up as the final fruit of this luxuriance are "critical" in two related senses of the word. First, they practice literary criticism, embedding readings of the poems within the narrative of the poet's life. Second, they are critical in the more popular sense of the word; critical biographers feel free, that is, to point out weaknesses, inconsistencies, and lapses of various kinds in the poet's life and in his work.

As Allen notes, each of these two qualities had already appeared by the end of the century. Both Burroughs and Bucke mixed biography and interpretation. And some of Whitman's friends—including Burroughs, as well as John Townsend Trowbridge and Edward Carpenter—were at least occasionally willing to call attention to the poet's weaknesses (Allen, *Handbook* 29-33; see also Barrus). Among Whitman's defenders, Burroughs's critical capacity was the most pronounced. In *Whitman: A Study*, for example, he notes Whitman's "lack of humor," though he excused it as the "price paid for his strenuousness and earnestness" (169). More suggestively—in a point that Edward Carpenter, Henry Bryan Binns, and ultimately Esther Shephard would make much of—Burroughs admits that "Whitman showed just enough intention, or premeditation in his life, dress, manners, attitudes in his pictures, self-portrayals in his poems, etc., to give rise to the charge that he was a *poseur*" (*Whitman: A Study* 107-108). In addition, Burroughs was not inclined to withhold criticism of Whitman's other friends. For example, he complains that O'Connor's writing lacks "the perception of identity": "What is common to all [great authors], he sees clearly enough, but what is peculiar to each . . . he totally fails to see. Thus Aeschylus and Rabelais, Hugo and Whitman, all awaken the same emotion in his mind, and he applies the same epithets to each" (qtd. in Freedman 203). In this summation, Burroughs insightfully locates O'Connor outside the organic tradition, which requires critics to identify differences, individualities. According to the view implied in Burroughs's more radical organicism, O'Connor belongs to the Victorian tradition of mechanization, which demands the perception of similarities and leads ultimately to quantifiable uniformities (see Botkin 27).

If, in contrast to Burroughs, writers like O'Connor, Bucke, and the literary executors Traubel and Harned often seem to idolize Whitman, their tone can be explained by the context in which their writings appeared, as Allen argues (*Handbook* 5). These "Whitmaniacs" wrote first to stave off attacks upon their friend, and their last efforts were designed to ensure the survival of a strong readership into the next generation. From first to last, then, their work was intended to sustain Whitman's reputation, and only rarely to correct and improve upon their subject.

What happened in the next generation of biographers and critics was the gradual fading of the poet-prophet image of Whitman. First critical biography, then psychoanalytical criticism attempted to exorcise the mystic Whitman and to shade over into the various schools of close critical reading that tended to emphasize the artful Whitman, with his shifting poses and personae (a movement I discuss more fully in chapter 3). By retaining an overweening interest in the person Walt Whitman, however, both critical biography and psychoanalysis preserve from the first generation the core of a genetic theory—the belief that, either through research into biographical facts or through deep analysis of behavioral traits keyed against symbolic expressions, study of the person will reveal the ultimate meaning and significance of the poems, or vice-versa, study of the poems will reveal the personality of the poet. Thus the critical tradition continues to be concerned with what makes Whitman unique, unusual, or indeed strange.

Henry Bryan Binns's *A Life of Walt Whitman* (1905) represents a transition toward critical biography. An Englishman, Binns came to the United States to research his subject in an effort to write the first comprehensive life of Whitman, a complete birth-to-death narrative. His research was only partially successful, however; and, faced with gaps and inconsistencies, Binns commits an error against professionalism that later biographers have found difficult to forgive. He accepts Whitman's claim, in a letter to John Addington Symonds, that "Tho' always unmarried I have had six children"; "My life, young manhood, mid-age, times South, &c: have all been jolly, bodily," the letter boasts, "and probably open to criticism" (*Correspondence* 5.73). On the questionable basis of this letter, Binns concocts a romance that puts Whitman to bed with a southern woman during the few months he spent working as a journalist in New Orleans in the late 1840s. To make matters worse, Binns falls victim to the biographical fallacy, citing the poem of remembrance "Once I Pass'd through a Populous City" as support for this story and thereby creating an irony that only later critics could appreciate: The manuscript of the poem eventually surfaced to reveal that the object of the poet's lyrical affection was originally a man, not a woman. The line "I remember only a woman I casually met there who detain'd me for love of me," for example, had originally read: "But now of all that city I remember only the man who wandered with me, there, for love of me" (*Leaves: Norton* 110n.).

Later critical biographers have looked upon Binns's story with amused detachment. In *The Solitary Singer* (1955), for example, Gay Wilson Allen says of Whitman's alleged progeny, "no trace whatever has been found of any of these children, and it is extremely doubtful that any evidence ever will be found. They were, in all probability, 'the children of psychology'" (*Solitary Singer* 536). Most recent scholars have agreed with Allen and have understood Whitman's letter as a ploy to set Symonds off the track of the poet's homosexuality. But readers in Binns's day—from Léon Bazalgette and Basil De Selincourt down to Emory Holloway—took the story seriously, and William Carlos

Williams repeats it in an essay on Whitman written as late as 1960 and published in 1971 as the introduction to *The Illustrated Leaves of Grass*. Binns's biography thus had a clear and lasting effect.

Binns uses the New Orleans adventure not only to explain Whitman's response to Symonds's questions about the nature of the "Calamus" poems, but also to speculate on the mysterious eruption of *Leaves of Grass* in 1855. Having discovered that the earliest manuscripts of the poems must have been written around the time of Whitman's brief southern excursion, Binns reasons that sexual experiences may have precipitated the "emancipation" of the great poet from the holds of convention and quotidian (Binns 50-53). This liberation permitted "illumination"—which, according to the Quaker Binns, is the key to understanding the *Leaves*. This reading of Whitman's work in light of the Quaker tradition comprises Binns's main contribution to the interpretive side of critical biography. Indeed, the interpretation nicely anticipates the recent historicist emphasis on liberation and the connection of personal freedom, political liberty, and intellectual illumination that emerged around the time of 1848 (see Hutchinson 7-8; L. Reynolds 125-52). However, the sensationalism of the New Orleans romance tends to overshadow Binns's critical accomplishments.

Whitman's next biographer, Bliss Perry, would be more cautious and less adoring of his subject than his predecessors, though he owed a number of insights to Bucke and much more to Burroughs, including the loan of unpublished manuscripts as well as the assignment to write the Whitman volume in the American Men of Letters series (Perry v). As for Binns's New Orleans romance, Perry accepted the story, though his scholarly caution urged him away from an overt retelling of it. After dutifully noting the lack of evidence about this obscure period of the poet's life, he writes in a passage full of echoes from Binns, "Whitman's wonderful book ... is a reflection of an inner illumination, of a mystical sense of union with the world, and this in turn had its reinforcement, if not its origin, in sexual emotion. The book was a child of passion. Its roots are deep down in a young man's body and soul" (47). Perry offers one off-handed indication that he even accepted Whitman's claim to have fathered illegitimate children. One of Whitman's likenesses to Rousseau, says Perry, was that "each man wrote superbly about paternity, and each man deserted his own children" (322). In the second edition of his biography, urged by correspondents who knew Whitman and who doubted the story about the children, Perry revised the sentence to read: "Each man wrote superbly about paternity, although neither, as far as is now known, ever acknowledged or supported the children which he says were born to him" (278).

Capitalizing on the religious and mechanical meanings of illumination and reflection, Perry tries also to preserve an organic metaphor in his comments about the roots of *Leaves of Grass*. The organic tendencies in his study are elaborated further in his frequent comparisons of Whitman to the older romanticism of Wordsworth and to transcendentalism. Organic metaphors also prevail in Perry's forthright treatment of what he considered to be flaws in Whitman's character—flaws which, like those noted by Burroughs, nevertheless bore fruit in poetic practice. In his view, Whitman suffered from "an excess of emotional endowment" and was subject to "the innate selfishness of a born sentimentalist" (19-20). Yet out of these (almost literally) genetic qualities came both the poet's sensitivity to nature and his love of human closeness among family and comrades. Perry thus distinguishes between Whitman's lyrical beauty and his moral and philosophical banality, which appears to derive from the poet's lack of emotional maturity. Whitman's "desire to glorify everybody equally," for example, Perry judges to be "touching in its naiveté" (294). This judgment would prove quite durable in the critical tradition. In 1926, opening the field for an orthodox Freudian interpretation of artistic discourse, Emory Holloway balances Whitman's "profound and far-reaching faith" against his "childish naïveté" and argues that Whitman's self-proclaimed contradictions are "often more fundamental than he realized," arising as they do from "the undisciplined emotionalism of the child rather than the complex cerebration of the normal adult" (*Whitman* x). As late as 1975, Gay Wilson Allen also picks up the theme in *The New Walt Whitman Handbook*: "*Leaves of Grass* is one of the most personal, and in many ways the most naively frank, collections of poetry ever written" (1).

In yet another influential move, Perry goes farther than anyone before him in covering Whitman's period of literary apprenticeship, focusing mainly upon the early stories and poems. He rejects the idea of a sudden inspiration and poetic flowering in 1855, and, in the Emersonian vein of organicism, insists upon a "slowly-shaping impulse toward some form of literary expression" (22). Apparently, Perry worried that Whitman's reputation would rise and fall with the fortunes of the free verse that he invented. He thus concedes, in a sentence now famous among Whitman scholars, that "Whitman's measures have been used as a megaphone to shout out essentially prose exclamations; freaks and cranks and neurotic women, with here and there a hot little prophet, have toyed with it" (285-86). Perry argues that, unlike the work of careless versecrafters, *Leaves of Grass* is "in no sense . . . an impromptu" but rather "the result of a purpose that had been forming for years" (68). Having carefully analyzed the early stories and poems, though, Perry finally agrees with Burroughs (and with Whitman himself) that none of the early works has much in the way of lasting literary merit (28-29).

Perry also accepts the views of Burroughs and Bucke on the matter of Whitman's readership, though not exactly for the same reasons. Whitman, he suggests, requires an audience sophisticated enough to sort the wheat from the chaff, to forgive the poet for his occasional lapses in language, thought, and morals. For this reason, Perry predicts that "Whitman's audience will . . . be limited to those who have the intellectual and moral generosity to understand him" (308). In this view, which tends to elevate the critical reader over the inspired poet, Perry would be followed by most of the rising professionals in the new field of American literary scholarship.

After Perry, Holloway's *Whitman: An Interpretation in Narrative* (1926) added strength to the critical tradition and detail to Whitman biography. Like Perry, Holloway explores the early writings in a full treatment of Whitman's literary apprenticeship. In particular, he pioneers the study of Whitman's journalism and early ventures in politics, work that would be taken up by Joseph Jay Rubin and more recent historicists.

Ironically, his close study of Whitman's journalism and unpublished manuscripts did not save Holloway from the kind of interpretive indiscretion that had made Binns seem out of touch with the growing caution of professional scholarship. In fact, Holloway comes to agree with Binns about the poet's romantic experience in New Orleans and even contributes a new twist to the story. Whitman's lover, he surmises, was a "Creole octoroon" (67). Like Binns, Holloway takes Whitman at his word in the Symonds letter and uses, as support, the feminine version of "Once I Pass'd through a Populous City." However, Holloway's appropriation of the little poem is yet the more curious, for he had not only discovered the original manuscript with the masculine nouns and pronouns but had even included the manuscript version in *Uncollected Poetry and Prose*, which he edited and published in 1921 (2.102). As Gay Wilson Allen shrewdly notes, Holloway appears to have known "more than he dares to tell" (*Walt Whitman Handbook* 57). Against the current of literary modernism, Holloway also interprets the "Calamus" poems not as expressions of homoerotic desire and vision, but as pure and simple specimens of the Victorian "friendship tradition" (compare Lynch). With a fervor that would now be considered "homophobic," Holloway worked his entire career to "prove" that Whitman had heterosexual relations with at least one woman (as if this would "prove" that he was not a homosexual). His last book on Whitman, *Free and Lonesome Heart*, is a kind of detective story that reveals what Holloway believed to be his ultimate discovery—actual evidence of Whitman's offspring, indeed the very grave site of a son. Unfortunately for Holloway, scholars have been as skeptical of this story as they were of Whitman's original tale in the letter to Symonds.

A much more influential legacy of Holloway's *Interpretation in Narrative* is his suggestion that the views of the elderly Whitman differed considerably from those of the younger poet of 1855 and that, consequently, the different editions of the *Leaves* reflect a change not only quantitative but also qualitative. If the early editions were marked thematically by a deep concern with physical and political life, the later *Leaves* dwelled upon the personal and spiritual. In that later verse, Holloway writes, "we have a different Whitman. Here is no longer the youthful feeling of immortality born of high animal spirits, nor even the agonized realism of the war-time verse; here is the aspiration of the pioneer soul" (244). In noting this passage from romantic rebelliousness to sober realism to mature religious awareness, Holloway takes a progressive slant on the story of growth. Though the poet of the body had withdrawn in the late poems, "the mystic survives" and "makes rendezvous, not with the Great Companions, but with the Comrade perfect" (245). Moreover, he argues, the influence of the poet would provide further "compensations" for the loss of physical intensity: "His leaves of grass grew from hardy, democratic roots; and now those roots begin to spread. Other hands will water them, till they shall have refreshed with their greenness every part where poets dwell" (252-53). The final touch in this organic line of reasoning would prove the most robust of all. Commenting on the "heat" with which Whitman responded to Symonds, Holloway develops a thesis that ties the concept of sublimation to that of compensation, arguing that, given the "tragic peculiarities of Symonds's nature," which are "well known," it is not surprising that the Englishman longed to take Whitman as his master; in "Calamus," Holloway asserts, Symonds "thought he recognized a kindred but more heroic spirit, and in them he glimpsed a possible spiritual sublimation of emotional tendencies which to his highly civilized intelligence were, when observed in themselves, obnoxious" (255).

Holloway's unwillingness to countenance Whitman's homosexuality thus amounts to a reluctance even to use the word *homosexual*, to name what an early reviewer of *Leaves of Grass* likewise had referred to as *Peccatum illud horrible, inter Christianos non nominandum*, the horrible crime not fit to be named among Christians (qtd. in Hindus 33). In an age that saw homosexuality emerging from the underground, such a reaction was not uncommon. What is interesting is the power of this reaction over the empiricism that, for the most part, guides Holloway's scholarship. Critical biography nevertheless preserves much of Holloway's pioneering effort, but finally develops a more "scientific" attitude toward Whitman's sexual preferences, substituting scholarly distance for Holloway's sense of mortification over the poet's departures from the dominant sexual mores of the early twentieth century.

None of these later biographies has had more of an impact than Gay Wilson Allen's *The Solitary Singer*, published in 1955 on the hundreth anniversary of the first edition of *Leaves of Grass* and still widely held to be the standard biography of the poet. At once the most comprehensive in its command of biographical detail and the most critical

of the critical biographies (in both senses of the term), Allen follows
Traubel and Binns in his attention to detail, but selects anecdotes and
evidence with a clear eye for effective narrative and solid proof; he follows Holloway in interpretive enthusiasm, but benefits from the
nearly thirty years of modern critical practice that had intervened since
the publication of *Whitman: An Interpretation in Narrative*. During
that time, both psychoanalysis and the New Criticism had evolved as
separate but complementary arts of close reading. Though Allen
mainly avoids the characteristic jargons of the Freudian and formalist
schools, he had clearly absorbed the general lessons of both, as well as
comprehending the growth of Whitman biography.

The Solitary Singer develops according to a fairly scrupulous ad-
herence to chronology, telling the story of Whitman's life from childhood to death, and seeking along the way "clues to the developing
mind and character—and genius—of the poet of *Leaves of Grass*" (16).
Gradually there emerges a definite characterization of the poet. In
many ways, it is close to the self-portrait Whitman gives in *A
Backward Glance O'er Travel'd Roads*. Allen agrees, for instance, that
Whitman forged a career in literature out of failures in business, journalism, and politics. But Allen's Whitman differs from Whitman's
self-portrait in at least one key feature. In Allen's view, Whitman was a
loner—a solitary singer. If not exactly a misfit, he was, in Allen's estimate, hardly representative of the common citizen. In the working
world, he was not a team player; he was hard to get along with and not
inclined to follow the standard party line even when the political
bosses and newspaper owners prevailed upon him. In his artistic career, however, the very stubbornness and individuality that cursed
him in day-to-day social life became the wellsprings of originality; they
provided the sources for his greatest distinctions—his antinomian
mysticism, his personalism, and his formal experimentation in the poetic craft. His family puzzled over his book, as did most of the critics
and reviewers of his day, but, with the early encouragement of
Emerson and the occasional acquaintance from New York's bohemian
underground (such as Henry Clapp), Whitman stubbornly persisted in
trusting his inner lights until he could be discovered and lionized by
the "choice circles" of readers in the 1860s.

Allen clearly admires Whitman's strong (protomodernist) commitment to himself, though the radical empiricism and skeptical outlook of modern critical biography keep him from fully accepting
Burroughs's claim that Whitman heroically discovered deep human
nature beneath the sediments of civilization imposed upon his character. Nevertheless, Allen does put some stock in the genetic view that
Whitman found his inspiration deep within his own character. But he
takes the analysis a step further, arguing that Whitman transformed
these psychic raw materials into art only through a rigorous process of
poetic composition. Like Perry, Allen denies that *Leaves of Grass* was

an impromptu. Rather, it was, at its best, a slow-maturing and rather transient accomplishment, revealing both organic and technical qualities of the highest order.

Moreover, Allen argues that Whitman's personal quirks and shortcomings were never entirely sublimated in his art. Under the critic's close scrutiny, they persistently show through poetic expressions that are sometimes merely awkward and that other times reveal deep problems. Confronting the mingling of erotic and religious language in section 5 of "Song of Myself," for example, Allen suggests that "what made Walt Whitman symbolize his concept of the union of body and soul in sexual terms" is "a problem for the psychoanalyst" (158). Satisfied only to hint at solutions to psychological puzzles, Allen is more willing to confront directly the literary problem of what the symbolic language "means in the context of the poem"; dismissing interpretations of the passage as either "an esoteric description of some physical experience" or an hallucinatory outcome of some kind of trance, Allen offers a cosmological reading that emphasizes the technical, literary qualities of the passage. "Whitman was dramatizing his doctrine that 'a kelson of the creative is love,'" Allen says; he "was a mystic [only] in the sense that intellectually and spiritually he believed love to be the creating, unifying, and life-giving principle of the universe, and as a poet he tried to illustrate this principle in visible analogies" (159). From Allen's literary perspective, then, Whitman's success lies in his ability to dramatize and illustrate rather than to think original thoughts or bring forth deep emotions.

Writing in the 1950s, Allen clearly felt the influence of New Criticism as the dominant school of the day. Since *The Solitary Singer*, with varying degrees of self-consciousness and methodological purity, applies most of the five major doctrines of New Critical practice summarized by Cleanth Brooks in the *Princeton Encyclopedia of Poetry and Poetics* of 1974, it may be useful to rehearse them here, at least briefly (following the example of Vincent Leitch). First, according to Brooks's redaction of the formalist method, the critic should focus on the literary object itself, viewing as irrelevant the "extrinsic concerns" of source study, sociology, politics, and cultural or intellectual history. Second, the critic should deal with the structure of the work itself, not the mind of the author ("intentional fallacy") or the response of the audience ("pathetic fallacy"). Third, the critic should espouse an "organic theory" of art, which, in this approach, means a refusal to divide form from content, so that "each word contributes to a unique context and derives its precise meaning from its place in the poetic context" (Leitch 28). Fourth, with strict attention to meanings of words and figures of speech, the critic should seek a unity of meaning within the individual literary work. Finally, the critic should maintain the distinction of literature from both religion and morality and should refuse to substitute one realm of inquiry for another (Leitch 28-29).

How could a biographer, even a critical biographer, participate in such a program? Allen's solution is partly to compromise and partly to make a serious dialectical effort to reconcile historical/empirical research with formalist criticism. In a bow to New Criticism, he demonstrates a strong reluctance to pause too long over the religious and psychological aspects of Whitman's poems (as we have seen in his treatment of "Song of Myself," section 5). He is likewise suspicious about the political significance of the *Leaves*. Whitman was a failed politician, Allen reminds us, and a successful poet not only in spite of this failure but probably because of it. Indeed, the success of the poems becomes problematical when the New Critical principles are applied most directly, as in Allen's discussion of Whitman's first-person persona. "Whitman's symbolical 'I' is usually esthetically successful; his personal 'I' less frequently successful," he argues: "Many of the impassioned confessions and outcries of self-betrayal have lyric power and beauty, but the general effect of them in the poem is to give the reader the impression that the poet vacillates between sublimity and pathos, between self-control and abandon, and consequent order and disorder in his esthetic form" (161-62). The measure of "success" here is distance and the ability to resolve in art what cannot be resolved in "extrinsic" life—Holloway's "sublimation" again, now substantiated with the powerful formalism of the 1950s.

Allen thus manages an exquisite tension in his book. Within a stream of biographical and historical narrative, he provides readings of the poems that respect fairly closely—but not absolutely—the limits established by the New Criticism. These islands of explication may hint at psychological or sociological significances, but Allen never expands the hints into full-scale readings of the poems; rather, they become sources only of biographical insight. In the psychological vein, for example, he reveals clearly the role that fantasy must have played in Whitman's art. Against the sometimes sordid details of Whitman's mundane life, Allen sketches the rich imaginative world of the poet: "What Walt Whitman wanted most in his life of the imagination was to immerse, to bathe, to float (these were to become the key images in his poems). . . . Having attained these mystical insights and intellectual concepts, Whitman was emotionally and mentally equipped to write the great book he had been dreaming of since his 'Sundown Papers' from his schoolmaster's desk" (144). But, in a quick turn away from psychology, Allen's phrase "emotionally and mentally equipped" hints at the view of poetry-making that underlies much of the critical biographer's drift toward New Criticism.

Though the New Critics often inveighed against science and technology, they fostered a decidedly technical view of poetic composition. The poem was seen as an artifact, its maker long since dead; or a machine, perpetually making meaning without requiring the direction of a maker or the operations of a user. In these dreams of a perfect technology—free from human labor and representing a world outside of history, a world of beauty, meaning, and wholeness—the New Critics nourished their paradoxical vision (or hope) of an organic utopia somehow disconnected from the organic world of nature and history. The main difference between the peaceful artistic world and the messy natural world is change, which is the one thing that cannot be allowed in the realm of the beautiful. Poems may be added, but they only reinforce eternally valid aesthetic laws. Thus, the notorious political conservatism of the New Criticism is part and parcel of what John Dewey called the "quest for certainty," the desire to create a realm of thought and art that functions predictably according to immutable laws. New Critical organicism applies only to this ideal world, not to the noisy world of political engagement and historical contingency. Whitman's celebration of this latter world would earn him the contempt of most New Critics. As Vincent Leitch notes, they preferred "complex, freestanding poems filled with intricate semantic interrelations," such as the works of the metaphysical poets and high modernists like T. S. Eliot, while they either condemned or ignored the poems of "Walt Whitman and other 'loose' romantics" (30).

Within this context, Allen attempts a tenuous resolution, forging a kind of double organicism. On the one hand, there is Whitman's historical existence, open to the findings of empirical research and inviting the biographer's narration of life processes—the birth, growth, and death of the poet himself and, by extension, the "life" of his book. On the other hand, there is the world of the artist, which yields to the explications and analyses of the formalist. Successful poems originate in the fantasies of the biographical subject, but, having been admitted into the realm of art, such fantasies lose their psychological significance and submit to the transforming, eternizing effects of aesthetic objectification. If the poems succeed, they can be approached through the laws governing the realm of the eternally beautiful. However, if biographical motives and themes continue to intrude upon the poems, the result can only be a failure of unity and sublimation, which invites the return of the psychoanalyst and the biographer.

If the poet's works betray their links to other literary and philosophical works, they also fail. For example, Allen faults the preface to the 1855 *Leaves of Grass* for revealing too much the influence of Emerson and earlier romantics, such as Shelley. The preface therefore lacks the original force of the poems, a force issuing forth from an "imagination . . . superheated by a secret volcano that threatened at any moment to burst forth and overflow" (156). In the 1855 Preface, as Allen reads it, "this inner pressure was under control, and as a consequence the literary form was disciplined to a much greater degree than in the long dithyrambic, and unrepressed poems that followed" (156). Emerson could have written the preface, Allen suggests, but not the poems, for "Whitman's temperament and expression were basically different" from Emerson's (156). Echoing Burroughs, Allen thus implies that Whitman produced his best results when he "let himself go." But, unlike Burroughs, Allen stakes out a fairly narrow field of success. Between repression (which leads to conventionality and submission to influence) and self-indulgence (which seeks to replace art with confession and sentimental self-display) lies the high ground of sublimation—the goal of technical perfection and organic unity.

Tracing and exposing the biographical and historical impurities in the artifacts of *Leaves of Grass*, Allen practices a kind of archaeology, ever seeking the core of high artistic accomplishment. His considerable research into the social and historical contexts of the *Leaves* and the life of the poet he thus consigns primarily to the background. The empirical facts may illuminate Whitman's failures, he suggests, but they do not explain the poet's successes. To do that, the biographer must alternate with the critic in a kind of self-imposed division of labor.

This method does much to enable Allen's influential explication of the changes wrought by Whitman's method of composing the *Leaves*. If Allen's reading of the growth of *Leaves of Grass* is correct, no edition could have been predicted from what had gone before. Individual poems may have organic unity, but the project as a whole suffered the contingencies of history along with fairly violent shifts of interest and outlook in the poet's experience. Nevertheless, Allen persists in framing his discussion with organic metaphors, as in the following passage that concludes his discussion of the 1856 *Leaves*: "With this 1856 edition *Leaves of Grass* had proved itself a hardy perennial, but many seasons of growth would yet be necessary before it could reach maturity" (190).

Separated only by the space of a year, the first and second editions were significantly different, in Allen's judgment, the growth of the book following some of the genetic trajectories rooted in 1855, but also departing along new lines of development. The poet's purpose appears to have shifted to include not only expressive aims—which Allen, following the romantics, tends to value highest—but also more strident rhetorical aims, direct appeals to the readership of the day. Allen argues that the rapidly changing historical scene of the pre-Civil War period joined with Whitman's worries about family matters and disappointment over the critical reception of the 1855 *Leaves* to produce "pressures from without and within, political and psychological." These pressures kept Whitman from artistically exploiting in 1856 the volcanic emotions of the first edition. Instead of the confident power of the 1855 *Leaves*, the poet submitted to self-consciousness and sentimentalism in the 1856 book. He displayed "erratic judgment," for example, in his prefatory letter to Emerson (a public reply to Emerson's private letter of congratulation, one line of which, to make matters worse, was printed on the spine of the volume—"I greet you at the beginning of a great career—R. W. Emerson") (179-80). The weak judgment extended to many of the poems. "Some of the new poems," says Allen, "are little more than prose statements of general ideas"—and not very good prose or stimulating ideas at that. Whitman's attempt to convert the 1855 preface into "Poem of the Many in One," for instance, resulted in a "confused poem" tormented by a "new nationalism" that diverged from the strong democracy of 1855 by being "provincial, fatuously self-sufficient, [and] isolationist" (180-81). Nevertheless, Allen grants that a few of the new poems—notably those now known as "Salut au Monde" and "Crossing Brooklyn Ferry"—"escaped from the confining themes of [Whitman's] personal life and the American nation into the freedom of time and space on the cosmic scale" (183-84).

The implication is that Whitman's strength is connected to his ability to tap the organic depths of his emotional life. When he let the inspiration flow, as Burroughs had suggested, good results followed, but when he worked too hard at channeling, directing, or managing the work, he produced a monstrosity. It is little wonder that—writing in the 1950s, an age that had seen technological warfare, scientific management, and bureaucratic complexity carried to heights never before imagined—Allen cultivates Burroughs's romantic celebration of Whitman's expressive individuality and implicitly dismisses the architectonic vision of Bucke. Following this line of interpretation, Allen searches each edition of *Leaves of Grass* for signs of new growth, on the one hand, and artificial impositions on the other. The "Calamus" poems of 1860 represent the former, an artistic encapsulation of the "smouldering fires" that indicate Whitman's having "passed through an experience—or a series of experiences—that threatened to destroy him" in the late 1850s (222). Allen hints that this was a homosexual adventure, but, with the caution of the empiricist, refuses to take the speculation too far. Nevertheless, in considering lines like "Hours of my torment—I wonder if other men ever have the like, out of the like feelings / Is there even one other like me—distracted—his friend, his lover, lost to him?" (*Leaves: Norton* 596)—lines from a poem later removed from *Leaves of Grass*—Allen asserts, "This, surely, was neither imaginary nor symbolical, but written out of shame and remorse" (225). Though hardly approving of Whitman's homosexuality, Allen faces it squarely and, applying again the New Critical doctrines, argues, "The redeeming feature of these poems motivated by unsatisfied homoerotic yearnings is that the poet was able to transcend his personal suffering. He would never be able to escape the torment of his emotions, but he could generalize them"; he could show "that what he feels within himself is analogous to some terrible force in the Earth, 'ready to break forth,'" as he says in one of the "Calamus" poems; and could finally "become a teacher of 'friendship'" beyond "the esoteric frenzy of the earlier, more obviously homoerotic lyrics" (225-26).

Later criticism both extends and refutes this interpretive line. Clark Griffith, for example, builds an entire interpretation of the "Calamus" poems on the notion that they were motivated by homosexual guilt. Robert K. Martin, on the other hand, opposes Allen's judgment and claims that, in fact, the best of the "Calamus" poems are not the sober performances on friendship, but rather the frenzied confessions where Whitman, once again, lets himself go. Both Martin and Charley Shively take issue with Allen's assertion that Whitman's emotions arose from "unsatified homoerotic yearnings." Martin and Shively develop external and internal evidence strongly suggesting that Whitman regularly satisfied his yearnings with real physical action and that therefore his emotions were homosexual and not merely homo-erotic. Nevertheless, Allen's work was surely a step in this direction, away from the homophobic denials of writers like Holloway.

To take another instance, Allen's discussion of Whitman's homo-erotic attachments with the soldiers he attended in the Civil War hos-pitals, as revealed in Whitman's letters and notebooks of the period, clearly anticipates and paves the way for Shively's treatment of the sol-diers' letters to Whitman and his consequent conclusion that the poet joined a number of the young men in a working-class network of ho-mosexual connections, complete with secret codes and special insider knowledge—the possible source for what Allen calls the "esoteric" homoerotic language of "Calamus." Such language is not as apparent in *Drum-Taps*, the poems that Whitman wrote out of his war-time ex-perience, though Allen admits that "Whitman had not conquered all his inner 'perturbations'"—as the poet claimed in a letter to O'Connor: "he was, in fact, engaged in a life-time struggle with them." Allen goes on, however, to apply again the rationale of sublimation that ties his biographical project to New Critical doctrine: "But one means by which he controlled [his homosexual 'perturbations'] was through the trans-mutation of his private yearnings for affection into a universal philos-ophy of love as a social force." Allen then adds, "He had attempted that, too, in the 'Calamus' poems, but sporadically and inconsistently" (339).

Later critics have disagreed with Allen's apparent preference for *Drum-Taps* over "Calamus," a preference which seems to derive from New Critical theories about the transcendental functions of art. But re-cent critics tend to agree with another of Allen's theses—that Whitman's tinkering with the later editions of the *Leaves* did little to improve the book. "For twenty years, "Allen writes in a discussion of the 1881-82 edition, "he had been trying to mold his collection of po-ems into an organic unity. Since one of his greatest ambitions . . . was to be the poetic voice of his country in the nineteenth century, and at the same time to put his own life on record . . . , the logical arrange-ment would have been a simple chronological one" that would suggest "the journey through life from procreation through young manhood (for him the 'Calamus' emotions dominant) to intellectual maturity (expressed in the sea-shore lyrics), and on past the war ('Drum-Taps,'

'Memories of President Lincoln') to old age ('Autumn Rivulets') and intimations of death ('Whispers . . .')" (496-97). But Whitman had "blurred the chronology" in earlier editions and "demolished" it utterly in "this final arrangement, to be kept in all future editions, with instructions to the executors to preserve it" (496). Moreover, the new editions failed to emphasize "the sex poems," which were among Whitman's most distinctive achievements, and added "new allegorical group titles" that "tended to submerge" the poetry of the body, placing "more stress on the journey of the soul through life into eternity" (498), a theme that had not progressed much since the publication of "Passage to India" in 1871—"the absolute summit of his poetic life" (430). Images of decline dominate Allen's treatment of the last twenty years of Whitman's life. Natural enough for a biographer, such tropes are applied to the the poetic production as well, suggesting a decline of artistic power and an ebbing of the book's aesthetic value that paralleled the slipping away of the poet's physical life. Thus, Allen does what Whitman did not do in his final arrangement of Leaves of Grass; he aligns the poems chronologically to suggest the cyclic patterns of Whitman's own life.

Allen's book appeared nearly at the same time as another narrative that offered a cyclic reading of Whitman's life and work—Roger Asselineau's Evolution of Walt Whitman. Together, these two studies establish the metanarrative based in cyclic organicism that remains the major shaping force in the critical tradition of Leaves of Grass. The English version of Asselineau's book was published in 1960, six years after the French version (L'Evolution de Walt Whitman après la première édition des "Feuilles d'herbe"), which appeared in Paris the year before The Solitary Singer. The similarities between Allen's and Asselineau's books are remarkable, though Asselineau finds different ways of combining criticism and biography. Unlike Allen, who builds a highly suggestive theoretical framework for the job, Asselineau may appear to have kept the two modes of inquiry separated in the manner of French academic writing, devoting volume 1 (subtitled The Creation of a Personality) to the life of the poet and volume 2 (The Creation of a Book) to the works. The organic parallels, obvious in the subtitles, represent the same tensions that Allen faced—above all, the tension between evolution and creation. The former implies a natural growth or spontaneous development, whereas the latter implies an action carried out by an agent, a creator (human or otherwise). The two volumes actually overlap considerably in their use of biography and psychology to explicate and criticize the poems (and vice-versa: their use of the poems to explain the life) as well as in their attempt to balance the "natural" organicism of inspired growth with the "technical" organicism of control and unification. The main difference is organization. The first volume proceeds chronologically, or "diachronically," while the second is organized "synchronically" around major themes and artistic problems (style, language, and prosody). In volume I, Asselineau establishes his main arguments as he tells the story of how *Leaves of Grass* grew. In volume 2, he adds few new arguments, but mainly substantiates points hurried over in the narrative of volume 1, thus filling out the details of his explications.

Asselineau is less interested than Allen in writing comprehensive biography. In the narrative, he pauses hardly at all over Whitman's youth and literary apprenticeship, for example. From the start, his main goal is interpretative, and he implies that what happened before the gestation of *Leaves of Grass* had little bearing on the book's development. Walter Whitman the journalist, for example, had to "die" so that Walt Whitman the poet could enter the scene. The poet was "born on the fourth of July 1855" (1.48). On this day, according to legend, *Leaves of Grass* first appeared on the bookstands (though Allen, with his usual skepticism, casts doubt on this mythic publication date [*Solitary Singer* 149]).

Arriving quickly, then, at the crucial point in Whitman's poetic career, Asselineau takes up the mystery of the poet's "birth." He begins by dismissing the New Orleans affair as a sentimental fabrication without evidence to support it. Indeed, a rereading of the notebooks leads Asselineau to conclude that the personal changes that brought forth *Leaves of Grass* in 1855 "had been in preparation for a long time" and had probably begun as early as 1847, well before the poet traveled to the South (1.48-49). He is also skeptical over other theories about the origin of the *Leaves*—including Bucke's idea of cosmic consciousness (which he finds more "attractive" than the New Orleans tale, but no more convincing), Edward Hungerford's suggestion that Whitman was emboldened to take up his new career by a flattering phrenological reading, and Trowbridge's hypothesis that Whitman's reading of Emerson provided "the spark that made it possible for him to achieve at one stroke the synthesis of hitherto inert elements" (1.49-55). The intensity of *Leaves of Grass*, Asselineau implies, could not have have arisen merely from the poet's reading, no matter how strongly he may have responded to Emerson, Carlyle, or George Sand. In final analysis, "all the hypotheses that have been suggested for the origin of *Leaves of Grass* prove equally unsatisfactory" (1.61); each theory "is too partial and accounts for only one aspect of the question" (1.61). In an empirical mood, Asselineau joins Allen by admitting "an inability to penetrate the mystery" (1.61). *Leaves of Grass* emerged from a "supersaturated solution"—the mind of the poet in the 1850s—that "remained amorphous until a sudden crystallization occurred": "No one has discovered the crystal which served as a 'germ,' and probably no one ever will" (1.61-62).

Borrowing from the language of science in this passage (and in others throughout the book), Asselineau follows the practice of European humanists of his day (and our own—as any reader of

Foucault, Habermas, and Derrida can attest) in appearing to seek rhetorical support for his "scientific" skepticism. The rhetoric notwithstanding, he does not sustain an empirical approach to the poems for very long, relenting first of all to critical evaluation (ever a subjective art, even when technical matters are considered) and then to speculation on the mingling of psychological and artistic effects.

He shares with Perry and Allen a willingness to pass judgment— often quite harshly—upon Whitman's poems. Though he finds the "content" of the 1855 *Leaves* "already extremely rich," for instance, Asselineau goes further than most scholars in criticizing the poems of the first edition, which he considers "a heterogeneous and rather poorly constructed book," not yet possessing the maturity of the later work (1.63). Like Allen, he finds much that is distasteful in the second edition as well. By 1856, buoyed up by the praise of Emerson, Whitman was "no longer . . . an amateur," but a professional author. Verging on "delusions of grandeur," the poet of 1856 shifted his stance; no longer content to "sing" himself, he strove to become the "Bard of Democracy" (1.85). No longer "an anonymous pamphlet," the book took on a "commercial character"—complete with a blurb from Emerson and a bona fide publisher. And yet, true to the tradition of critical biographers from Burroughs on down, Asselineau tempers his criticism with a strong measure of praise. Although the 1856 *Leaves* had been "vulgarized," in Asselineau's estimate, it was also "considerably enriched" by new poems, many of them on a theme "close to his heart"—sexual liberation—which in this new edition would be connected yet the more strongly to associated themes, the idea of the spiritual journey and "the theme of the universe contemplated in its totality or in its perpetual becoming" (1.80-84). Asselineau is somewhat less forgiving in his assessment of the poems added to the *Leaves* after 1871. He suggests that Whitman was less successful in his efforts at sublimation than Holloway and Allen seemed to think. "The new poems show him tired of life and of its perpetual struggles," says Asselineau; "He would like to escape from his body and launch himself with his soul in search of God" (1.189). But this "spiritual solution," Asselineau implies in an influential reading, lacks the artistic honesty of the poems published in the 1850s and 1860s (1.190). The "quiet labor of self-censorship" that began in 1871 would continue to affect not only his production of new poems but also his revisions of old ones, with the result that the power embodied in the early poems gradually faded along with the poet's declining health and spirits (1.247). Asselineau refuses to hedge about what he thinks it was that the poet felt he had to censor in the poems: It was the expression of his homosexuality.

In developing this daring thesis, Asselineau departs from the more cautious biographers in his readiness to approach gaps of evidence with a speculative spirit and the flair of a story-teller. The result is a biographical study that, while lacking Allen's accuracy and authority, avoids the occasional vagueness of phrases like "emotional pressure," "perturbations," and "homoeroticism," to which Allen had to resort in the absence of hard evidence. By contrast, having dismissed the New Orleans story and drawing on a neglected reading suggested by Edward Carpenter (*Some Friends of Walt Whitman* 9), Asselineau substitutes another romance—this time a story of homosexual love—which eventually emerges as Asselineau's explanatory principle of Whitman's poetic productivity. Conceding that it is "impossible to arrive at any certainty" about the "obscure period" of the late fifties, Asselineau speculates, mainly from internal evidence, that Whitman experienced at the time "a severe moral crisis." His continuing concern with "sexual problems" surfaced in his newspaper editorials ("in spite of the reprobation which he was sure to encounter") and, with renewed emotion, in the 1860 *Leaves*, "which shows unequivocal traces of a painful emotional disappointment" (1.107). The inescapable conclusion, for Asselineau, is that Whitman "experienced in 1858-59 . . . a great passion for a man about whom nothing is known," a passion "so violent and so exclusive that it superceded everything that concerned him previously" (1.107-8). "Drunk with love," Whitman experienced the "exaltation" that inspired his mystical performances of the third edition as well as the sense of adventure expressed in the celebrations of the "open road" (1.108).

Throughout his life, Asselineau's Whitman experienced the cycles of emotion hinted at in the "Calamus" poems in their 1860 version, periods of "disillusion, doubt, and despair," followed by a recovery of the "fervor" he needed to produce his best poems (1.161). Out of these cycles of passion came the wavering emotion that could account for the unevenness of the poet's productivity, both quality and quantity. "The most difficult battle . . . was . . . with his wild homosexual desires, which never left him at peace and constantly menaced his balance," Asselineau writes (2.259). From this emotional war came both good and ill. An archetype of the alienated artist, Asselineau's Whitman was driven to write *Leaves of Grass* by the very struggle with his homosexuality, yet his "anomaly . . . also explains his inability to renew himself as he grew older—unlike Goethe" (2.259-60). Whitman "lived too much alone, too much wrapped up in himself," and finally the solitude, out of which came the great poems, "drove him to despair" and left "at the very core of himself, a sense of defeat and frustration" (2.260).

Dealing with Whitman's struggle against his homosexual desires, Asselineau repeats a key conclusion, looking back on his biographical study in a 1974 essay: "Without a doubt it was his art which saved him by permitting him to express (literally) the troubled passions which haunted him. His poetry was a means of purification. It was not the song of the demi-god depicted by the hagiographers, but the sorrowful pouring forth of a sick soul which sought passionately to understand itself and recover its self-possession" ("Walt Whitman" 241). In Asselineau's *Evolution*, then—a work which anticipates the contributions of psychoanalytical criticism—the modernist demystification and secularization of Whitman's accomplishment is almost complete, as is the development of a cyclic organicism that traces the poet's progress through periods of growth and decline—defined holistically and including the physical, psychological, and artistic elements of the poet's life and work. All of this Asselineau manages without submitting to the psychoanalyst's demand for clinical distance and without forfeiting entirely genetic organicism's hope of discovering a key to the poet's character. Despite his empiricist tendencies, Asselineau remains faithful to his interpretive key—his perception of Whitman's homosexual struggle with himself. Gay readers may take offense at Asselineau's sympathetic but somewhat illiberal pronouncements about Whitman's "sick soul," but they can hardly deny the originality and importance of the biographical critic's claim that Whitman's homosexuality was central to his life's work and that Whitman faced the consequences of his sexual tendencies throughout his career, not merely during the time that he wrote "Calamus" (a key point that Charley Shively preserves even as he strips away Asselineau's strong implication of homosexual guilt).

Nearly twenty years would pass before other critical biographers would follow in the impressive wake of Allen and Asselineau. When they did, they could add little in the way of biographical detail, new anecdotes, or even new interpretations of the poems. But biography is often a signal for the shifting tides of generations in literary studies. Not surprisingly, then, as the New Criticism gave way to the explosion of historicism in the late 1970s and the 1980s, new biographical studies came forward to support the revival of research into the historical and political contexts of *Leaves of Grass* (a movement covered in chapter 4).

Joseph Jay Rubin's *The Historic Whitman* (1973) gives the fullest discussion available of Whitman's politics during the 1840s and 1850s, but abruptly ends just at 1855, when the first edition of the *Leaves* is published. The exact connection between the themes (and even the form) of the poems and their historical context would have to be established by the further study of later critics (notably Wynn Thomas and Betsy Erkkila).

Justin Kaplan's *Walt Whitman: A Life* (1980) explores somewhat more fully than Allen and other predecessors Whitman's relation to the popular culture of Victorian America—the cranks and snake-oil sellers as well as the more respectable literary figures. Kaplan's treatment of urban life and of the spiritualists, phrenologists, free lovers, and penny-press journalists who flourished in Whitman's day provides a biographical accompaniment or prelude to the work of writers like Harold Aspiz and David Reynolds.

Paul Zweig's *Walt Whitman: The Making of the Poet* (1984) works the same territory, but offers what was, at the time the book appeared and with the possible exception of Schyberg (see chapter 3), the most detailed study of how, in notebooks and multiple draft manuscripts of the poems, Whitman reveals his transformative power. Having heard "the din of the national temperament," the poet took the "vulgar symbols" of popular press and political forum and "filled them with his own meanings." In the process, he became "a masterful poet of personal change" (244-45). If Rubin leaves Whitman at the beginning of his poetic career, Zweig leaves him at the zenith, the end of the 1860s. Anticipating the conclusion of Michael Moon's recent study, Zweig writes, "During the Civil War, Whitman's 'language experiment' had ended in a violent commingling of life and art" (345).

Psychoanalytical Criticism

This "violent commingling of life and art" has absorbed no group more fully than Whitman's psychoanalytical critics. Paralleling the growth of critical biography, psychoanalysis developed an interest in Whitman as early as the 1920s and has continued to produce its characteristically probing and provocative criticism ever since, occasionally overlapping with more traditional biography, but not so much as one might expect.

The reasons for the distance between the two practices are mainly methodological. The psychoanalytical critic brings an elaborate theoretical framework to the task of interpreting the life and work of the artist that few biographers, caught up in their narrative task, can afford to review, explicate, or justify. Critical biography and psychoanalysis certainly share an interest in a "scientific" approach to literature and a professional ethos, complete with ironic distance and a skeptical outlook, but they appeal to different authorities. Critical biography takes solace in empirical historiography, with the ultimate goal of giving precedence to verifiable facts, even if that means abandoning cherished theories and interpretive frameworks. To the outsider, psychoanalysis appears to do the opposite. The most orthodox practitioners seem to force subjects into rigidly defined theoretical categories, aiming not so much to illuminate the life and writings of the individual artist as to use the artist as a "case" to demonstrate certain truths and problems in psychological theory. In its more subtle and complex modes, however, psychoanalytical criticism cultivates a dialectical relation between theoretical concepts and the individual case, allowing one to engage and transform the other. Over the years, Whitman scholars have produced both varieties of psychoanalytical criticism. Practitioners of this approach have taken a special interest in the two critical-biographical problems that Malcolm Cowley calls "The Secret" and "The Miracle."

The Secret refers to Whitman's homosexuality, and the Miracle refers to the apparently sudden eruption of *Leaves of Grass* in 1855.

The stage was set for the study of the poet's sexual inclinations by the clinical tradition in the European human sciences. Indeed, Whitman's name and "case" appeared in the earliest treatment of homosexuality as a clinical condition late in the nineteenth century— Havelock Ellis's landmark study *Sexual Inversion* (1897). The book was co-authored with John Addington Symonds, the homosexual scholar who had tried to get Whitman to go on record about the true nature of his sexual preferences, only to be greeted with the story of the poet's heterosexual adventures and illegitimate children. In his own *Walt Whitman: A Study*, Symonds refuses to go against Whitman's authority; instead, he suggestively aligns Whitman's "Calamus" and *Drum-Taps* with the Greek tradition of heroic male friendship. He is not much less inhibited in the statements he makes as one of Ellis' anonymous informants in the study reported in *Sexual Inversion*. Nevertheless, in the latter context, the attribution of homosexuality to Whitman comes through clearly enough. Not only Symonds, but other of the informants (including Whitman's correspondent Edward Carpenter), use Whitman's term *comrade* to refer to homosexual lovers, thus indicating also the degree of influence Whitman had on the burgeoning homosexual awareness movement in England at the turn of the century (Sedgwick 203-206).

Ellis opened the way for a brisk interchange among European readers of Whitman in the early twentieth century. The German critic Eduard Bertz, in *Der Yankee-Heiland* (1906), debunks the "Yankee-Saint" image of Whitman and reveals what he considers to be the psychopathology of the homosexual artist. "The feminine and even hysterical *Grundton* of his being is obvious to any observant reader," Bertz writes; "No one familiar with modern psychology and sex-pathology is in the slightest doubt that the erotic friendship, which is found in the poetry and life of our wonderful prophet, is to be explained in any other way than by his constitutional deviation from the masculine norm" (qtd. in Allen, *Handbook* 38-39). Along the same lines, although with considerably less critical fervor, W. C. Rivers published a study in 1913 on what he called "Walt Whitman's anomaly." Like Bertz, Rivers emphasizes the "essentially . . . passive" and "feminine" character of Whitman's homosexuality (64).

Whitman's admirer and imitator Edward Carpenter was the first to take issue with these critics, and he did so, at least partly, on methodological grounds. In *Some Friends of Walt Whitman: A Study in Sex Psychology* (1924), he argues that Rivers's book "embodies again the same defect" found in the continental critics—namely, "a certain vulgarity of view. The author . . . accentuate[s] the petty or pathological marks but fails altogether to realize that the feminine characteristics in such a case *may* have a most important meaning as pointing to the evolution of a *higher* type of humanity . . . a form inclusive of the feminine as well as the masculine" (13-14). Carpenter longs for an "investigation of homo sexuality [sic], not as a sin or a crime, but as a natural phenomenon"; and, in a rebuke that has become something of a tradition in gay criticism, he faults Symonds for rudely confronting Whitman with questions too direct for the old man to answer candidly, thereby undermining his own and Ellis's plan to provide the first truly scientific study of homosexual human nature (12).

By the time Carpenter wrote, though, Freud and his followers had begun to dominate the psychiatric scene in Europe; and, in the most direct application of Freud's system up to his time, Jean Catel turns away from what seemed to be becoming an easy diagnosis of an effeminate homosexuality in Whitman. In *La naissance du poète* (1929), Catel offers an interpretation of the sudden emergence of the *Leaves* that would prove extremely attractive to later biographers and critics (notably Allen, Asselineau, and Stephen A. Black). Rejecting both the New Orleans romance and the story of prophetic inspiration, Catel argues that Whitman was primarily *autoerotic*. Drifting toward melancholy and becoming increasingly self-absorbed, the poet steadily withdrew from the world of social contact to live in a fantasy world of his own creation, according to Catel. The poet was "born" when the moody and withdrawn Whitman of the late 1840s and early 1850s discovered that out of his fantasies he could form a literary link with the outer world again and thereby save himself as a social being. The exuberance he found as a result of this salvation rang forth in the rhetoric of political and sexual freedom.

Whatever the strength and subtlety of Catel's argument, however, its presence did not dispel altogether the fascination among psychoanalytical critics with Whitman's passive "femininity." In an article published in 1951 and reprinted as late as 1967, Gustav Bychowski confidently asserts, "Because of his prenatal, narcissistic and maternal fixation, Whitman's masculine ego never fully developed" (159). With this diagnosis—and despite Bychowski's professed admiration of Whitman's poems—we come full circle, returning to Bertz's early-century unmasking of the poet he presumed to be a pathological homosexual masquerading as the bard of democracy.

Such orthodox Freudian criticism extends the genetic branch of the organic tradition by seeking a central psychological motive for Whitman's poetic production and character. Picking up the themes introduced by Catel, however, and drawing further upon Erik Erikson and post-Freudian ego psychology, the two most original of Whitman's psychoanalytical critics shift toward the cyclic version of organicism. Although both Edwin Haviland Miller and Stephen A. Black preserve the normative conservatism of psychoanalysis to some degree, they focus not so much on rigidly defined psychological types and symptoms, but rather emphasize psychological processes. Their informing metaphor is not the gene or the germ, but the journey.

The journey motif is particularly useful because it allows for a balance between the classical motives of passion and action. On his journey, the poet experiences growth both passively, as he is beset by urgings from instinct or the unconscious, and actively, as he attempts consciously to control his world and to create an alternate poetic world by mapping out new paths of development. His work is partly conscious, partly unconscious; it is organic both in the sense that he lets his inner nature lead him where it may and in the sense that he attempts, in the manner theorized by the New Critics, to construct a form that unifies the disparate elements of his experience—a "stately pleasure dome" whose builder, like Coleridge's Kubla Khan, strives to harmonize the natural and the technical.

Edwin Haviland Miller cogently summarizes these points in the preface to *Walt Whitman's Poetry: A Psychological Journey* (1968). Extending Asselineau's concept of Whitman's life as continual struggle marked by cyclic periods of growth and decline, Miller emphatically denies a continuous or progressive march toward higher poetic attainment; he writes, "to say that the journey is from darkness to light or from innocence to awareness is unsatisfactory, since it removes Whitman's journey from the psychic terrain in which it takes place and conventionalizes his insights into the human personality" (vii). To conventionalize Whitman, Miller argues, would be to destroy that which makes him unique among his contemporaries. Most nineteenth-century writers "were in one way or another examining the nature of the self," but none so courageously and unconventionally as Whitman; "he alone explored frankly the sexual origins of art and attitudes, the physical nature of the soul, the enduring significance of infantile needs and aspirations, and the endless quest not for intellectual consistency but for emotional security" (vii).

Like Catel, Allen, and Asselineau, Miller understands Whitman's work as an attempt to reconcile himself to his own inability to break out of himself into a world of satisfying social contact. "Song of Myself," for example, Miller reads as "the reverie of the outsider, the isolate, the perennial American protestant, who struggles to reassert the collective dream, only to end, as Whitman does, in a retreat into the self that copes with, or, perhaps more precisely, evades, reality through imaginative transcendence into the timelessness and harmony of art"; thus, the "serio-comic tone" of the poem "serves as a protective mechanism to disguise the poet's uncertainty and disenchantment from his audience and probably from himself," which in turn gives rise to "another characteristic device," his "amorous dialogue with his audience—'And what I assume you shall assume.'" Miller is impressed less with the artfulness than with the "trickery of the device," which "reveals not only society's failure but Whitman's too: although many people appear in the poem, no one converses with the protagonist, who is, in final analysis, as thwarted as the old maid who in her fantasy caresses the bodies of twenty-eight swimmers" in section 11 of "Song of Myself" (86-87).

The cycles that Whitman undergoes on his journey tend to follow a fairly explicit pattern, in Miller's reading. The poet encounters a point of psychic tension and discovers a defensive means for coping with it, but the apparent resolution is tenuous, and the tension returns at various stages, often indicated by compulsive repetitions and rhythms that bespeak the needs of the body and the mind more than the needs of artistic unity. Thus, while Miller shares with the New Critics a concern with the resolution of tensions, and with an artistic world isolated from the extrinsic forces of the "real world," he explains the world not by the universal laws of aesthetic beauty, but rather by the laws of psychic dynamics. In other words, Whitman's "genius" and his rare "greatness" have less to do with the usual concerns of criticism—"genres, traditional structure, rhetoric, and so forth"—and more to do with psychology: "the tensions in his poems are . . . psychic," and the resulting "inner drama" displays "an inevitable progression and its own psychic laws, for tensions and conflicts must find some kind of resolution or release" (vii-viii).

For Miller, then, "the long foreground" that preceded the "miracle" of *Leaves of Grass* did not emerge from a context of literary life, but rather from a context of thwarted family relations. Whitman compensated throughout his life for an unhappy childhood. He not only created an ideal family in his poems—which on frequent occasions betray the reality of the unhappy life experienced by a disaffected son—but he also tried to manipulate his "real" social environment so that it would satisfy his unmet needs. Throughout his life, for example, he surrounded himself with young men of the working class, the "roughs" whose relation to Whitman the middle-class Burroughs could never understand. Instead of following Cowley in jumping to a homosexual hypothesis about Whitman's relation to these young men, Miller inserts a number of graduated stages, in which the roughs fill the role of Whitman's substitute family members, whom he can identify with as a neglected son and can love as his mother never really loved him (8-11).

Against this background of emotional struggle, as Miller conceives it, Whitman's politics can only seemed forced and ranting. Sliding from a discussion of Whitman into a general pronouncement, Miller writes, "Ideology, political or otherwise, is the work of a harried mind at work vainly seeking to fill emotional needs through cerebral evasion of those needs' (12). Whitman's forte, Miller insists, is not the "noisy evangelism" of political, religious, or programmatic verse, but lyricism, the work of a "passive comptemplator, an observer who more successfully than most men [and women] handles his emotional needs by honestly searching for self-understanding" (12).

And yet, though Miller is concerned primarily with psychological causes and effects in Whitman's poems, he is not averse to dealing, at least tangentially, with cultural factors, such as "the anomaly and isolation of the artist in a materialistic society, the ambivalence of protestantism toward women, and ... the weakening of patriarchal concepts in a land which demanded almost heroic sacrifices from those who wanted to conquer and to fulfill the American dream" (149). In Whitman's day, a code of behavior arose that, "like all codes, camouflaged the insecurity which gave rise to it and crippled individualism in the name of phony masculinity" (150). Against this background, Whitman wrote "Calamus" perhaps as a compensation for lost homosexual love, but more poignantly, in Miller's view, as "a lament for the loss of love" in a more general sense—the loss of the very possibility of love.

In his conclusion, Miller writes, "*Leaves of Grass* is not ... a unified work; the poet's arrangements and rearrangements demonstrate that it did not grow organically but was arbitrarily contrived according to a vague scheme" (223). The growth of *Leaves of Grass* from one edition to the next does not reveal what Miller understands as the contours of poetic and psychic formation, nor does the chronological sequence of the poems accomplish the unification, as Allen suggests it might. Because Whitman encountered the psychic tensions that produced his poems in a structure characterized by a temporary resolution followed by a return of the repressed—a structure which took different forms as the poet aged and adjusted his relation to the social rearrangements taking place around him—Miller's reading of the poems follows an allegorical arrangement emphasizing the various stages of the poet's psychic and behavioral development. The 1855 "Song of Myself," says Miller in a typical reading, is no less "homosexual" than the 1860 "Calamus," in which the poet of 1860 claims to step upon "paths untrodden." Miller argues that, contrary to the poet's claims, "He explores no new 'paths' in 'Calamus'; he merely uncovers with fewer indirections the narcissistic and homosexual bases of his art" (142). He is able to bring himself to do so, Miller asserts, because by the time he composed the poems of 1860 his father, who was still alive while Whitman composed the 1855 poems, had died.

Thus, armed with the tools of ego psychology and empowered further by the perspective of time and distance, Miller weighs unconscious revelations against conscious purposes to arrive at a reading that the poet himself could not have constructed, no matter how free and bold he may have been. The psychoanalytical method suggests that only through the interpretive efforts of close readers can the growth of *Leaves of Grass* be completed in the transformation of lyric into allegory of life and work—a journey with universal appeal and significance.

Stephen A. Black's *Whitman's Journey into Chaos* (1975) shares this outlook with Miller's book and reveals interpretive similarities as well. The "patterns and conflicts" that Black identifies are quite similar to those with which Miller is concerned—above all Whitman's portrayal of "a futile wish for a father's love, the [spiritual] death of a child, [and] the covert attack on a seductive mother" (Black 19). But Black's book has more of a phenomenological cast than Miller's. He is deeply concerned with how fully the poet comprehended his own sexual relation to others as well as the larger relation of the self to his psychic and social environment. Thus, of "Song of Myself," Black writes, "What begins as a celebration of the self becomes a troublesome question: who and what am I?" (93). Unlike Miller, who was, according to Black's reading, "convinced that Whitman was overtly and actively homosexual and generally conscious of the sexual meanings of his poems," Black believes (with Catel) that Whitman was "chiefly autoerotic" and that the poet "tended to keep hidden from himself both his homosexual impulses and his sexual confusions" (5). Black also insists that Miller overstates Whitman's power to resolve his psychic crises, but I think this is a misreading of Miller, who, though he greatly admires Whitman, often to the point of heroizing him, carefully maps the return of the repressed in Whitman's work. Naturally enough, Black appears somewhat anxious to distinguish his work from Miller's, which appeared only a few years before.

It is quite clear, however, that Black does depart from the traditional tendency of psychoanalysis to tie interpretations exclusively to past events from the analysand's childhood. Instead, Black focuses on psychic events in process at the time the poems were written, giving special attention to the poems published during the crucial decade of 1855-1865. Nevertheless, he suggests that Whitman's early writings should not be neglected. The fiction is especially useful, for it reveals "in naïve simplicity the subtle and complex psychological patterns and conflicts underlying *Leaves of Grass*"; where *Leaves of Grass* succeeds, however, the early writings fail, in Black's estimate, "because when Whitman employed stock situations and devices of characterization his own unconscious attitudes and assumptions intruded upon the material. Unconscious forces conflicted with the intent to be conventional" (16-17). The "original energy" that the poet was able to muster and channel into the creative process leading up to the 1855 *Leaves* involved, by contrast, a descent into the chaos of the unconscious, from which Whitman emerged with a temporary and very tenuous, though frequently exhilarating, command of his key symbols and unconventional language.

The poet of the 1850s thus achieved a "catharsis" in the Freudian sense (not the Aristotelian sense), which allowed him to feel that he had resolved the main conflicts of his inner life (47-48). But with each such exploration of his own unconscious, fearful thoughts emerged ever more clearly. Before the late 1850s, for example, Whitman was only vaguely conscious of the homosexual import of many of his symbols, according to Black. By the time he wrote "Calamus," he had begun to see them ever more certainly and was horrified. Thus, he had to balance his near confessions with his political vision of brotherhood. When this defensive strategy no longer seemed to work, he dropped the theme of comradeship altogether.

With this step, he may have saved himself considerable psychic pain, but ironically, in Black's view, he destroyed himself as a poet. Black writes, "As the poet increasingly sought to fulfill in real life the ideals and fantasies underlying his poetry"—in his role as "wound dresser" during the Civil War, for example—"his creative excursions into the regressive, unconscious world, the source of his poetic power, became fewer and more superficial" (221). And thus, the creative effort that had gone into his poems now went into his life, his attempt to live up to the image provided mainly by others, most especially William Douglas O'Connor's ideal of the "good gray poet."

Black's and Miller's use of the journey motif and their appropriation of cyclic organicism allow them to synthesize insights from both psychological and cultural analysis—two approaches to literature that, in an oversimplified and methodologically stilted criticism, could seem mutually exclusive. A similar synthetic approach is employed by two later psychoanalytical critics who also make use of the insights that come from historical study—Michael Moon (whose work is considered in chapter 4) and David Cavitch.

Picking up Black's suggestion that "nearly all of the important poems were composed before 1860" (Black 3), Cavitch argues that "by the outbreak of the Civil War [Whitman] was virtually worn out as a poet: undermined morally not by public neglect of his poetry but largely by his culture's massive repudiation of the meaning of his inner life" (44). Cavitch, who also draws upon phenomenological analysis, joins Black in delineating Whitman's anxiety over his accomplishments—not just his poetic achievements, but his very ability to maintain a clear sense of selfhood: "He could not glorify himself without also anticipating annihilation" (71). In the manner of Emily Dickinson, he "constantly glances ahead beyond the limits of personal experience to the abyss of death in which he finds no one at all in the emptiness: imagine there is nothing, he taunts himself, imagine there is no self" (71). Thus: "Even during the first splendid upwelling of his creative genius, his ascent to imaginative freedom and joy had to be weighted by his deep habituation to anxiety and depression" (71).

With this outlook before us, we have come a long way on a quick journey through the biographical criticism of Whitman's poems—from the first writings of Whitman's friends, who hailed the charismatic poet as a personal savior, down to the later psychoanalytical writers, who show us a Whitman barely able to save himself.

Appearances to the contrary, however, these later writers have not lost sympathy for the poet. What they reflect is rather the modern sense of the precariousness of selfhood in a fearful world. In other words, they have not lost their admiration for Whitman so much as they have lost the confident optimism that O'Connor, Burroughs, and Bucke had in confronting the natural and social world. For modern readers, selfhood is no longer a rock-hard certainty, but has become a struggle, a process of becoming, a journey beset by the worry that, in real life as well as in poetry, one's identity constantly drifts toward "maya, illusion," to use the terms suggested in a dark "Calamus" moment (*Leaves: Norton* 123).

In the next chapter, I explore how literary modernism, which Whitman himself anticipated, conspires with the professionalist division of labor to continue this movement, all but eliminating considerations of the person in its examination of the poem and thus pressing literary criticism toward "textualism," a full identification of life and art (Rorty). Art comes to serve as the model for how everyone constructs the world in the absence of a bona fide reality. In a world dominated not by people but by texts, the poet survives mainly as a name, a convenient linguistic marker for a body of literature. Or, in a related way, the name "Walt Whitman" refers not to an exemplary person, but rather to that specialized, functional entity, the literary figure—with a pun on figure, indicating in the case of Whitman a persona, a character who in 1855 names himself as the subject of his own poem—"Walt Whitman, an American, one of the roughs, a kosmos" (*Leaves of Grass [1855]* 50).

3: The Poet

In his 1932 book *Discusión*, Jorge Luis Borges offers a negative assessment of critical writings on Walt Whitman. Repeating his point some twenty years later in his "Note on Walt Whitman," Borges complains that the commentators on Whitman's work always resort to "the senseless adoption of the style and vocabulary of [the] poems"—including, presumably, the vocabulary of literary organicism—and, in a still more bothersome and related "error," the critics persist in confusing "Whitman, the man of letters, with Whitman, the semidivine hero of *Leaves of Grass*" (144). Would anyone so confuse Homer with Odysseus, Borges wonders, or Cervantes with Quixote?

In defense of the critical tradition, we may reply that no author before Whitman plays quite so elaborate a game with autobiography and poetic rhetoric. This difference has strongly affected the way critics have gradually come to grips with the nature of Whitman's contribution to the history of letters. Their cycling of his language and concepts back through their own work is part of the process of incorporating him into the tradition of Western literary study. Their treatment of the identity of person and poet can only remain problematical even as it seemingly grows in complexity and sophistication.

We have seen how, in *A Backward Glance O'er Travel'd Roads*, Whitman actively encourages his readers to think of his book as an attempt to "express in literary or poetic form ... [his] own ... Personality," to give "one man's—the author's—identity, ardors, observations, faiths, and thoughts, color'd hardly at all with any decided coloring from other faiths or other identities" (*Leaves: Norton* 563). Certainly, in their studies of this "Personality," the biographical critics appear to have followed the poet—but not as far as Borges suggests. Beginning in the 1950s, the very time when Borges reiterates his critique, critical biographers were fashioning a kind of double organicism that hypothesized a strong distinction between the organic networks of living systems (nature and history) and the organic unity of poems. According to one version of this theory (Allen's), Walt Whitman the person intrudes upon the world of his poetic creation only at the risk of spoiling the effects of his art. In another version (Asselineau's and later Black's), Whitman's finest poems are those that betray the heaviest personal investment of emotions; the quality of the work diminishes as it drifts toward conventionalism, with the self remaining outside, an observer and maker of a poetic world. Both approaches require an understanding of the potential difference between Whitman the man of letters and Whitman the hero of the poems, though both deny an absolute separation of the two beings.

On the question of the identity of his poetic character, Whitman himself resorted to this doubleness. At one point, he appears to have dropped his famous "personalism" altogether. He found himself in an awkward position, defending against a reader who had taken his heroic self-assertions more seriously and more literally than he would have wished. Not an irate reviewer, but an admirer, the Englishwoman Anne Gilchrist, after reading *Leaves of Grass*, proposed to become the author's wife and bear his child. Whitman recoiled from the proposal, falling back upon a critical position that separates the poetic hero from the writer—and the writer from the reader with whom the hero, by contrast, warmly identifies ("every atom belonging to me as good belongs to you" [*Leaves: Norton* 28]). "Dear friend," the man of letters replies on 20 March 1872, "let me warn you somewhat about myself—& yourself also. You must not construct such an unauthorized & imaginary ideal Figure, & call it W. W. and so devotedly invest your loving nature in it. The actual W. W. is a very plain personage, & entirely unworthy such devotion" (*Correspondence* 2.170). The letter shifts the interpretive responsibility away from the author, toward the reader who is charged with "constructing" an "imaginary ideal Figure" that is "unauthorized," devoid of the poet's authority. The man of letters escapes as a "very plain personage" in a move that no doubt would have pleased Borges.

Other instances suggest that, in escaping Gilchrist's proposal, Whitman was not merely theorizing under the pressure of an embarrassing moment. In one of the "Calamus" poems of 1860—later titled "Are You the New Person Drawn Toward Me?"—he shows that he had already considered a position similar to the one implied in the 1872 letter to his admirer. The reader of the poem ("you") is advised to "take warning." The speaker ("I") claims he is "surely far different from what you suppose." "Do you suppose you will find in me your ideal?" he asks; "Do you suppose yourself advancing on real ground toward a real heroic man?" Then, with a tone of cool distance, all but foreign to the poet of 1855, he challenges the reader's faith in his poetic ethos: "Have you no thought O dreamer that it may be all maya, illusion?" (*Leaves: Norton* 123).

In oscillating between a personalist and a somewhat more rhetorical understanding of the relationship between author, reader, and poetic character, Whitman becomes an early participant in what Robert C. Elliott describes as a "massive shift [in the early twentieth century] ... away from ... the confessional style of much nineteenth-century writing" (13). This view—"popularized by Ezra Pound, given impetus by Yeats, [and] institutionalized by Eliot"—"holds that the 'I' of a poem is a dramatized 'I,' no more to be identified with the actual poet living in history than the Bishop ordering his tomb is to be identified with Robert Browning" (16). This understanding of the literary persona appealed strongly to the New Critics. As a means of theorizing the difference between the poetic "I" and the "man of letters," it is an especially useful way of reconciling seemingly autobiographical elements with an organic theory of art purified of extrinsic influences. If nothing but internal evidence can be summoned in a "close reading" of a poem, then the concept of the persona provides a way to discuss characters indicated by words like "I" and "you." In ordinary discourse, such words shift attention to the outer context of the discourse. "I" relates to the speaker, "you" to the listener. But the idea of the persona as a figure of speech allows a critic to read "I" and "you" as invented characters confined by the narrow context of the poem's structure.

Accordingly, when we read Whitman's famous lines, "Camerado, this is no book, / Who touches this touches a man" (*Leaves: Norton* 505), we know that we are in the realm of a literary transformation; and when the trope shifts to a yet more personal suggestion—the assertion that "It is I you hold and who holds you"—the "I" we read is obviously not a real man in our hands, but a figure of speech, a metaphor portraying the book as a man—the author who, like a departed lover in one of Poe's poems, comes back from the dead to haunt our reading. And what about "you"? That must be the ideal reader, portrayed as a lover who caresses the traces of the author's presence (the corpus of his poems). Both "I" and "you" are therefore constructs to be explained not by reference to the world beyond the text but by an economy of figural relations contained within the poem (to be exact, a special instance of poetic apostrophe or prosopopoeia).

Of course, the poem could also be explained (in the biographical mode) by reference to the poet's need for companionship, which, frustrated in real life, breaks forth in poems that create an ideal community of readers to meet emotional needs unfulfilled by real companions. Or we could say (in the historicist mode) that this community is constructed to model the kind of genuine face-to-face interchanges threatened in Whitman's day by the onset of a literate, specialized, incorporated culture that the poet resists in favor of the kind of social life he sees slipping away—an older village culture, whose values are artisanal and radically democratic. Or, yet again (now following the prophetic line of interpretation), we could say that the poem is a kind of incantation against the onset of an impersonal, bureaucratic America, the prospects of which the poet-prophet cannot tolerate.

None of these approaches, however, is satisfactory in the view of a criticism that strives to become exclusively literary, that attempts to explain artistic success in purely aesthetic and structural terms. If the biographical, historical, and prophetic modes treat the poem as an open system, with meaningful links connecting the text to various points in the life of the author (and the life of the audience), the aesthetic mode treats the poem as a closed system with its own internally generated laws of operation. The world outside is merely an environment, a background, a source of resonances perhaps but not of meanings comprehensible within the semantic structure of the poem.

Literary studies in the first half of the twentieth century came to favor readings of poems as closed texts. In many ways, this change represented a correcting force directed against the dominant preoccupation with historical philology and biography. In the eyes of the New Critics, the literary profession was becoming a footnote factory with no appreciation for the beauty of poems and no understanding of how poems really work. By drawing upon the practices of popular critics and by developing their own theories out of the texts of classical poetics and rhetoric, the New Critics labored to return attention to the act of reading by eliminating "noise" in the system, the preoccupation with "background" that interfered with the critic's direct experience of the poem.

Despite its attractiveness, this purified literary criticism never really caught on in Whitman studies, partly because, as Borges suggests, Whitman scholars have never been able to rid themselves of the idea that Whitman really meant what he said about singing himself. But there are other reasons as well, which have to do with the character of Whitman's poetic composition. To read *Leaves of Grass* as a closed system tends to impoverish it. It is a book that, at its best, turns the reader's attention outward from itself. Moreover, in its many editions, it refuses to stand still long enough to become an artifact to be lovingly admired and analyzed by interpreters seeking the principles of internal structure and logic. Its insides keep going out again. Thus, even the most devoted formalists among Whitman's critics have to discover the means of compensating for the swirl of process that seems ever to attend the product that Whitman offered. In Whitman studies, the New Criticism has yielded, for the most part, to rhetorical criticism, an analysis of how meaning flows (consciously or unconsciously) from an author to an audience through the mediating patterns and structures of the poems' language, a medium that shifts according to the exigencies of a changing rhetorical situation.

This literary criticism—with a somewhat attenuated stress on literary—divided during the 1950s into two branches. The first—the analytical branch—developed most strongly under the direct influence of the New Criticism. Practitioners of this approach, such as James E. Miller, Jr., and Howard J. Waskow, have applied various types of close reading to *Leaves of Grass*, seeking internal principles of organic unity—the key themes and stylistic or generic trends of Whitman's art. The second branch—the literary-historical—is best represented in the work of Gay

Wilson Allen and Floyd Stovall and in the more recent writings of Jerome Loving, Kenneth Price, and Ezra Greenspan. These authors have maintained closer ties with critical biography than the analytical critics while nevertheless focusing upon the professional, literary life of the poet rather than his private psychological journeys. Instead of close readings that attempt to harmonize the inner workings of the *Leaves*, the literary-historical critics produce influence and reception studies, comparative criticism, and career studies.

With the analytical interest in poetic technique and the literary-historical interest in the career and reputation of the man of letters, these two branches of Whitman studies reflect the twin forces of technical expertise and professional specialization in twentieth-century American culture, which matured in the years after World War II. Before that time, the two branches had not divided. Instead they existed incipiently in the critical movement that defended Whitman against charges of primitivism and artless crudity. Contributors to this movement sought to establish Whitman's reputation as a true poet and a rightful subject for the best literary scholarship. This early work, then, paved the way for the development of both analytical and literary-historical criticism.

Defending the Poet

The defense of the poet was directed first against the early reviews of *Leaves of Grass*. Among the first reviewers, the common complaint that Whitman's poems were crudely ignorant of the principles of high art anticipated the New Critics' reaction against Whitman's "loose" romanticism (Leitch 30). In 1865, for example, Henry James—then an all but unknown magazine writer, but later one of the gods of modern formalism—calls *Drum-Taps* "an offense against art" (qtd. in Hindus 113). If you are to be a poet, young James lectures Whitman, you must reach beyond personal and prophetic enthusiasms to attain distance and control: "Your personal qualities—the vigor of your temperament, the manly independence of your nature, the tenderness of your heart—these facts are impertinent. You must be *possessed*, and you must strive to possess your possession" (qtd. in Hindus 114).

James echoes the judgments of other negative reviews, which seem to divide equally between angry condemnations of Whitman's "licentiousness" and more sophisticated censures of his artlessness. In the latter vein, one reviewer cites Whitman's "carelessness," "impertinence," "nonchalance with regard to forms," and "indifference to the dignity of verse" arising from "an overweening confidence in the value of what is said" (qtd. in Hindus 53). Another reader finds "neither wit nor method in [Whitman's] disjointed babbling" and can only suggest that the poet "must be some escaped lunatic, raving in pitiable delirium" (qtd. in Hindus 61). Even relatively appreciative critics demurred on the issue of style and poetic form. Charles Eliot Norton, for example, says that the poems of the 1855 *Leaves* "are neither in rhyme nor blank verse, but in a sort of excited prose broken into lines without any attempt at measure or regularity, and . . . without any idea of sense or reason"; the result, in Norton's eyes, is an odd "mixture of Yankee transcendentalism and New York rowdyism" (qtd. in Hindus 24-25). Charles A. Dana, another critic favorably inclined toward Whitman's work, nevertheless declares that the *Leaves* "cannot be especially commended either for fragrance or form," though "the taste of not overdainty fastidiousness will discern much of the essential spirit of poetry beneath an uncouth and grotesque embodiment" (qtd. in Hindus 23).

The most creative early defense against such charges is found in the work of John Burroughs. Having said that Whitman is not at fault but at his best when he "lets himself go" in *Leaves of Grass*, how could Burroughs address the reviewers' complaints against the poet's artlessness? In effect, he argues that Whitman's work requires a new and bolder set of standards than those usually mustered by his contemporaries. Because conventional poetics runs toward "the precise, the exact, the methodical," it cannot comprehend the organic power of *Leaves of Grass*. The book is "not a temple" but "a wood, a field, a highway" (*Whitman* 149, 136). "In saying . . . that [Whitman] was not begotten by the literary spirit," Burroughs writes, "I only mean that his aim was that of the largest art, and of the most vital and comprehensive literature. We should have heard the last of his 'Leaves' long ago had they not possessed unmistakably the vitality of true literature, 'incomparable things, incomparably well said,' as Emerson remarked" (190).

Burroughs is justified in quoting Emerson in this connection. In the famous 1855 letter to Whitman, the language of which Burroughs appropriates, Emerson praises *Leaves of Grass* as "the most extraordinary piece of wit & wisdom that America has yet contributed." He grounds his praise in his own organic theory of literature: "[*Leaves of Grass*] meets the demand I am always making of what seemed the sterile and stingy Nature, as if too much handiwork or too much lymph in the temperament were making our western wits fat & mean" (qtd. in Hindus 21). For Emerson, then, Whitman's "free and brave thought" is, among other things, free from an excess of "handiwork"; it is not overwrought or excessively artful. Although in other statements made later Emerson follows Norton more closely—as in his joke that *Leaves of Grass* is an odd mixture of the *Bhagavad Gita* and the New York *Tribune* (qtd. in Zweig 8)—he would likely have agreed in 1855 with the broadly organic reading of the poems offered later by Burroughs. Thoreau certainly would have. In his 1856 letter about Whitman's book, he writes: "Though rude and sometimes ineffectual, [*Leaves of Grass*] is a great primitive poem,—an alarum or trumpet-note ringing through the American camp. Wonderfully like the Orientals, too" (qtd. in Hindus 68).

Beyond the transcendentalists, few of Whitman's early defenders took up this line of argument, despite its cogency. Most of the poet's friends seemed inclined to go in the other direction, head-on against the attack, insisting that Whitman ranks with the greatest poets, no matter what critical standards are applied. This approach dominates O'Connor's broad comparisons in *The Good Gray Poet*, for example, and leads Symonds to read Whitman in light of the high heroic tradition of the Greeks. Going a step further in this direction, at the turn of the century, Basil De Selincourt gives an extended and technically detailed account of Whitman's "prosody," using rules and terminology commonly applied to the analysis of traditional western poetry. Along similar lines, William Sloane Kennedy, in *The Fight of a Book for the World* (1926)—arguably the first Walt Whitman handbook—pastes together the loose ends of a reception study, a brief account of Whitman's revisions (entitled "The Growth of *Leaves of Grass* as a Work of Art"), and a few "elucidations and analyses of difficult poems." Taken together, the notes in Kennedy's "companion volume to *Leaves of Grass*" comprise an argument for the status of Whitman's work as high art and an attempt to open the way for further study by the emerging professional class of literary scholars in America and England. Whether following the comparative method of criticism, applying the technical analysis of classical philology, engaging in literary-historical research on reception, or encouraging the founding of new interpretive traditions, these appreciative commentators could not rest satisfied with readings—even favorable readings—that likened Whitman's accomplishments to those of "primitive" (read: "non-Western") poets. Their poet was an artist worthy of popular adoration and scholarly attention.

The first interesting twist in the trend toward professionalization of the poet and his critics came with Esther Shephard's 1938 book *Walt Whitman's Pose*. Picking up a hint from Burroughs (*Whitman: A Study* 107-8), Shephard argues that, more than artful, Whitman is cunning; not only in his poems, but also in his life, he is primarily a poseur. With the embittered tone of a disappointed admirer or a disillusioned cynic (reminiscent of Eduard Bertz), Shephard disregards the professional ethos of objectivity even as she presents a carefully researched source study, revealing that, from 1855, Whitman's life and major poems verge on a too-close-for-comfort correspondence with the story line and characters of George Sand's novel *The Countess of Rudolstadt*. Shephard argues that, since Whitman modeled his book and his own public persona on a character invented by the French novelist, whom he confessed to admire, the antiliterary strain in Whitman's work is a giant hoax. *Leaves of Grass*, not to mention the very person of Walt Whitman, is all literary.

With the publication of *Walt Whitman's Pose*, Shephard became persona non grata among Whitman scholars, a role she filled for decades afterward (see Asselineau, "Walt Whitman" 239-40). Her real faux pas, I would argue, is not so much that she dared refuse to worship at the poet's shrine (though certainly this may have contributed to the reaction against her work), but rather that she misread the signs of the times. The values she espouses, the romantic values of artistic honesty and confessional intensity (perhaps even personal integrity) were, under the influence of formalism, giving way to a stronger emphasis on poetic craft (and maybe craftiness as well). Few would accuse Whitman of plagiarism—Sand's novel, great and influential as it was, could not have filled both its own place and the place of *Leaves of Grass* in literary history—and, if Whitman were a poseur, according to the new lights of the twentieth century, all the better; at least he escapes naiveté. Indeed, Shephard's Whitman conforms nicely to one perfectly acceptable model of the modern poet: Out of literature, he made a life for himself, and out of that life, he made poems. In her attempt to undermine Whitman's reputation, Shephard may have helped it.

A book that appeared a few years before Shephard's (in 1933) catches the spirit of the modern era more successfully in a far-ranging treatment of *Leaves of Grass* that, while scholarly and critical, yet remains appreciative. *Walt Whitman* by the Danish critic Frederick Schyberg would prove quite influential, especially after the appearance of the translation by Evie Allen introduced by Gay Wilson Allen in 1951. Early in his study, Schyberg strikes a modernist note, asserting that "Walt Whitman is not so much an individual, interesting for his remarkable peculiarities and his many American traits; rather he is a trend in world literature, like Zola, Dostoyevsky, or Nietzsche, and is therefore of especial interest to the literary historians, who are more concerned with the connecting links of literary history than with individuals" (3). Schyberg's concept of "world literature" reflects the globalization of consciousness in the twentieth century, also evident in the emerging idea of world government or the notion of a world-wide "scientific community," a kind of "abstract society" (Popper 1.174-75). With Schyberg's pronouncement, Whitman enters the global society of modern literature not as a person, but as a literary figure, and a prominent one at that—a genius who "generates an epoch" (3). In this extension of the genetic tradition, Schyberg creates the protomodern Whitman who, in his willingness to "praise the erotic in poetry with complete frankness" and in his "revolt" against the conventional forms of literature, provides the genetic impetus for the onset of the modern temper in literary history (9-10).

Schyberg begins with a brief cultural history of America in 1850 and a biographical sketch of Whitman in the years just before he published the *Leaves*, drawing a connection between man and milieu that anticipates both the literary-historical and the ideological criticism of later

Whitman studies. He makes much of the early influence of the Quaker philosopher Elias Hicks, who encouraged his followers to "develop the inner Christ"—an influence Whitman acknowledges in his prose writings. And, while acknowledging the importance of Whitman's trip south as the poet's first opportunity to grasp the fullness of America, Schyberg dismisses the possibility of a New Orleans romance. He follows Clara Barrus and other scholars in discounting the story in the letter to Symonds and depends more fully upon the account of Catel in describing Whitman's experience at midlife—not, however, as a birth, but as an awakening. "Whitman was thirty when be began to wake up," he writes (57). Schyberg allows some credence to Bucke's hypothesis about the onset of cosmic consciousness, a development of mind and spirit supported, in Schyberg's reading, by biographical and historical forces: "For Whitman this inner stimulation to write poetry was supplemented by a series of events in the crucial years preceding 1855," including the Crystal Palace Fair in New York in 1853; the frequent lectures and sermons of abolitionists, transcendentalists, and all manner of inspirational speakers; popular musical performances; and other results of a swirling cultural ferment (59-63). Schyberg also surveys the potential effects of Whitman's reading in the 1850s, from Burns to Carlyle and Emerson. From the latter, he most likely took the important idea of "the poet as the minister of the new era," the root idea of his "cosmic democratic poetry" (71-73). Ultimately, Schyberg's survey of Whitman's life, cultural milieu, and literary experience "reveals among other things that the myth about Whitman as . . . a sort of Atlas in the poetic ranks has no basis"; rather, he was "a dreamer and a mystic" with "traits of both sensuality and effeminacy" who was nevertheless struck at mid-life by an overwhelming ambition to write poems and, on this basis, put into action the multitude of influences at play in his mind.

In addition to this balanced, if eclectic, approach to the origin of the *Leaves*, Schyberg offers what continues to be one of the fullest accounts of the growth of *Leaves of Grass* from 1855 to 1889. Working from the manuscripts as well as the many editions, Schyberg takes the cyclic view in connecting the poet's biography with his poetic production. The Washington period in the 1860s, he argues, "was a peak in Whitman's life" (186), during which time he discovered a humane mission for his life among the wounded soldiers, found himself among a circle of admiring friends, and in *Drum-Taps* "transformed his Calamus idea into patriotism" in an effective "sublimation" of his hitherto troubling (homosexual) emotions (191). Despite the implied decline which always follows such a peak, Schyberg concludes his survey not tragically or comically but "scientifically," treating the growth of the book and the man as an evolution: "Whitman was not successful in conquering the conflicts in himself or in his book, but he did succeed to a remarkable degree in becoming identified with his book, which affected all its characteristics good or bad" (246-47).

Schyberg closes his book with a literary-historical chapter on "Whitman in World Literature," which connects *Leaves of Grass* not so much to its immediate influences as to the works of literature it most resembles in theme, tone, and form. Schyberg treats both western and nonwestern resemblances, discovering, for example, "traces of neo-Platonism, Persian Sufism, and Jewish Chassidism in Whitman, all covered with the common pantheistic characteristics" (251). Having begun with what is most particular and peculiar in Whitman, then, Schyberg's book ends with a chapter that opens outward toward what the poet has in common with the great tradition of world literature. The overall effect of the Danish scholar's work may best be described as canonization, a late and sophisticated attempt to defend Whitman's art and reputation as a worthy subject in the scholarly enterprise.

The same effect arises from the phenomenally influential work of F. O. Matthiessen. His *American Renaissance: Art and Expression in the Age of Emerson and Whitman* (1941) sets a high tone for American studies in general and did as much as any other book to stimulate the explosion of Whitman studies in the years after the second world war. Matthiessen concentrates on the single half-decade of 1850-55, which saw the publication of major works by Emerson, Hawthorne, Melville, Thoreau, and Whitman. Leaving aside a broader look at either literary or socio-political history (in the narrative mode), Matthiessen proposes to study the books of this period "as works of art," to consider "their fusions of form and content" (vii). The reference to "fusion" indicates Matthiessen's taste for dialectic, which guides much of his commentary on individual writings and his evaluations of the writers' overall accomplishments.

Occasionally ranging beyond the limits of his chosen period—to locate influences among the five master authors and to indicate connections in the broader tradition of western poetry—Matthiessen assesses the theories of the writers "concerning the function and nature of literature" in terms of how well "their practice bore out their theories" (vii). He concedes that this approach "may make their process [of composition] sound too deliberate," but he tries to gain some distance by a second critical move comparing the authors' theories and practices with "our own developing conceptions of literature," thereby placing "these works both in their age and in ours" (vii-viii). Quoting Vernon Parrington's famous disavowal of concern with "aesthetic judgment" in *Main Currents of American Thought* (see chapter 4), Matthiessen declares that his own "concern has been opposite" (ix). Whatever the historian may think, says Matthiessen, "the common reader . . . does not live by trends alone; he [or she] reads books, whether of the present or past, because they have an immediate life of their own" (x).

Matthiessen is interested, then, in revealing in each of his major writers "the immediate life" of each poetic work, or what Harold Bloom has called "the irreducibly *aesthetic* dimension in plays, poems, and narratives" (*American Religion* 36). In Whitman, Matthiessen locates this poetic core in the attempt to discover a special language for bridging a conceptual gap that Emerson frequently pondered but left unbridged—the gap between the material and the ideal. Surveying not only the poems but also the neglected prose writings on language (such as *An American Primer*), Matthiessen seeks evidence that Whitman succeeded in his dialectical quest. He finds the proof he needs in the poet's treatment of the body as a foundation, but not a substitution, for linguistic expression: "Whitman's language is more earthy because he was aware, in a way that distinguished him not merely from Emerson but from every other writer of the day, of the power of sex" (523). No one before the protomodern Whitman understood the body's "immediate bearing upon a living speech," Matthiessen argues (523). At his best, Whitman's "words adhere to concrete experience and yet are bathed in imagination" (526). However, in Matthiessen's view, the poet does not always succeed in this powerful blending: "On the one hand, his desire to grasp American facts could lead him beyond slang into the rawest jargon, the journalese of the day. On the other, his attempts to pass beyond the restrictions of language into the atmosphere it could suggest often produced only the barest formulas." And yet, these "inordinate and grotesque failures in both directions throw into clearer light his rare successes, and the fusion upon which they depend" (526).

Moving from words and phrases to poetic forms, Matthiessen explores possible theoretical motives for Whitman's eccentric lines and rhythms. On this topic, the critic's guiding principle appears at first to be analogy, but this eventually revolves back again to his favorite mode of dialectic. Matthiessen reveals "three recurrent analogies" that appear in "Whitman's evolving sense of what he meant by a poem"; he compares poetry "with oratory, with Italian music, and with the sea" (549). Examining the notebooks, conversations, and poems, he finds that Whitman "made only the loosest distinctions" between speech and writing (553) and concludes that the poet was driven in this direction (driven, again, to both successes and failures) by his philosophy of "personalism": the "compelling charm of the voice was the ultimate token of personality" (554). "In such a way," writes Matthiessen, "he arrived ... at the bodily and spiritual oneness which he wanted his poems to convey" (555). Just as he attempted to manage the dichotomy of body and soul by "bathing in imagination" the words of bodily existence, and as he tried to overcome the difference in writing and speech by his efforts at "vocalism," so Whitman also tried to synthesize music and writing, producing poems that, "in spite of being unsingable," still "have music 'at their heart'" (563). Finally, Whitman's most ambitious analogy was the comparison of poetry with the sea. Matthiessen argues that Whitman "wanted to absorb [the ocean's] elemental power by identifying himself with it" (567). "In this breakdown of the distinctions between [humankind] and nature," writes Matthiessen, "can be read also the reason for the deliquescence and disintegration in his work of the controls of traditional poetic movement"; thus, "his fertile discovery of the physical grounding of rhythm . . . came to him first in the rising and falling of the waves" (567).

Despite the occasional, almost arbitrary, appearance of terms like "evolution" and "development," Matthiessen's interpretations of Whitman's poems and prose exhibit an organicism more deeply genetic than that of any critic that preceded him. This remarkable originality appears to stem from an attempt to demonstrate how Whitman differs from Emerson. In Matthiessen's reading, the key difference is that Whitman's poetic experience was rooted in his own body—not in his person or in his psyche, but in his actual physical body. Matthiessen's Whitman—having touched, heard, tasted, and smelled the world—struggles to bring the rhythms and sounds of physical experience into the medium of language, thus to resolve what seems to be for Matthiessen the ultimate dichotomy—the word and the flesh. For Matthiessen, Whitman's poems work best when they overcome the tension between body and language to create a rare poetic moment in which words live. Like the formalists of his day, Matthiessen accepts the possibility of a pure aesthetic experience; but, unlike many other aestheticists of his generation, he seems to have a deeper respect both for the power of material being and for the difficulty of creating a world apart that somehow remains anchored in the physical realities of existence. What he respects in Whitman is the effort—a strenuous effort that extended over a lifetime—to face a difficult synthesis that other writers of his age were content to leave unresolved or to ignore altogether.

On its way to locating a major period of literary productivity in the United States, *American Renaissance* canonizes Whitman as a literary figure whose poems—not to mention his occasional prose and notebook jottings—deserve the closest attention of the best professional scholars. Matthiessen's treatment of Whitman's ideas on language—as revealed both in neglected theoretical writings and in his poetic practice—looks forward to some of the most recent contributions to Whitman studies, such as that of Hollis, Larson, Warren, and Bauerlein, which I will discuss in chapters 4 and 5. More important for this chapter, Matthiessen's discussion of the form of Whitman's poetry anticipates the work of the analytical critics. His analysis of Whitman's relation to opera and the visual arts—competing somewhat with his emphasis on the physical root of Whitman's poetic practice—establishes *Leaves of Grass* as a work of fine art rather than some kind of primitive effusion. And the location of Whitman as a unique figure among the masters of the American literary flowering—Emerson, Thoreau, Hawthorne, and Melville—suggests that the poet's reputation should be tied to the fortunes of these other master authors, his accomplishments measured against theirs and not against the nineteenth-century figures with whom he was once unflatteringly contrasted—such as Longfellow and Fanny Fern, now reduced to minor curiosities by the sweep of Matthiessen's critique (x).

Encouraged no doubt by the example of Schyberg and Matthiessen, and by the work of scholars like Jean Catel, Emory Holloway, and Harold W. Blodgett (who produced the first modern reception study, *Walt Whitman in England*, in 1934), Gay Wilson Allen brought out his *Walt Whitman Handbook* in 1946. Updated in *Walt Whitman As Man, Poet, and Legend* (1961) and *The New Walt Whitman Handbook* (1975), this book is a forerunner of almost every strain of critical inquiry to emerge in the following four decades. Along with the 1955 biography *The Solitary Singer*, the *Handbook* guaranteed Allen's reputation as the dean of Whitman studies. It also did much to ensure Whitman's reputation at a time when American literature itself was still on shaky ground as a subject for serious scholarship. (The preface to *The New Walt Whitman Handbook* tells of Allen's difficulties in convincing publishers about the original project.)

Moreover, the *Handbook* institutionalizes organicism as the dominant metanarrative in the critical tradition of Whitman studies. The chapters on "The Growth of Whitman Biography" and "The Growth of *Leaves of Grass* and the *Prose Works*" reveal the plot of organic development that dominates the biographical criticism. The chapters on "Whitman's Fundamental Ideas" and "Literary Technique in *Leaves of Grass*" hint at the means whereby Whitman achieved a different kind of organic unity within the poems themselves—a thematic or formal unity, the search for which occupies analytical critics of the two decades following the publication of the *Handbook*. The chapter on "Social Thought: Ideas in Action" anticipates the revival of ideological and historicist criticism of the 1980s. And the chapter on "Walt Whitman and World Literature" follows Schyberg in setting the stage for a full-blown literary-historical criticism of Whitman's writings. With the publication of Allen's *Handbook*, then, in the immediate aftermath of World War II, the ground was not only broken, but fully furrowed and seeded for Whitman scholarship. An explosive growth quickly followed.

Analytical Criticism

Of course, Allen himself was a chief contributor to this new growth, as was Roger Asselineau. Allen's and Asselineau's works mixed together various approaches to the poems (in critical biography or in the necessary eclecticism of the literary handbook). Other new studies tended to specialize, concentrating either on critical analysis or some aspect of influence or reception. Under the pressure of the New Criticism, which dominated the American critical scene in the 1950s, a number of new studies were built upon the foundation of close readings of the poems. The first and most influential of these were two very different books—Richard Chase's *Walt Whitman Reconsidered* (1955) and James E. Miller's *Critical Guide to Leaves of Grass* (1957).

Chase's book is a watershed of Whitman criticism. It transforms the eclecticism of earlier books into a truly pragmatic or holistic argument about the relationship of artistic, biographical, and cultural elements of *Leaves of Grass*. The occasion of the book is the centennial of the first edition of the *Leaves*, on which, says Chase, "I have wanted to treat Whitman lovingly and to place him, if possible, where he ought truly to be in our culture and our feelings" (7). In addition to "looking fairly directly at his most interesting works," Chase thus spends some time "comparing him with other authors, in seeing him in relation to national attitudes, and to noticing some shifts of opinion about him" (7). But the book is not merely an "appreciation," because, Chase asserts, "you can't treat Whitman lovingly without offering him considerable opposition" (7). This opposition takes the form of close attention to the conflicts and struggles embedded in the poems, though Chase resists "the kind of rigorous linguistic analysis . . . now practiced by many critics" (7). Although it is not his aim, he says, "to brandish Whitman at the New Critics" (185), he does hold their method at arm's length, for such work is "doomed to be insulative and disheartening"; works of art regarded formalistically, says Chase, in a typically organic turn of phrase, "seem to wither before our eyes to the extent that we see them only as forms irreparably severed from the imperishable sources of being" (98). Thus, Chase avoids New Critical methods not because he supposes "(as some people do) that Whitman's poetry disappears like chaff before the wind when subjected to a rigorous criticism" but because such an approach violates what is deepest and most original in *Leaves of Grass* (7).

Chase turns from formalism to a special version of rhetorical and generic criticism. He modifies, he says, but does not seek to replace the image of Whitman as "the supreme poet of American optimism and pragmatism, the rhapsodist of our material and spiritual resources, the unabashed celebrant of the self at home in an open, dynamic universe" (7-8). He concentrates on "Whitman the comic poet, the radical realist, and the profound elegist" (8). In a strong application of cyclic organicism, he sees the three dominant genres of *Leaves of Grass*—high comedy, realism, and elegy—as corresponding to three stages of the poet's successful career, beginning with "Song of Myself" and ending with "Lilacs." The poetry that appeared after the period of the Civil War, in Chase's view, "bespeaks a mind in which productive tensions have been relaxed, conflicts dissipated, particulars generalized, inequalities

equalized" (148). In an openly biographical reading, then, Chase anticipates the psychoanalytical interpretation of Stephen A. Black.
Whitman's hospital visits, Chase writes, "became a substitute for poetry and not the inspiration of it"; thus, "the war was Whitman's salvation as a man, but his doom as a poet" (136, 149). For Chase, Whitman's
life was "an ordeal rather than . . . merely a happy excursion through
nineteenth-century America, with a pause now and then for a bracing
sexual or mystical experience" (8).

Chase therefore departs from the New Critics in his treatment of
the text as an open system, reflecting the rigors of a difficult life in a
narrative modeled on cyclic organicism, but he retains their interest in
conflict and resolution both in his view of Whitman's career and in his
readings of individual poems. Conflicts unresolved are not to be admired, but conflicts resolved too easily, so that tension is totally re-
leased or evaded, are equally inadequate, the stuff of poems without
energy or power. Nevertheless, what counts as resolution is a great deal
broader for Chase than for the formalists. With a brand of historicism
that would flourish among the critics of the 1980s (particularly in the
work of Wynn Thomas and David Reynolds and in my own
"Whitman and Motherhood"), Chase admits that "Whitman was different from us"; in fact, Chase celebrates his difference: "Walt
Whitman was a product of those decades just before the Civil War, of
the freshness, the large-mindedness, the complex versatility, the general vigor and adventurousness which the war and the Gilded Age did
not much to destroy." And he suggests further, "Perhaps it is the variousness of Whitman's character, its free multiplicity as contrasted with
our sameness or our specialization, that first strikes us as being attractive" (15). The poems seek to contain this "variousness" and
"diversity"—as well as a tendency to be "sexually versatile" (39-40)—
within a fluid, yet clear sense of identity, the formation and mainte-
nance of which was Whitman's "lifelong concern" (27).

Chase's treatment of the problem of identity leads to a major contribution to persona theory. He picks up (where Esther Shephard had
fallen) on the notion that Whitman's ability to pose and model new
identities constitutes a great strength in a poet whose chief genre is not
the romantic lyric with its confessional intensity (as Shephard must
have supposed) but rather the hybrid forms of the comic-epic ("Song of
Myself"), the realistic image poem (as in the best of *Drum-Taps* and in
many of the 1860 poems of observation), and the elegy (the "Sea-Drift"
poems of 1860, as well as much of *Drum-Taps* and of course "Lilacs").
All of these benefitted from a strong dramatic overlay, the great result
of Whitman's being "one of those writers who, like Mark Twain,
Shaw, Dostoevsky [sic], and Yeats, present themselves through their art
and their public life in the guise of more than one self" (41). Whitman
"presented not one but several personalities," which he transferred to
his poems from his life: "the worldly, dandified young metropolitan

journalist of the early 1840s; the homely, Christlike carpenter and radical of the 1850s; the full-bearded, sunburned, clean-limbed, vigorously
sexed, burly common man of the later fifties and early sixties; the male
nurse and good gray poet of the Washington period; the sage of
Camden of the late years" (42). The "strain of insincerity in Whitman"
is no flaw, for Chase, for the "masks are not assumed merely to fool the
public" (42). Rather, in Chase's interpretation, they are the masks of the
"American humorist . . . quirky, ironic, 'indirect,' guileful" and of "the
modern personality . . . the divided, multiple personality . . . suffused
with yeasty eruptions from unconscious depths, turning uncertainly
from self-assertion to self-recrimination and despair" (43). Despite his
"difference from us," then, Whitman exhibited the modern tendency
toward a varied presentation of the self, in life as well as in art—a tendency treated systematically in the sociological classic *The Presentation
of the Self in Everyday Life* by Erving Goffman and carried to its farthest extremes in the deconstructionist critique of the "metaphysics of
presence," which raises the possibility that the self is endlessly generated not upon a basic ground of identity, but merely as a succession of
tropes upon tropes, under which lies the abyss (see Goffman; Derrida;
on Whitman, see Bové and Blasing; and compare Byers).

But Whitman did not go quite so far as to accept the ultimate
emptiness of the self, except in moments of deep despair, according to
Chase, who leans toward the view of Whitman's emergence that
would be fully developed in the work of Black. Chase suggests that, in
the early 1850s, Whitman discovered what Emerson calls "the aborigi-
nal self . . . the last fact behind which analysis cannot go," where "all
things find their common origin"—namely the unconscious. This discovery coincided with political and biographical factors and literary influences to produce the 1855 *Leaves*. In Chase's reading, the process of
the poet's emergence is dramatized in "The Sleepers" and "Out of the
Cradle" (53-57). In fits and starts, it is this discovery that carried the poet
through the Civil War. Each new edition of the poems, however, betrays a decreasing confidence and a corresponding decline in poetic
power, according to Chase (99). By *Drum-Taps*, the reader senses the
poet's striving toward "a more taut and often a more conventional
versification, a less luxurious verbal texture, and a sharper, more realistic imagery" (133). Despite his progress in the war years toward a new
"imagistic realism" growing out of a pattern of "alternating regressions
and thrusts outward to reality," the poems begin to show the "signs of
having been written by a poet whose visionary grasp of things is weakening" (133-37). The final decline commences when Whitman "comes
to think that he is alienated not only from the world but from himself
and that this alienation can no longer be felt as a challenge to be met by
aggressive poetic expression or in contemplative elegiac verse but is
felt, rather, as a threat which can only be met by extra-poetic means—by

becoming, that is, the hospital visitor, the self-publicist, the good gray poet, the sage and master" (46).

Chase therefore provides a link between the critical biographers with their cyclic metanarrative and the emerging formalists with their revised organic theory. He appears to accept the idea of organic unity within individual poems, focusing primarily on the final authorized version of each poem, sidestepping the problem of the different editions even as he characterizes the general rhetorical traits of each new version of the *Leaves*. The unifying force within each poem, he argues, comes from a manipulation of poetic genre, with a strong stress in every genre on the dramatic development of the poem's persona. Chase also accedes to the possibility that poems can ascend to otherworldliness; however, in anticipation of later historicists, he politicizes this outlook in a way that resists the "apolitical" stance of the New Critics. In *Leaves of Grass*, Chase argues, "Whitman does not content himself with deploring society and taking to the woods with his bachelor companions. He entirely destroys society by imaginatively transfiguring it so that it becomes, as it were, merely the particular locus of the innocent pastoral world" (79).

For all of his admiration of Whitman's political and poetic strength, Chase borrows heavily on the old hypothesis of Whitman's naiveté and "primitivism." He says, for example, that the Whitmanian self is "a preternatural being, a numinous presence which is felt with all the wonder the primitive . . . feels in the presence of [a] god or tutelary spirit" (86) and that, in his "ideas about words, as in his poetic practice, Whitman is paradoxically extremely civilized and extremely primitive," at once the semanticist and the bard—"a kind of primitive I. A. Richards and a sophisticated Orpheus" (92).

In contrast to Chase, who modifies the old hypothesis, R. W. B. Lewis hints at a complete revival of the primitive Whitman in his influential history of ideas *The American Adam* (1955). In *Leaves of Grass*, Lewis sees the fullest embodiment of the archetype of the New Adam—"the liberated, solitary, forward-thrusting personality . . . with conventions shed and the molting season concluded," replacing "sinfulness" with "innocence" as "the first attribute of the American character" (28). According to Lewis's ironic perspective, "the creative act" for Whitman was a "lust for inventiveness," "the groping after novel words to describe novel experiences" (41); the poet's aim was to "find and assert nature untroubled by art, to re-establish the natural unfallen man in the living hour" (43). The latter-day Calvinism and modern scientism implicit in Lewis's critique appear to be offended by the notion that the poet can create a world rather than merely discover and reconstrue the matter of an already created if chaotic existence (51-53).

This critique ran against the grain of a growing critical movement in the 1950s that stressed the conscious artistry and control of materi-

als—the technical excellence—evident in *Leaves of Grass*. The clear
leader of this movement was James E. Miller, Jr., who came closer than
any critic of the 1950s to producing an appreciative full-length study of
Leaves of Grass based on New Critical principles. In addition to besting
Chase in the practice of close reading, he accepts many of the prohibi-
tions that characterize high formalist criticism in his *Critical Guide to
Leaves of Grass* (1957). Miller's preface has the ring of a manifesto,
asserting a clear decision to avoid reading the *Leaves* in either the biographical or the literary-historical mode. He says that he will neither
"use the poetry as a basis for speculation about the life," nor "place
book or poet on the psychoanalyst's couch," nor "search the economic,
social, or political milieu for causes of the volume of poetry," nor
"attempt to make Whitman the poet of some particular cause—science,
democracy, sex, or religion," nor even "search in the earlier editions
and the manuscripts for the primary evidence for criticism" (vii). What
he does intend to do is examine the *Leaves*—in their final authorized
form—as artifacts whose structures are governed by their own internally consistent laws and principles. Interestingly, Miller shares with
the early defenders a polemic purpose, which he attempts to accomplish with the head-on strategy, directly confronting Whitman's formalist critics and the perpetuators of the naiveté hypothesis with the
claim that Whitman, whatever else he was, was most certainly a conscious artist with the ability to realize his aims in closely structured and
organically unified poems. Though Miller seeks "neither to worship
nor to ridicule the poet," he nevertheless wants "to help dispel the
common notion that Whitman was a formless, even a chaotic, poet"
(vii), a notion he aims to correct even if Whitman himself helped to
perpetuate it. The poet's constant assertions of originality and his pose
of country-boy (or Bowery-boy) contempt for sophistication Miller
reads as aspects of the poet's persona, arguing (à la Borges) that
Whitman "has 'taken in' . . . readers" who gullibly assume that the
poet practiced some kind of "automatic" writing that emerged from
"frenzied fits" of inspiration (3). Miller follows Burroughs and
Shephard in noting Whitman's dramatic flair and propensity for the
calculated pose. But, he says, "all poets are frauds in that they diligently
attempt to palm off an imaginative as an 'actual' experience. The most
'fraudulent' poets are the most successful in persuading the reader to
'believe'" (4). Miller therefore follows Allen, as well as the New Critics,
in stressing the otherworldliness of the poetic creation.

Above all, Miller's Whitman is a dramatist: "His poems are plays;
he is the protagonist" (4). Who "he" is exactly does not much concern
Miller; the identity of the speaker in *Leaves of Grass* is implicitly resolved by the New Critical recourse to persona theory. This "I" is an ac-
tor, whom we follow through a kind of pilgrim's progress, a plot
repeated again and again in the best poems—in "Song of Myself," "The
Sleepers," "Out of the Cradle Endlessly Rocking," and "Passage to

India." The plot moves through conflict to resolution, always in a series of stages, which idealize and rarify action, thus separating it from ordinary experience: "Poems seldom 'record' but frequently 'transmute' events," Miller asserts (58). Likewise, the poems contain no "philosophical progression and conclusion," in Miller's reading: "Whitman was not stating philosophical truths so much as he was dramatizing himself and his life of the imagination" (4).

"Song of Myself," for example, is described as a "dramatic representation" of an "inverted mystical experience"—inverted because "the self is not, as in the traditional mystical experience, submerged or annihilated, but rather celebrated; the senses are not humbled but glorified," so that "only through the intimate fusions of the physical and spiritual" can one "come to know transcendent reality" (10). The inverted mysticism is analyzed into stages that roughly correspond to William James's treatment of the mystical experience: entry into the mystical state (sections 1-5), awakening of the self (sections 6-16), purification of the self (sections 17-32), illumination and the dark night of the soul (sections 33-37), union (in faith and love) (sections 38-43), union (in perception) (sections 44-49), and emergence from the mystical state (sections 50-52) (Critical Guide 7). As detailed in the Critical Guide and summarized in Miller's widely read Twayne volume on Whitman, this interpretation of the poem's structure and main themes makes a good case for the organic unity of what had been considered a loose poem with little or no structure. Miller shows that "the dropping and subsequent return to a particular subject" follows definite patterns of thematic development and is justified by reference to dramatic progression. Thus, "in the emotional state imposed by the mystical experience, something approaching ecstatic frenzy, it is natural that the poet's thought should lack logical continuity" (16). If logic is lacking, however, organic unity is not.

Squaring Leaves of Grass with New Critical theory and practice, Miller arrives at similar readings of other major poems. "The Sleepers" he reads as a "psychological dramatization of a flow of images with only eccentric relationships one to another," which nonetheless form a coherent structure with four movements: "sections 1-2, identification; sections 3-4, ocean and death; sections 5-6, time and love; sections 7-8, union" (130). In noting the resemblance between Whitman's method of development and "the stream-of-consciousness technique of a later era" (130), Miller connects Whitman's art to that of the formalist deities Joyce and Faulkner, as well as again recalling the connection to another figure from the literary-philosophical mainstream, William James (compare Chase 88-90).

Miller's Critical Guide uses cyclic organicism not as a means of unifying the poet's overall career or poetic production, but rather as a structural principle for demonstrating the internal unity of individual poems. Thus, in Miller's reading, "When Lilacs Last in the Dooryard

Bloom'd" traces the movement from grief to reconciliation: "The movement is cyclic, not smooth but halting, not logical but emotional" (111). Likewise, "Passage to India" becomes a dramatic interplay of the concepts of space and time, treated not as dialectical abstractions but as concepts rooted symbolically in human achievements—technological achievements (improvements in transportation and communications) as well as, and foretold by, poetry and religious prophesy.

In "Calamus," however, Miller discovers the limits of the formalist approach. He first muses over an odd fact from the history of the poems' reception: "It is indeed strange that the very element in Whitman's poetry that gained him nineteenth-century praise for his 'purity'"—his treatment of male friendship—"should bring him twentieth-century condemnation for his 'immorality'" (52-53). Faced with the need to "test the validity of the prevailing belief that ... Whitman gave stammering utterance to a doctrine whose implications he did not fully comprehend," Miller decides reluctantly to violate New Critical principles and look to the "extrinsic" evidence. In so doing, he throws over any scruples about the intentional fallacy, obviously more determined to pursue his polemic purpose of proving Whitman's conscious artistry than to preserve the formalist purity of his approach. "Abundant evidence as to the intended meaning of 'Calamus' exists in Whitman's prose works," he writes, continuing with a bow to New Criticism: "and, though not conclusive, as external data never is, such evidence is highly revealing and surely relevant" (54). It is relevant because it supports Miller's rhetorical point about Whitman's purposeful craftsmanship: In "Calamus," Miller says, "intentional ambiguity— ambiguity used consciously as a poetic device—abounds, resulting in a language always something more or something less than appears on the surface" (54). Supporting his readings with statements from the prose works, Miller ends up approximating the nineteenth-century view of "Calamus," asserting the "purity, innocence, and spirituality of the 'Calamus' concept" (55). The concept has, according to Miller's reading, "two facets—personal and social"; the merging of "particular individuals in a deeply personal, yet purely spiritual attachment" precedes, then joins with "a multitude of such attachments interpenetrating and binding a nation ... a democratic state rooted deeply in genuinely moral human character rather than in convention or law" (56).

Miller's decision to ground his reading of "Calamus" in extrinsic sources appears to arise from a perceived need to defend Whitman against charges of homosexual obscenity. In later writings, he forthrightly elaborates and energetically celebrates the "omnisexual" character of *Leaves of Grass*, which includes (though perhaps transcends) homosexuality (see "Whitman's Omnisexual Vision" [1973]). However, the *Critical Guide*, written in the 1950s well before the "sexual revolution" in American popular culture, is more circumspect and even defensive. Miller reacts specifically against Fredson Bowers's implication, in a 1955 study of the manuscripts, that "Calamus," in its original form, depicts the story of a "specific emotional experience"— meaning a homosexual affair—which Whitman tried to cover over in his revisions of the poems. In Miller's view, Whitman revised "not for biographical but for poetic or dramatic reasons" (59). The group of poems, as it was finally published, achieves the organic unity that the original manuscripts lack, Miller argues, by centering on the key theme of democratic and spiritual brotherhood.

Later critics have both built upon this reading and objected to it. Even by the time Miller wrote, Asselineau was already in the camp of Bowers, arguing that the "quiet labor of self-censorship" that haunted the poet's work had its roots in homosexual anxiety (*Evolution* 1.247). A decade later, in "New Light on *Leaves of Grass*," Arthur Golden rejects the self-censorship thesis with the claim that the textual evidence does not bear it out; while, in *Whitman's Poetry of the Body* (1989), I use evidence from the Variorum edition of the *Leaves* to revive Asselineau's argument that Whitman anxiously sought to spiritualize homosexual references in his revisions and, in the process, undermined his liberatory sexual politics (Killingsworth 144-54). However, David Kuebrich, in *Minor Prophecy: Walt Whitman's New American Religion* (1989), returns to a reading that comes close to Miller's original position. He argues, "The more recent scholarship which interprets the 'Calamus' motif as a celebration of gayness repeatedly distorts the poetry by attempting to discuss Whitman's alleged gayness as a separate theme that can be considered apart from his religious vision" (131). Kuebrich thus recapitulates the notion that "Calamus" is unified not by homosexual emotion but by principles of spiritual brotherhood. The dispute is not likely to end on this note.

The crucial point here is that "Calamus," at least to some extent, frustrated Miller's determination to prove the poems' unity while avoiding the use of external evidence. The attraction of the manuscripts was strong enough to tempt Miller into considering the evidence they offer for biographical intrusions into the aesthetic realm. Even if he finally discounts this evidence, he does so only by using the prose works as a balancing force. However, in the critical tradition overall, once the gate of the closed text is opened, it becomes difficult to stop the influx of competing external data.

Miller also drops the principles of formalist organicism when he considers *Leaves of Grass* as a whole. In search of a structural principle that explains the organization of the poems in the final order authorized by Whitman in his last years, Miller rejects the possibility of a logical order and considers a metaphorical structure, "a structure resembling some object other than a book of poems" (168). He explores several possibilities, both organic and mechanical, but finds none altogether conclusive or comprehensive: "Grass, house, Bible, music, journey, man—perhaps *Leaves of Grass* is a composite of these several metaphors," he suggests; "each of them in turn influenced the structure of *Leaves of Grass* so that it is proper to say, although none is fully applicable or suitable, together they illuminate and reveal, contradictory as some apparently are" (172).

On this note of irresolution, Miller turns to the task of framing a metanarrative for the growth of *Leaves of Grass* in a chapter called "Evolution of a Structure." The result is partly cyclic and partly progressive. It is cyclic in the sense that Miller outlines three successive periods of growth in *Leaves of Grass* that correspond to three periods of intensified creative activity in the poet's life. The first period ends with the 1860 *Leaves*, the second with the 1871-72 *Leaves*, and the third with the 1881 edition, which remained essentially unchanged, at least in its arrangement of the poems. Each period of creativity was sparked by events in Whitman's life history—the original burst of energy in 1855, which carried him up through the third edition of 1860; then the new impetus provided by the emotions of the Civil War; and finally the sense of incompleteness engendered by the poet's ultimate realization that he must keep writing to realize his greatest goal—the embodiment in his book of the New World personality, as represented in the person of Walt Whitman.

At each of the three points—1860, 1871, and 1881—the poet had a sense that the book was complete, only to enter a new cycle of creative interest. What is progressive about Miller's interpretation of this biographical-literary evolution is that, in his view, the work accomplished its purpose—not a purpose that was established from the start, as Bucke had argued, but rather a purpose that grew and changed with the poet's vision and experience. The proof of the achieved purpose is the structure of the final *Leaves of Grass*, which Miller obviously admires. It is basically a three-part structure that, like the rings of a tree, reveals the external impact of the poet's mood at the time the parts were composed and arranged. Though not exactly chronological, it follows more or less the same progression identified by Emory Holloway's *Interpretation in Narrative*—"the youthful feeling of immortality born of high animal spirits," followed by "the agonized realism of the war-time verse," leading finally to "the aspiration of the pioneer soul" (Holloway 244). Like the growth of a tree, then—which, at least from a human perspective, is increasingly impressive—the growth of *Leaves of Grass*, as conceived by James Miller, moved steadily toward the monumental accomplishment represented in the death-bed edition.

This reading of the book's growth and structure (which is much more fine-grained than I suggest in this brief treatment) implies that Whitman was ultimately successful in his life-long quest. This argument provides Miller with an implicit rationale for his decision to analyze the individual poems in their final versions. More importantly, it leads Miller to a significant conclusion about genre. In its final form, *Leaves of Grass* is a New World epic, he argues, complete with invoca-

tions, local deities, wars, journeys, and, above all, broad cultural significances. "In insisting on being the poet of science and democracy and,
above all, of 'religion,'" Miller writes, "Whitman was not clinging to
personal attitudes but was rather defining the nineteenth century's
view of the universe and itself and reflecting it in his epic, as the epic
poets of the past—Homer, Vergil, Dante, and Milton—reflected their
own times in order to become epic spokesmen for their ages" (261).

Miller's *Critical Guide to Leaves of Grass*, like its subject, thus appears to undergo an evolution from beginning to end. Its structure resembles an unfolding, beginning with readings of individual poems as
closed texts, but ending with a treatment that shows how the text as a
whole opens out onto the cultural scene of nineteenth-century
America. In his later work, Miller pursues his hypothesis about the
epic nature of *Leaves of Grass*. His book *The American Quest for a
Supreme Fiction: Whitman's Legacy in the Personal Epic* (1979) exam-
ines what Miller perceives to be the central tension in Whitman's
work—the tension "between the lyric (private) and epic (public) roles
the poet assigned himself" (43)—and traces this pattern through a set of
remarkable correspondences in the work of Stevens, Pound, Eliot,
Crane, Olson, Berryman, Lowell, and Ginsberg. By this time, Miller has
abandoned the need to work within the confines of the closed text.
Though he retains his New Critical verve for structural analysis, he
moves toward a rhetorical criticism that emphasizes the effects of individual poems within radically transformed genres and that accepts a
literary-historical framework for examining further relations among
works of art.

Miller thus lays the groundwork for criticism that treats the poems
as open textual systems. Ironically, he does so not only in his broader
claims about Whitman's experimentation with the epic genre and his
omnisexual vision, but also in his readings of individual poems, despite his stated aim to keep within the boundaries of the texts' own
structural principles. His emphasis on the drama of the public and private in his readings of "Song of Myself," "The Sleepers," and "Lilacs"
has special significance for the growth of psychoanalytical criticism (E.
H. Miller; Black; Cavitch), socio-historical study (Martin; Hutchinson;
W. Thomas; Erkkila), and linguistic analysis (Hollis; Warren). Miller's
penchant for analysis and interpretation sets a strong precedent for future studies, which, however strongly they may react against other
New Critical principles, enthusiastically embrace the practice of close
reading. The zeal for such criticism in Whitman studies—among critical biographers, psychoanalysts, historicists, and poststructuralists as
well as more traditional analytical critics—is fully demonstrated in
Edwin Haviland Miller's recent book *Walt Whitman's "Song of
Myself": A Mosaic of Interpretations*, which assembles an astounding
number of comments for each line of the poem. Clearly, explication of

Leaves of Grass has not suffered on account of the biographical-historical focus of the critical tradition as a whole.

This penchant for close reading was reinforced by other critics who followed James Miller in the analytical task of locating key structures, genres, and themes of the poems. One of these, Thomas Edward Crawley's *The Structure of Leaves of Grass*, overlaps considerably with Miller's *Critical Guide*, perhaps because, as the preface tells us, the book was mostly finished when Crawley submitted the manuscript as his dissertation in 1955, though the book itself was not finally published until 1970. Crawley implies in several places that Miller does not go far enough in breaking the hold of biographical studies and criticism of the poems based on readings of the prose. What Crawley attempts, then, is a study of *Leaves of Grass* that conforms even more completely to the New Critical ideal. The resulting book sets forth Crawley's "revelation" that *Leaves of Grass* is more than "a handy one-volume edition of the collected lyrics of the poet"; rather, it is "a unified work . . . a single poetic achievement, lyrical, and yet in its totality not without an epic quality and direction" (3). The religious overtones in Crawley's description of his revelation are entirely appropriate in light of the thesis that he gradually develops: "Out of Whitman's organic theory of art grew naturally his concept of the poet-prophet; in much the same way his development of the Christ-like prophet as the central figure of *Leaves of Grass* led to his involvement with the great national themes. The Christ-symbol, then, has a unifying effect reaching far beyond the fact that it is the most fully developed and frequently recurring symbol in *Leaves of Grass*" (78).

It is little wonder that, having offered this thesis, Crawley contends, "In any study of the structure of *Leaves of Grass* the seventh [sic] edition, published in 1881, is the key volume" (80). I have already mentioned my contention that Whitman worked for a decade and a half to spiritualize his book, smoothing the edges of his rough democratic politics and removing passages that are distinctly un-Christlike, such as the 1855 line, "Thruster holding me tight and that I hold tight! / We hurt each other as the bridegroom and bride hurt each other" (see *Whitman's Poetry of the Body* 152). With such lines purged, the 1881 edition is more likely to support Crawley's thesis. Even as an argument for that edition, however, it has not enjoyed wide appeal among Whitman scholars. The reasons for this neglect lie largely in the bad conceptual fit between New Criticism and Whitman's poems.

Like Miller, Crawley tries to "subordinate" external evidence to internal evidence (ix). Though following the critical tradition in devoting a chapter to the "evolution" of *Leaves of Grass*, Crawley stays clear of Schyberg's tendency to link changes in the book to changes in the poet's life and way of thinking and Miller's dependence upon prose sources as evidence of Whitman's intentions in his revisions (48-49, 166). The changes in the poems' style, according to Crawley, are more "the result of the development of the subjects than the detached development or disintegration of artistry or expression on Whitman's part" (221). In other words, Whitman did not progressively improve his artistry from edition to edition (as some defenders want to argue), nor did he lose heart and give in to conventional expression in his later poems after surging with unconventional energy in 1855, 1856, and 1860 (as Chase suggests, among others). In Crawley's view, Whitman's artistry was consistent; the style of the poems changed to accommodate the changing subject matter of each edition—the wild passions of the early books, the sad and stately topics of the war poems, and the elevated themes of Whitman's exploration of the spiritual dimension of life in his later years. Thus, the finished structure of *Leaves of Grass* represents "the final vindication of Whitman's organic theory of poetry" (225). Whereas Allen the biographer was disappointed that Whitman's book does not adequately follow a perceivable chronological sequence, Crawley the student of poetic process sees a "striking correlation between the chronology of composition and the final arrangement of 1881" (225). "Certainly one of the striking dimensions of his poetic vision," writes Crawley, "is his exalted, mystical view of the poetic process itself, that process upon which he saw *Leaves of Grass* as a profound comment" (225). As in Miller's work, the tree analogy guides Crawley's conclusion: "As the oak tree unfolds out of the folds of the acorn, so Whitman's *Leaves* of 1881 unfolded out of the folds of the acorn of 1855" (225).

At this point in the argument, as the organic theory takes hold and narrative overwhelms analysis, the poet emerges as an active agent. If Crawley avoids biography in the technical sense, he nonetheless begins to write a kind of ideal biography, whose poetic hero succeeds in a single-minded quest toward a mature book that reflects the stages of artistic growth. In an argument common in the textualist mode of interpretation, *Leaves of Grass* becomes a poem about poetry. Like many of the New Critics (especially those educated in the southern United States), Crawley was absorbed by two topics—art and Christianity—topics which, for all the determination to keep external concerns out of readings, somehow manage to appear frequently, either separately or in tandem, in New Critical investigations, not merely as background, but as unifying themes. Though it signifies his solidarity with the school of New Criticism, Crawley's view of *Leaves of Grass* as poetry whose primary purpose is to present a theory of poetry and whose unifying center is the "Christ figure" has had little impact on the development of Whitman studies. *The Structure of Leaves of Grass* is rarely cited and almost never discussed at length, even in books and articles that focus on Whitman's formal concerns or spiritual inclinations.

A tighter, if not much more influential, case for the unity of Whitman's work is made by Howard Waskow in his 1966 study

Whitman: Explorations in Form. Waskow, like Miller and Crawley before him, complains that too few studies have addressed the problems of form in *Leaves of Grass* in close readings of the individual poems (1-2). He also makes clear his decision to begin his own readings from the latest versions of the poems, "appealing to earlier ones where they are helpful" (4). He sticks with the 1892 poems, he says, mainly for practical rather than theoretical or aesthetic reasons, since they are the most readily available versions, but he also implies a preference for these later versions: "Whitman's editing was occasionally wrongheaded," Waskow admits, but "was more often right than wrong" (5).

Explorations in Form is primarily motivated by what Waskow sees as a major gap in Whitman studies: There has been, he says, "no real success in identifying Whitman's creative center, the unity that generates his different kinds of poems, as distinguished from the constructed unity of *Leaves of Grass*" (3). Conceding that a poet need not have such a center, Waskow asserts that Whitman does. It is not a theme or some kind of fixed idea that serves as the generative principle of Whitman's poems (as Crawley suggests), but rather a "habit of mind" (3-4). In making this claim, Waskow builds upon James Miller's idea that Whitman was above all a dramatic poet, but he censures Miller for using the phrase *dramatic structure* "so loosely that very different sorts of poems . . . are all included under the rubric" (3). The term Waskow puts forward as a description of Whitman's informing center comes from Emerson—*bipolar unity* (22). Much less shy about using cultural sources than either Miller or Crawley, Waskow places Whitman in the history of ideas by showing how he continually balances an organic and a mechanical world view and theory of poetry. Noting a main current of dispute in Whitman criticism over whether the poet was primarily a monist and an organicist in the romantic tradition identified by M. H. Abrams or a dialectician in an older, more rationalistic and dualistic tradition, dating to Descartes, Waskow says that the poet was both—and neither (9-12). In his view, Whitman does not merely vacillate between monism and dualism, symbolism and rationalism, but "lives in both a mechanistic world and an organic world" in a state of bipolar unity, with creative tension surging between the two poles.

Each of these "worlds," according to Waskow, brings forth a distinctive poetic form. The organic favors a poetry of indirection, which produces imagism; while the mechanical favors a poetry of direction, which tends toward didacticism. Neither of these is distinctly Whitmanian. Though either impulse may dominate a particular poem, it is their combination and interplay that creates the special effects of Whitman's poems. While some poems move toward one pole or the other, most "fuse the characteristics of imagism and didacticism," giving rise to three distinctive forms of Whitmanian verse—the narrative (exemplified by "Out of the Cradle Endlessly Rocking"), the monodrama (such as "The Sleepers"), and the poem of reader engagement (such as "When Lilacs Last in the Dooryard Bloom'd") (114).

Waskow's argument tends toward a bipolar unity of its own. In speaking of the "fusion" of imagism and didacticism, the critic capitalizes on organic and mechanical connotations, at once suggesting the merging of organisms through natural processes and the welding of materials in mechanical labor. (One thinks of nuclear fusion, which appears also to combine organic and mechanical traits, at least as it is carried out in human-constructed nuclear reactors, or bombs.) The detailed readings of the poems offered by Waskow likewise merge two images of poetic practice—the one leaning toward the organic model of inspired genius (Burroughs's Whitman who lets himself go), the other favoring the mechanical model of the skilled craftsman (Bucke's master builder). And finally, Waskow seems to draw upon both the organic impulse toward extending and completing the poet's work (bringing it to fruition) and the more mechanical tasks of selection and judgment.

The very originality of this approach may lie behind the lack of influence that Waskow has had among Whitman scholars. He does precisely what Borges implies Whitman's commentators have not done. He creates a system of inquiry that comprehends Whitman's writing in terms other than those the poet himself preferred. The structure of *Whitman: Explorations in Form* is sophisticated, analytical, and systematic, beginning with the core idea of bipolar unity and developing outward in concentric circles until the conception is broad enough to encompass the largest part of Whitman's poetic corpus. It differs from the most influential studies in lacking a narrative sequence. Even Miller's and Crawley's books—which also depart from the sequential presentation characteristic of most Whitman studies—nevertheless provide a narrative foothold in chapters on the "growth" or "evolution" of *Leaves of Grass*. Waskow's analytical experiment eschews narrative altogether and thus cuts itself off from the critical mainstream.

It is curious that, of all modern critics, Miller, Crawley, and Waskow—those closest to the New Criticism—tend to recover a genetic version of organicism or to imply that a progressive narrative lies behind Whitman's poetic accomplishment. They appear to be driven in this direction by two forces, one historical, the other methodological. The historical reason is that the progressive outlook puts the analytical critics in a better position to defend their poet against the prevailing view that Whitman was a "loose" romantic; if they can show that his work got better and better, they can more easily demonstrate the ever-tightening artistry of the poems. The methodological reason is connected to the formalist preference for genetic organicism. Just as biographical geneticism seeks an informing motive in the author's character, the formal geneticist seeks a unifying theme or structural principle—a textual replacement for the author's intention or the reader's response, a meaning machine powerful enough to generate the energy to sustain the closed system of the internally unified text. The progressive quality of this approach arises from the critic's need to demonstrate the pervasiveness of the germ (theme or structural principle) that has been identified. If at any point in the evolution of the poems the germ ceases to be an informing principle, then it fails the test of generativity. At this point, the critic must concede that some other force is at work that would direct our attention to extrinsic influences.

The one critic who both extends the analytical tradition and slips free of some of these complications is Ivan Marki. In *The Trial of the Poet* (1976), Marki manages to revive the formalist concept of unity by limiting his discussion to the first edition of *Leaves of Grass*, taking his inspiration from Malcolm Cowley's 1959 judgment that "the long opening poem" of 1855, the earliest version of "Song of Myself," is not only "Whitman's greatest work" but also "one of the great poems of modern times" and that "the first edition is a unified work" (Cowley, "Introduction" x; Marki ix). Dividing his monograph into three parts— the first on the 1855 preface, the second on the 1855 "Song of Myself," and the third on the remaining poems—Marki sets out to substantiate what Cowley only asserts.

Marki claims that he is driven not by New Criticism but by "common sense" to rely on internal evidence, for the long tradition of Whitman criticism has, in his opinion, yielded no cogent insights into how and whence the *Leaves* emerged: "The 'long foreground' has kept its secret," he says (5-6). Following the lead of Matthiessen, Marki turns to the prose preface to discern a theory of poetry and then to the poems to see how well the theory works in practice. His findings lead him to the thesis that "so far as Whitman had a consistent theory of art, that theory . . . was a version of organicism, and in the literature of organicism vegetable growth is the master-analogy and 'leaves' the favorite metaphor" (8). Marki builds upon Matthiessen's identification of the dialectical power in Whitman's thought and Waskow's invocation of the Emersonian bipolar unity in his interpretation of the structure of *Leaves of Grass*: "The 'bipolar unity' that ensues is the principle of coherence in the paired opposites Whitman could devise with such prodigious facility: body and soul, one and many, identity and distinction, universal and particular, male and female, human and deity, land and sea, life and death. . . . Out of the configuration of such complementary opposites . . . a characteristic pattern of 'dialectical triads' emerges" (39). Thus, the "central Whitman" that Marki works out in close readings of the 1855 poems is "constituted of the tension between 'centrifugal' and 'centripetal' forces, that is 'self-shunning' and 'self-seeking' impulses" (41). While avoiding the progressivism of the other analytical critics, then, Marki joins them in their preference for a rather mechanical view of the organic unity of the 1855 *Leaves*, resorting finally to the language of physical motion to describe the key patterns of the poems.

The main problem with Marki and his formalist predecessors is suggested in a comment on Waskow's work offered by Roger Asselineau in 1971. While praising Waskow's deft explications, Asselineau argues that, in final analysis, "the contents of the poems tend to be underestimated . . . in favor of New Critical ambiguities" ("Walt Whitman" 264). This comment foretells the reaction against the New Criticism among historicists of the 1980s, who (implicitly or explicitly) dismiss the formalist tendency to gut the poems of referential power. Typical of a major disciplinary trend in academic studies, the relationship of the analytical critics and the historical revisionists parallels developments, for example, in the field of technical logic. As the science writer Jeremy Campbell explains, a "contentless" modern version of logic has gradually given way to a content-based view of thinking based on the work of cognitive scientists: "In general, modern logic, like modern art, is not 'about' anything but itself. A painting ceased to portray nature and life, and became part of a theory of painting. In much the same way, logic turned inward and explored its own foundations"; in the last thirty years, however, cognitive research has revealed that "general intelligence is . . . not based on rules, whether universal or makeshift" and "is not blind to content, as logic is" (Campbell 38, 67). Just as the logician's internally consistent systems of rules and relations are declared existentially irrelevant by the cognitivist's contention that thinking is content-dependent, modern criticism's closed world of art, its textualism, is challenged by the historicist's insistence on the openness of textual reference.

Literary-Historical Criticism

The literary-historical approach to *Leaves of Grass* steers free of the tendency of formalist criticism to reduce the poems to structural and formal patterns and to avoid extrinsic evidence. This approach nevertheless shares with formalism the modernist emphasis on the professional life, the literariness of the poet. As Schyberg puts it, "Walt Whitman is not so much an individual" but rather "a trend in world literature" (3). The poet is thus canonized—rendered appropriate as a subject for scholarly work—by being defended as a product of high culture and a strong representative of intellectual life.

Following the work of Schyberg and Allen in this vein, two books appeared in 1951 that attempted to demonstrate the range of Whitman's intellect and his inheritance of a sound cultural tradition. In *Walt Whitman and Opera*, Robert D. Faner argues that Whitman was heavily influenced by his exposure to the opera, especially Italian opera; this influence, according to Faner, accounts for many of the most original developments in the form and structure of *Leaves of Grass*. In

Walt Whitman: Poet of Science, Joseph Beaver traces the poet's references to scientific topics in order to demonstrate Whitman's solid grasp of scientific learning. The overall effect of such work is to dispel the lingering tendency among both biographical and analytical critics to accept at face value Whitman's own claims to a kind of anti-literary primitiveness. For the literary-historical school, as for the analytical critics, such claims are but part of the poet's artfulness, his pose.

Much of the historical criticism in the fifties and sixties was carried forward in critical biographies and handbooks, as well as in introductions and notes to the various editions of the poems. The most influential single book in this genre did not appear until 1974. This was Floyd Stovall's *The Foreground of Leaves of Grass*, which still stands as the broadest and most complete survey of Whitman's reading. Stovall shows that, while Whitman was obviously not a systematic scholar, he was certainly a devoted reader and throughout his life was in search of other authors who, either by contrast to his own work or by likemindedness, could help shore up his own self-image as a literary figure. Though he covers Whitman's exposure to the theatrical arts, science, and popular literature, Stovall's main focus falls upon Whitman's comprehension of the canonical literature of the United States, Great Britain, and Europe, and, perhaps most interestingly, upon the poet's reading practices, especially his tendency to follow closely reviews and summaries of books in magazines and newspapers and to preserve such notices in clippings and notebooks.

As the title suggests, Stovall takes seriously Emerson's guess about the origins of *Leaves of Grass*, arguing that "there was nothing sudden or very remarkable about the transition between 1845 and 1855 from Walter Whitman, the first-rate journalist but third-rate poet and fictionist, to Walt Whitman, the original genius and accomplished poet of *Leaves of Grass*. There was a change, to be sure, but no such revolutionary change as to be called a new birth, and no illumination that cannot be accounted for by a normal, if unusual, intellectual and spiritual growth" (13). For the historian, as Morris Berman suggests, "miracles don't just happen, they have contexts" (164). No wonder, then, that the literary historian Stovall prefers a gradualist interpretation of the growth of *Leaves of Grass* over one that emphasizes the miraculous. By such lights, Whitman's development as a poet appears not as dramatic and sudden, but as a slow and painstaking work involving reading, note-taking, and experimentation within conventional genres—a literary apprenticeship or adolescence. For Whitman, this period was quite long, lasting into his early middle age, with *Leaves of Grass* not appearing until his thirty-sixth year of life. According to Stovall, even the "flowering" that occurred then was a "gradual opening of latent faculties under the stimulation of his reading combined with a growing confidence in himself" (14).

Not surprisingly, Stovall (referring to Anne Gilchrist's proposal to Whitman) insists upon "a clear distinction between the imaginary figure in *Leaves of Grass* and the real man," while nevertheless admitting that the "ideal" man "evolved from the real," just as the "latent" or "innate" qualities of Whitman the poet evolved under the guidance of the self-educating reader (15-16). Even the apparent "primitivism" of the *Leaves* has roots not only in the poet's primeval self, but also in his more conscious literary wanderings, especially in his acquaintance with Hebrew and bardic poetry as well as literary theory in the tradition of German romantic philosophy (184-204). But Stovall ultimately (and judiciously) concedes that Whitman's reading of other poets had only a marginal effect upon his own writing. His "critical sense developed more slowly than his intellect and his imagination," Stovall argues, finally agreeing with other modern critics who argue that poems like "Out of the Cradle" and "Lilacs" are "less characteristic of Whitman than 'Song of Myself' because they have been more influenced by the musical qualities of poets like Shelley and Tennyson" (258). In the earlier poems, Stovall suggests, the British poets exerted an influence "more on the substance of [the] poems than on their verse form" (258). Moreover, he argues, "Even for the substance of *Leaves of Grass* Whitman's debt was almost wholly to prose works—to those of Carlyle and Emerson among others—and to the social and political thought developed in America from Revolutionary sources before 1850" (258).

The influence of Emerson is important enough for Stovall to devote his last chapter to the topic. Interestingly, however—and, I would argue, as part of the process of canonization whereby the poet's originality, his personal contribution to the literary tradition, must be stressed—Stovall highlights not the similarities but the differences between Whitman and Emerson, aligning a long series of passages from the writing of the two authors, in which the content is similar but the style quite different. In Stovall's view, Whitman's originality consists primarily in the development of a new verse form for his prophetic utterances; his realism ("both as a philosophical principle" to be distinguished from Emersonian idealism and "as a basis for poetic style"); his stress on urban life and a social theory deriving therefrom; his "crudeness in imagery and language' and "emphasis on sex as the basic principle of creativity"; his "love and appreciation" of music, theater, and the performing arts; and his firm belief in "the immortality of the individual self," which Emerson appears on several occasions to have questioned (304). "The fundamental difference between Emerson and Whitman," Stovall concludes, "was in their personalities," but he gives a historian's or sociologist's account of "personality" with an emphasis on educational and environmental influences: "Emerson was a somewhat over-refined product of New England Puritanism, overlaid but not obscured by philosophical idealism drawn from many sources," while "Whitman was a comparatively unrefined product of a working-class country and small-town democracy, overlaid with a thin coating of Quaker and Evangelical piety and a thick coating of big-city worldliness" (304). If Emerson was an "intellectual" and an "aristocrat," Whitman was a "man of feeling" and a "democrat" (304). It is interesting that, even in the literary-historical project of canonization, Whitman's primary distinction, especially as it is foregrounded in this pointed comparison to Emerson, is to have brought a nonintellectual element into the American intellectual and literary tradition, thereby creating a new tradition of strongly emotional and democratic literature. As a literary figure, then, in Stovall's impressively honest appraisal, Whitman remains, at least to some extent, antiliterary.

Stovall thus ends by substantiating Matthiessen's assertion that "the whole question of the relation of Whitman's theory and practice of art to Emerson's is fascinating, since, starting so often from similar if not identical positions, they end up with very different results"—a statement which becomes the epigraph for Jerome Loving's more detailed analysis of the two writers' work in *Emerson, Whitman, and the American Muse* (1982). If Stovall's survey exhausts what may be considered the most traditional version of literary-historical investigation in Whitman criticism—the attempt to connect Whitman to a literary tradition via source study—it certainly does not close the field entirely. Loving's book is one of several original works that go beyond Stovall by combining an interest in influence and reception with a treatment of Whitman's career as an emblematic figure in the history of American poetry.

In what turns out to be a strong assertion of cyclic organism, Loving traces the intertwining career paths of Emerson and Whitman, arguing (against Stovall) that "despite the difference in their backgrounds or culture," the two authors were much alike in "temperament and talent," a "similarity which accounts for their complementary roles in the literature of the American Renaissance" (12). Discounting "theories that have tended to stereotype Emerson as the 'gentleman' and Whitman as the 'rough' of American literature," Loving argues that both writers "overcame the stifling influences of their cultures to accept the challenge of producing a literature that was uniquely American because it reflected the spontaneity of 'becoming' in the New World" (12). Thus: "Emersonian self-reliance became 'original energy' in Whitman's *Leaves of Grass*" (12).

Implicitly, Loving follows Matthiessen in attempting to determine the success of literary practice by how well it embodies the dominant literary theories of the authors. He draws, for example, upon Whitman's own analysis of Emerson's character (from his conversations with Horace Traubel) to explain the tendency of literary historians to overlook the similarities in the two writers. In Emerson, Whitman "perceived two distinctly different selves" (13). One was a public, official self—the man of letters, the genteel figure of society, the cautious reformer; the other Emerson was the author of *Nature* and the early essays, a revolutionary and original thinker who "required more freedom, at times 'wildness'" (14). This private, deeper Emerson was, in Loving's reading, the author of the 1855 letter warmly receiving the "gift" of *Leaves of Grass* and praising its "free and brave thought," a letter that Emerson in his role as public figure would later have to explain and may have even regretted.

The distinction of private and public, or "natural and artificial" (15), a concept based upon Emerson's and Whitman's organic theory of art and life, becomes a major thematic concern, even a unifying principle for Loving. The great achievement of each writer, in Loving's view, was to gain after a "long foreground" a "crack in . . . conventionality," a fracture through which the private, deepest self could grow into the light of public expression. In the middle 1850s, the two writers experienced a momentary intersection during the prime of their careers, a time when they commanded a tenuous, yet powerful union of private conviction and public voice. By then, Emerson had thrown off the cloak of the minister to become the "poet-preacher" of the early essays (17). He had completed his "transformation from Unitarian to Transcendentalist," perceiving the "occult relation between man and the vegetable" that presents nature as "an end in itself" rather than as a mere rhetorical device of "anthropomorphic religion" (23, 32, 37). But he had not yet slipped into the role of "the sage of Concord" inspired by the hero worship of his disciples. The 1850s was also the time Whitman discovered his vocation as a true poet. Abandoning the "pose" of "journalist as moral paragon" and moving beyond "slavish imitation" of other writers, Whitman took what he had learned from his exposure to politics and natural science, his reading of Emerson and other romantics, and his "merging of his sexual preference [for men] with an understanding of the Neoplatonic concept of amelioration," then "simply discovered his character" (60, 67, 68).

While rejecting many of the particulars of John Burroughs's early study of Whitman—particularly the claim, probably inspired by Whitman's own anxiety of influence, that he did not read Emerson until 1856 (62)—Loving recapitulates and substantiates much of the spirit of Burroughs's work and of Whitman's self-interpretations. In particular, Loving's understanding of Whitman's (and Emerson's) discovery of a literary form suitable for the expression of the deepest self is quite close to Burroughs's idea that Whitman allowed Nature to speak through him (Burroughs, *Whitman* 169). In thus amplifying the concept of Whitman's "mediumship," Loving relies upon the robust tradition of geneticism, which reproduces the poet's own theory of expression. In "Calamus," for example, Whitman refers to his poems as "the blossoms of my blood" that spring from the inmost self, "the conceal'd heart" ("Scented Herbage of My Breast," *Leaves: Norton* 114).

If Loving's understanding of Whitman's and Emerson's success is largely romantic, however, his adoption of a cyclic thesis to round out his argument is thoroughly modern. The nearly miraculous coincidence of public and private, of nature and poetry, of rhetoric and expression—like the "intersection" of Whitman's and Emerson's career paths—was quite brief, in Loving's view. Like Chase before him, Loving argues that by the late 1860s both Emerson and Whitman experienced a failure of vision, substituting a version of "God-reliance" for the old program of "self-reliance," a "compromise" that Emerson initiated in his essay "Experience" and that Whitman began to accept in the 1860 *Leaves* and adopted in full by "Passage to India" (170). After 1870, Whitman busied himself with "playing the poet" rather than with writing as an inspired poet (186). Thus, the cycle of his career (like Emerson's) swung through a period of conventionality to a brief but glorious moment of originality and back again to conventionality (albeit a modified conventionality).

Ultimately, Loving's interpretation rests upon a strong assertion of the ethic of individualism. Following Asselineau and Edwin Miller, Loving admires the Whitman who ventures farthest in the quest for self-discovery. This figure dominates the poems of the 1850s, the peak of the poet's career, and passes out of sight with "Passage to India," after which, in addition to growing increasingly religious, "Whitman came to forsake self-reliance for the composite strength of a nation" (191). In Loving's work, then, the growth of *Leaves of Grass* is, as in critical biography, deeply tied to the growth (and decline) of the man Walt Whitman. But Loving avoids explaining the success of the poet by some psychological category (like "sublimation"). Nor does he account for success in aesthetic or rhetorical terms (such as the various "unities" of Miller, Crawley, Waskow, or Marki). Rather, the poet's success is seen as a kind of harmony between the inner self and the outward expression that may best be summed up by the concept of vocation. In accepting his "calling" (a voice from within), the great poet discovers his most effective public "voice."

While Loving's book ties literary-historical criticism closely to biography, the recent books of Kenneth Price and Ezra Greenspan cultivate alliances with analytical criticism and with a historicist criticism more closely attuned to sociopolitical issues. In *Whitman and Tradition: The Poet in His Century* (1990), Price argues that "Too often influence studies give the impression that authors live in an isolated and timeless realm of literary immortals," ignoring "the importance of book reviews and other minor writing, the power of publishers and censors, the role of immediate audiences of all kinds, and the significance of the academy" (1). Yet, in Price's view, these are the very materials critics must examine if we are "to understand how ideas, works, and reputations actually survive in transmission or how reputations rise and fall, sometimes to rise again" (1). The emphasis on "transmission" and "reputation," influence and reception, indicates Price's modernist concern with poetry as a profession, a specialized way of life, but his openness to the suggestions of a newer historicism is indicated in his determination to keep in view "a broader social field" (1). His interest in reputation and transmission links his work to James Miller's *The American Quest for a Supreme Fiction: Whitman's Legacy in the Personal Epic* and to Perlman, Folsom, and Campion's *Walt Whitman: The Measure of His Song*. At the same time, Price's interest in an expanded social context connects to the work of politically oriented critics like Betsy Erkkila (especially *Walt Whitman among the French*) and Robert K. Martin, whose concern with the transmission of Whitman's influence is clear in both *The Homosexual Tradition in American Poetry* and the recent collection of essays, *The Continuing Presence of Walt Whitman: The Life after the Life*.

Price's originality derives from his focus on Whitman's conscious artistry as the receiver and founder of a tradition. He maintains that "the 'rough' persona created by Whitman, as daring as it was memorable, has impeded critical understanding of his poetry" (148). Though a "denier of tradition," in Price's account, Whitman is also a poet who "possessed the enabling ego of a tradition builder" and who appears, moreover, as a surprisingly "erudite poet possessing a shrewd understanding of his literary heritage" (148-49). Price resists Whitman's own insistence on his originality, his determination to forgo literary models and literariness itself, his unprecedented "sweeping rejection of English poets," and his orientation toward the future as the starting point of a new tradition (which, as Price cleverly notes, "demonstrates the falsity of the widely held assumption that the tradition monger is inevitably conservative") (3). With the kind of independence that Whitman (ironically) encouraged in his readers, Price argues that "the sheer energy of Whitman's denials of connectedness with literary high culture . . . suggests that more attention should be paid to his defensive strategy" (4).

To this task, Price turns his attention. In a closely argued source study, he begins by building upon the work of Blodgett and Stovall in a reconstruction and explication of "the unacknowledged, suppressed, but nevertheless operative English heritage" (5). He traces the poet's ambivalent and shifting relation to writers like Shakespeare and Carlyle from Whitman's early denial and discreet incorporation of their influence to his more gracious acceptance of their greatness in late works like *Specimen Days*, a book that Price reads as calculated to ensure a public image of broad-mindedness and generosity for the elderly Whitman. In this reading, as well as in his treatment of Whitman's relation to Emerson (in which he sees more irony and artistic distance than other critics have noticed) and other American contemporaries like Poe, Bryant, and Longfellow, Price continually emphasizes the rhetorical quality of Whitman's engagement with other writers. His artful echoes of their work, just like his denials of their influence, appear to have been, according to Price, carefully calculated to appeal to the ideal audience Whitman spent a lifetime trying to create for his poems.

The best that can be said of Whitman's appeals is that, as Price quite adequately demonstrates, they worked. Though the poet may not have been as successful in creating a contemporary audience as he could have hoped, his efforts were rewarded in the next generation with an appreciative and sophisticated readership. Whereas others (like James Miller and Robert Martin) have demonstrated Whitman's presence among the modern poets, Price documents Whitman's reception during the onset of modernism in the generation of writers at the turn of the century and thus provides a missing link in the narrative of Whitman's influence. With concentration and care, he maps the subtle intertextual network that arose among novelists like Hamlin Garland, Kate Chopin, and E. M. Forester, and the Harvard poets George Santayana, George Cabot Lodge, William Vaughn Moody, and Van Wyck Brooks. Whitman's appeal for these writers, as Price shows, was associated with the very things that had been detested or ignored by his own contemporaries—especially his general iconoclasm in sexual mores and his more particular willingness to give voice to homosexual impulses. The Harvard group, for example, "spurned the messianic image presented by Horace Traubel and *The Conservator* in favor of the poet as writer and as the founder of a tradition of iconoclasts" (126).

Thus, Price concludes, "Later writers found assurance in the image of Whitman as founder: he was an author vilified then vindicated, mocked then admired. He managed to intertwine forces of literary prestige and anti-literary counter-culturalism by becoming himself a center of power while giving the impression that he stood outside all privileged positions" (150-51). In addition to perpetuating his own reputation, therefore, Whitman delivered on his promise (in "Song of Myself") to speak for "marginalized groups" (151), among them the homosexuals, the alienated women, and the literary bohemians who would break the cultural monopoly of the genteel tradition and create the milieu of literary modernism. Price's revised understanding of how traditions are created and transmitted thus places Whitman's work in a new, more organically rich relation to nineteenth-century culture (in Great Britain as well as America) and to the emerging culture of the present century.

A similar effect is achieved by Ezra Greenspan, who, like Price, takes as his starting point Whitman's attempt to create a reading public for his poems. In *Walt Whitman and the American Reader* (1990), Greenspan brings a yet wider-ranging historical perspective to bear on the fascinating question of the relation of "I" to "you" in *Leaves of Grass*. In keeping with the organic tradition, Greenspan conceives of the relation of Whitman and his audience as an evolving one. Its growth depended not only upon the early education and reading of the poet (as Stovall suggested in his more traditional literary history), but also upon Whitman's early experience as an apprentice printer and journalist, which prepared the would-be poet to enter the tightening nexus of author, publisher, and reader that was emerging at midcentury. It gave him an insider's position, which Greenspan illuminates more clearly than any scholar before him. From this position, Whitman gradually shifted roles from publisher (in the broad sense of both printer and publicizer, or journalistic reviewer) to publisher-author of the first edition of *Leaves of Grass* (which Whitman printed and publicized almost totally on his own), and on to his final position as professional author.

Of his approach to Whitman, Greenspan observes, "In contrast to the attention paid by much recent literary criticism to the privatized encounter between writer, reader, and text, my own attention has been drawn primarily to the historicity of these agents and of their patterns of interaction, to the ways literary culture—and in particular, the creation, production, distribution, consumption, interpretation, and critical evaluation of imaginative literature—is created out of and in response to the changing circumstances of human life lived in society" (vii-viii). In this manifesto, Greenspan moves in the direction that Jerome McGann says literary criticism must move if it is to become self-critical and truly historical—connecting formal, linguistic, and semiological study with "those other traditional fields of inquiry so long alienated from the center of our discipline: textual criticism, bibliography, book production and distribution, [and] reception history" (McGann 81). Taking his initial direction from Carroll Hollis, Greenspan provides an extended analysis of "the strongly reader-addressed quality of Whitman's poetry" (viii). In Greenspan's reading, Whitman's encounter with the audience constitutes "one of the most culturally significant and aesthetically cultivated features of [his] art" and, in addition, sets his poetry apart from that of earlier romantics who, in M. H. Abram's famous formulation, all but disregarded their real audience in an extended experiment with lyrical soliloquy (Greenspan viii, 107-8).

Greenspan (again like Hollis) asserts that "the primary influence on Whitman's style came from nonliterary sources," particularly from the language of journalists and orators of his day (viii). Faced with improvements in printing and the distribution of texts, as well as a rapidly expanding reading public, Whitman joined popular speakers, writers, and publishers in a brisk enthusiasm over the possibilities of democratizing the institution of literature. When therefore, in his open letter to Emerson that accompanies the 1856 *Leaves*, Whitman exults over the ever-increasing numbers of booksellers, printing presses, penny dailies, "story papers," "low-priced flaring tales," and "numberless copies" of sentimental novels, he is, Greenspan argues,

"describing . . . the school of letters in which he had received his education in the 1830s and 1840s and from which he exited the following
decade with the ambition to write first-rate poems for first-rate persons" (163). In his effort to give as complete a picture as possible of
Whitman's "education" in this peculiar "school of letters," Greenspan
is forced to cover much well-known territory in Whitman studies. Yet
his new emphasis on the culture of public literature throws everything
into a new light. In both his detailed examination of Whitman's literary apprenticeship and his readings of individual poems (especially poems like "Crossing Brooklyn Ferry" that employ the techniques of
direct address to the audience), Greenspan frames the story of
Whitman's professional growth with an attention to detail and a
thoroughness of contextualization that will not likely be matched in
the near future.

Greenspan also does his part to institutionalize the metanarrative
of sequential or historical organicism currently dominant in Whitman
studies. Along with Loving, in fact, both he and Price not only accept
but refine this model. Both critics note a change in Whitman that begins in earnest with the 1860 *Leaves*. Price points out a relatively gentle
"shift in style" that suggests "a writer less opposed to literary conventions" (61), while Greenspan sees a more profound shift: As "the old
expansive thrust of the persona outward toward the world of man, nature, and nation was reversed, was redirected inwardly toward a deeper
and more intense self-understanding," the 1860 poems began to exhibit
a turn toward narrative (indicating "the need to tell the story of the
self") as well as deep stylistic changes, such as those evident in the
"quiet restraint, . . . spare wording, and . . . tight formal symmetry" of "I
Saw in Louisiana a Live-Oak Growing" (199-201). The shifts of 1860
were, in the accounts of both Price and Greenspan, successful, but they
also suggested changes that soon thereafter led to a collapse of
Whitman's poetic enterprise. The "glittering prospects" of that "Year of
Meteors," says Greenspan, slipped all too soon into the oblivion of the
Civil War (213). The poet's former ability to recast tradition on his own
terms eroded, says Price, into mere conventionalization. "As early as
1865," Price argues, Whitman "turned increasingly to inversions, literary diction, and other poeticisms. He turned also to a more overtly al-
lusive style, signaling a renegotiation of his relationship with other
poets. . . . Forces of destruction and disorder stimulated his desire to become a joiner and a healer" (70).

Despite their view of the poet's declining powers, however, neither
Price nor Greenspan pictures Whitman as out of control or at odds
with himself. Rather, both adopt a traditional rhetorical model in presenting a Whitman in command of his poetic materials. His efforts to
create an audience and to turn tradition his way are viewed as the work
of a conscious artist. An index of their commitment to this model is
that, like the analytical critics Waskow and Marki—hearkening back

indeed to Bucke—Price and Greenspan draw upon mechanical metaphors to describe the poet's manipulations. Price speaks of the "transformations," "structures," and "techniques" Whitman used in his efforts to secure an effective "transmission" (59). Greenspan describes Whitman's poetic project as an "experiment . . . with the dynamics of poetic communication," borrowing Emerson's metaphor of the "galvanic circuit" to describe the poet's theories on the relation of author and audience (157, 173). The approach of the two historical critics thus represents a strong rejection of the psychoanalytical notion of the power of the unconscious mind over the artist's will, as well as the New Critical concept of the intentional fallacy and the "new historicist" trend to view history as a concept that somehow replaces (or "constructs") the will of the author. Though fully conscious and possessed of clear intentions, however, their poet is hardly infallible. Again and again, history finds him adjusting too early or too late to the demands of audience and tradition. More in line with the view of history offered by William James or John Dewey—or even Karl Marx, who said that men and women make history but not under conditions of their own choosing—Price and Greenspan give us a poet heroically, but not always successfully, confronting the contingencies and ironies of his situation.

In treating the poems within a story of growth and decline, Price and Greenspan also depart from the tendency of the analytical critics to seek a metaphorical, symbolic, or otherwise "intrinsic" principle of organic unity for *Leaves of Grass*. The unity they present is rather a narrative unity. As Paul Ricoeur explains—like metaphor, which joins two disparate objects in a new relation of thirdness—narrative is dialectical in its tendency to synthesize various elements into a dynamic whole, a plot. In favoring this approach, Price and Greenspan reflect the temper of their times. By 1990, historical and political criticism have come to dominate Whitman studies, as I show in the next chapter.

4: The Prophet of Democracy

In the 1855 preface to *Leaves of Grass*, Whitman repeatedly insists that "the genius of the United States" resides "most in the common people" (*Leaves: 1855*, 5-6) and that the place of the poet is to give voice to this "genius" and thereby make clear the path by which the spirit of the times may best be realized. This task involves a grave responsibility that puts the poet in a position similar to that of the biblical prophets, who combined spiritual and moral discourse with political injunctions for the chosen people of God and who have been echoed by countless jeremiads in American literature (as Sacvan Bercovitch has shown). "Folks expect of the poet to indicate more than the beauty and dignity which always attach to dumb real objects," Whitman writes; "they expect him to indicate the path between reality and their souls" (10). Hinting at the potential shortcomings of a purely literary or aesthetic approach to *Leaves of Grass*, he says (in one of the clearest instances of his own organicism), the poet should never take trouble with "ornaments" or even "fluency," for "the rhyme and uniformity of perfect poems show the free growth of metrical laws and bud from them as unerringly and loosely as lilacs and roses on a bush" (11). What then should poets do? They should show the way by which all people can become living poems. Here is the formula of 1855: "Love the earth and sun and the animals, despise riches, give alms to everyone that asks, stand up for the stupid and crazy, devote your income and labor to others, hate tyrants, argue not concerning God, have patience and indulgence toward the people, take off your hat to nothing known or unknown or to any man or number of men, go freely with powerful uneducated persons and with the young and with the mothers of families, read these leaves in the open air every season of every year of your life, re-examine all you have been told at school or church or in any book, dismiss whatever insults your own soul, and your very flesh shall be a great poem and have the richest fluency not only in its words but in the silent lines of its lips and face and between the lashes of your eyes and in every motion and joint of your body" (11).

Such thoughts and such purposes inform much of the writing in the first four editions of *Leaves of Grass*. The emotion the author inspires, or the response he appears to be seeking, is not intellectual sympathy or admiration of his technical ability (though mental sympathy and aesthetic admiration are likely to follow—as naturally as buds bloom in the Spring). The dominant feeling is rather devotion, discipline, and action. For some the feeling is "religious"; for others, "political." George Hutchinson probably comes closest to touching the heart of the matter in his suggestion that Whitman's poetic speech-acts are ecstatic performances that invite an ecstatic response or participation on the part of the reader. Very likely, in his period of "literary shamanism," Whitman saw little distinction between religious poetry (addressed to his readers' "souls") and political poetry (addressed to "the genius of the United States," the common people). In a line added to the 1856 version of "I Sing the Body Electric," the poet asks, "if the body were not the soul, what is the soul?" (*Leaves: Norton* 94). And, as sure as the connection of body and soul, Whitman creates a strong link between the individual's body and the body politic in this poem with its striking twin treatments of slavery and prostitution—and indeed the broader sociopolitical manifestations of buying and selling upon the suffering human body—"A man's body at auction" and "A woman's body at auction" (*Leaves: Norton* 98, 99). The interpenetration of body, soul, and political body is made yet the clearer by a remarkable vision (or "fantasy") recorded in an 1847 Whitman notebook, which becomes the point of departure for Lewis Hyde's original reading in *The Gift*. The notebook entry may well have been one of the first realizations of the synthesis that would unfold eight years later in the 1855 *Leaves*: "I am hungry and with my last dime get me some meat and bread, and have appetite enough to relish it all," the poet writes: "But then like a phantom at my side suddenly appears a starved face, either human or brute, uttering not a word. Now do I talk of mine and his?—Has my heart no more passion than a squid or clam shell has?" The passage ends with a probing conclusion, which, like the 1856 line on the relation of body and soul, takes the form of a question: "And what is it but my soul that hisses like an angry snake, Fool! will you stuff your greed and starve me?" (qtd. in Hyde 160-61).

If we accept the prevailing attitude of historical criticism (represented in the last chapter by the varied work of Chase, Loving, Price, and Greenspan) that the most vigorous and enduring poems of *Leaves of Grass* were composed in the first ten years of the book's "life" (between 1855 and 1865), then we must account for three intertwining phenomena prominent in those years—the spirituality of *Leaves of Grass*, the politics, and the remarkable blending of spirituality and politics. The need to explain one or more of these related phenomena—to take seriously Whitman's claim on the title of prophet of democracy—has driven a strong tradition of primarily historical scholarship in Whitman studies. This line of criticism stands as an alternative to the trend in modern professional criticism to portray Whitman primarily as a poet, a literary figure who somehow stands above or apart from the history and politics of his time.

The dissenting tradition of historicism, however, offers no single method for returning the poet to his place in history. A number of studies in this vein begin (almost ironically) with a consideration of spiritual matters. Quite popular among the first generation of Whitman commentators, mystical interpretations of *Leaves of Grass* fell into disfavor in the early twentieth century as professional critics, mounting their quest for objectivity, distanced themselves from "hagiographers" like O'Connor, Bucke, and Traubel. But then, in the 1940s, Henry Seidel Canby discovered a means of reinvigorating the spiritual Whitman. His insight was to foreground the sociopolitical implications of the prophet's ethos and thereby demonstrate that Whitman's spirituality was deeply connected with his vision of American politics. This approach caught on again in the 1980s, when such critics as Lewis Hyde, George Hutchinson, and David Kuebrich explored Whitman's political religion (or religious politics, depending upon the emphasis). Their works suggested, in turn, a strong connection with other, more ideologically oriented scholars (many of whom came of age in the era of the civil rights movement, Vietnam, and feminism). Exploring the connections between Whitman's texts and their historical contexts, these scholars extended the work of older historicists, especially those who wrote in the turbulent period between the world wars, notably Vernon Parrington and Newton Arvin. The historicist revival of the 1980s brought to Whitman studies an interpretive energy inspired by contemporary literary theory and an expansion of political inquiry informed by neomarxian, feminist, and gay criticism. This ferment resulted in books as different as those of Robert K. Martin, Harold Aspiz, Wynn Thomas, Kerry Larson, Betsy Erkkila, and Michael Moon.

Even though some overlap has occurred among the books, the diversity of scholarly perspectives and interpretation remains remarkable. In this chapter, I try to respect this diversity by avoiding general pronouncements about the "new historicism." (On the the problems of "new historicism" as a critical category, see Gregory Jay's *America the Scrivener* and Brook Thomas's *The New Historicism*.) Instead, I explore the profusive growth in Whitman studies by asking what has been added to the critical heritage and what has been imported, extended, or rejected.

Spiritual Politics

Richard Maurice Bucke is justly remembered as the main progenitor of the spiritual emphasis in Whitman studies. How far Whitman himself endorsed Bucke's hagiographical slant remains unclear and likely would have been different during different periods of his life. It is clear enough, however, that parts of the 1855 preface recommend the view, as does a famous note toward the third (1860) edition of *Leaves of*

Grass, in which Whitman speaks of his work as "the Great Construction of the New Bible" (qtd. in Bowers 45). Nevertheless, as shown in chapter 2, the poet was somewhat uncomfortable with Bucke's insistence that he was a special breed of human being, gifted with a deep insight into the nature of the cosmos. In his own contributions to Bucke's biographical study, Whitman balanced his admirer's enthusiasm by stressing the representative qualities of *Leaves of Grass*, his intention as poet to take the part of the common people whom he described in the 1855 preface as "the genius of the United States."

Unencumbered after the poet's death of the balancing influence upon his writing, Bucke gave free reign to his ideas about Whitman's spiritual status, not only in his work as one of the literary executors, but more famously in his book *Cosmic Consciousness*, which was first published in 1901 (and is still in print today, quite popular in fact among "New Age" enthusiasts in North America and England).

Bucke defines cosmic consciousness as a "higher form of consciousness than that possessed by the ordinary man [or woman]." Common mortals, he suggests, must rest content with self consciousness, an awareness which separates people from the other higher animals possessed only of "simple consciousness" (1). But mere self consciousness, he argues, can barely conceive of the "third form which is as far above Self Consciousness as is that above Simple Consciousness" (2). Cosmic consciousness includes not only the implied mental grasp of the whole "life and order of the universe," but also a special experience of "intellectual enlightenment or illumination," following which the enlightened one enters "a state of moral exaltation, an indescribable feeling of elevation, elation, and joyousness, and a quickening of the moral sense," and finally obtains "a sense of immortality, a consciousness of eternal life, not a conviction that he [or she] shall have this, but the consciousness that he [or she] has it already" (3).

Bucke's study ranges far and wide over intellectual and religious history, both Western and Eastern, in the search for exemplars of cosmic consciousness. But he concludes that none—not even the Buddha—fits the definition better than does Whitman, "the best, most perfect, example the world has so far had of the Cosmic Sense, first because he is the man in whom the . . . faculty has been, probably, most perfectly developed, and especially because he is, par excellence, the man who in modern times has written distinctly and at large from the point of view of Cosmic Consciousness, and who also has referred to its facts and phenomena more plainly and fully than any other writer either ancient or modern" (255). In *Leaves of Grass*, the key passage for Bucke comes from the 1855 "Song of Myself" (later section 5). The passage changes little from edition to edition and includes some of the most frequently quoted lines in all of Whitman's writing. It is thus worth quoting at length (in the original 1855 version with Whitman's eccentric use of ellipses and periods intact):

I believe in you my soul . . . . the other I am must not abase itself to
   you,
And you must not be abased to the other.

Loafe with me on the grass . . . . loose the stop from your throat,
Not words, not music or rhyme I want . . . . not custom or lecture,
   not even the best,
Only the lull I like, the hum of your valved voice.

I mind how we lay in June, such a transparent summer morning;
You settled your head athwart my hips and gently turned over
   upon me,
And parted the shirt from my bosom-bone, and plunged your
   tongue to my barestript heart,
And reached till you felt my beard, and reached till you held my
   feet.

Swiftly arose and spread around me the peace and joy and knowl-
   edge that pass all the art and argument of the earth;
And I know that the hand of God is the elderhand of my own,
And I know that the spirit of God is the eldest brother of my own,
And that all the men ever born are also my brothers . . . . and the
   women my sisters and lovers,
And that a kelson of the creation is love (*Leaves: 1855*, 30-31).

Bucke argues that the passage represents an actual experience that
probably occurred in 1853, in which "the old self" ("the other I am")
gave way to a new self ("my soul"). The new self, in Bucke's account,
came to Whitman on a June morning and "took (though gently) absolute possession of him," illuminating him with the knowledge of
God's brotherhood and of his corresponding familial (or sexual) relation to all men and women in the world (227-28). In strong contrast to a
literary-historical rendering of the passage—such as that given by
Bradley and Blodgett, who see in the lines a new setting for an old poetic genre, the debate between the body and the soul (*Leaves: Norton*
32-33n)—Bucke's reading connects the poem to the extensive literature
of mystical illumination (the New Testament story of Paul's conversion, for example) even as it allows for a biographical content that
stresses the historical uniqueness of Whitman's experience and writing.
    Bucke was hardly alone in suggesting that Whitman's message was
deeply religious (or mystical) as well as poetic. On this point,
Whitman's early defenders spoke in unison. Before Bucke, there was
William Douglas O'Connor, whose treatment of the prophetic
Whitman in *The Good Gray Poet* (1866) functions polemically.

O'Connor dismisses would-be censors and critics as failing to recognize and to comprehend the spiritual depth of the poet, much as the Pharisees could not understand Jesus (and therefore could not tolerate him). The analogy between Whitman and Jesus reappears in O'Connor's Christmas tale "The Carpenter," in which a strikingly Whitmanian figure plays the role of a modern incarnation of Christ (Freedman 208-15). In his meditations on Whitman's Christ-like nature, however, O'Connor merges his religious heroes all too completely, obscuring the traits that distinguish Whitman as a figure of nineteenth-century history. Above all, he underestimated (and perhaps shook Whitman's own confidence in) the earthy and at times shocking treatment of sexuality (see F. D. Miller, "Before *The Good Gray Poet*"; Loving, *Whitman's Champion* 145).

Other friends, like the naturalist Burroughs, were more inclined to accept the full implications of Whitman's "primitive" side. Nevertheless, in *Whitman: A Study*, Burroughs insists that "we must place Whitman, not among the minstrels and edifiers of his age, but among its prophets and saviors" (21-22). *Leaves of Grass*, writes Burroughs, "is like the primitive literatures . . . in its prophetic cry and in its bardic simplicity and homeliness" though "unlike them in its faith and joy and its unconquerable optimism": "It has been not inaptly called the bible of democracy. . . . It is Israel with science and the modern added" (83).

The same receptive spirit animates Henry Seidel Canby's *Walt Whitman: An American*, one of the few modern biographical studies to accept the full implications of Whitman's prophetic utterances. Published in 1943 in the midst of the second world war, Canby's book brings out the political dimension of Whitman's interest in the inner life (and the physical life) of his fellow Americans. Canby argues that *Leaves of Grass* celebrates "not a real America, though the real America was his background and the source of his inspiration," but "a symbolic America, existing in his own mind, and always pointed toward a future of which he was prophetic" (v). According to Canby, Whitman remained throughout his life a rebel against "the complacent and dangerous certainties of the nineteenth century" (325), who nevertheless remained deeply religious in his poems, sacramental even, giving freely of "his own self-revelations and the powerful confessions of a man whose inner life was incredibly rich though he lived only on common ground" (342). Above all, "he offered love," which, in Canby's view, was not love "in the abstract, but as a function of a healthy, beautiful body, which the common man [or woman] might possess as certainly as the aristocrat" (342-43). Canby dwells upon Whitman's tendency to praise "sexual organs with the moral elevation of hymns" (118-19), anticipating the work of Hyde and Hutchinson, as well as the later interest in Whitman's sexual politics. But Canby's focus remains primarily biographical, and, with his loose narrative structure, he skirts

the issue of the changes that Whitman made in *Leaves of Grass*, imply-
ing (like Bucke, O'Connor, and Burroughs) that Whitman's poetic
strength was ascending throughout his career. In one of the most appreciative modern analyses of Whitman's style, Canby concludes that
"Whitman seldom failed in execution, but only in inspiration," but he
demurs when it comes to demonstrating and chronicling the failures
in inspiration (323). In general, then, Canby joins the first generation of
Whitman enthusiasts in combining praise of Whitman's technical excellence, prophetic spirituality, political energy, courage in challenging
sexual mores, and open celebration of communal love. In espousing a
genetic or progressive organicism, he brings romantic values over into
the twentieth century. What makes Canby different is the tendency,
which he shares with the historicists, to treat Whitman's inner life as
dialectically related to nineteenth-century political history. His conception of Whitman's religiosity thus respects Whitman's insistence on
the republican nature of the *Leaves* in a way that Bucke's interpretation
of cosmic consciousness does not.

In his 1946 essay on Whitman biography, Gay Wilson Allen praises
Canby's treatment of the social and intellectual milieu of Whitman's
poems and more or less ignores the other half of the dialectic—Canby's
interest in the spiritual qualities of Whitman's vision. Very likely, this
omission was part of a plan to rescue the literary and intellectual
Whitman and to lay the poet-prophet interpretation to rest once and
for all. With deep irony (recalling the tone of D. H. Lawrence, another
representative of the high modern temper), Allen describes the viewpoint of Bucke, Traubel, and Harned (Whitman's literary executors)
thus: "In the publication of the first edition of *Leaves of Grass* [the executors say] the 'hidden purpose of [Whitman's] life was suddenly revealed. . . . From this time on they make the story of the book the story
of Walt Whitman. Everything is grist for the mill, even . . . self-adver-
tising; the poet's life and personality are observed to grow more
Christlike each day. . . . [Through] all suffering, disappointments, and
misunderstanding Walt Whitman grows more serene, lovable, and
triumphant over the world and the flesh" (*Handbook* 29). By associat-
ing the poet-prophet scheme primarily with the work of the Whitman
"idolaters," Allen contributed more than perhaps anyone else to modern scholarship's skepticism about Whitman's mystical aims. Indeed, it
appears to have been Allen, not Bliss Perry, who first applied Perry's
term "hot little prophets" to the early biographers and literary executors (see *Handbook* 23). Perry used the term to describe Whitman's imi-
tators in free verse—among them "freaks and cranks and neurotic
women, with here and there a hot little prophet" (Perry 285-86)—
though Allen's usage approximates the spirit of Perry, who occasionally
offended the literary executors and who also welcomed the demytholo-
gizing of the poet (see Perry 291).

However, Allen himself was enough impressed with Whitman's mysticism to treat it fully in nearly every book he wrote. In speaking of the poet's efforts to express "the mystical unity of all human experience," Allen relates the theme to his central concern with the organic quality of the poet's compositional practices. "The very mystical nature of [his] poetic ambitions," Allen writes, "explains why Walt Whitman did not plan, write, and finish one book but continued for the remainder of his life to labor away at the same book. He was not writing autobiography in the ordinary sense, . . . but was attempting to express the inexpressible. . . . Hence, so long as the afflatus moved him, he could not finish his life-work or feel satisfied with the tangible words, pages, bound volumes" (*Handbook* 106). By the time Allen wrote *The Solitary Singer*, he had found a way to limit the application of the term "mystic" to Whitman's verse—reducing the spiritual element to a subsidiary of a broader interest in human love (*Solitary Singer* 159)—but still the poet-prophet was a figure to be reckoned with.

Without dying out altogether, critical interest in Whitman's prophetic ethos lagged for nearly three decades after World War II. In recent years, however, interest has been rekindled in a movement that began with the work of Lewis Hyde. In *The Gift: Imagination and the Erotic Life of Property* (1979), a study that blends comparative anthropology and literary criticism in an effort to understand the conceptual relation of gift-giving, creativity, and communal life, Hyde devotes a long chapter to Whitman that makes a strong break with the dominant lines of professional academic criticism outlined in chapters 2 and 3 and represented in Allen's attack on the "hot little prophets." It should come as no surprise that Hyde is not a professor, but a novelist and essayist—like D. H. Lawrence, another critic who monitored Whitman's attempt to play the prophet (largely as an anxious literary heir and competitor for the title). Unlike Lawrence, Hyde treats Whitman's prophetic ambitions sympathetically, but he also exhibits a demanding critical edge missing in "idolaters" like O'Connor and Bucke.

Hyde begins with an exposition of two forms of gift-giving, distinguished by motive and structure. In a number of nonwestern societies, Hyde reveals, gift-giving follows a circuitous pattern; gifts are passed from one person to the next, with rules or taboos preventing the receiver from returning a gift directly to the giver. The practice of giving is a matter of circulating objects whose worth is often determined not by some objective standard (such as monetary value) but rather by ritual and tradition. By contrast, Western societies in general, and especially capitalist societies, follow a reciprocating logic in gift-giving, which requires the receiver to "repay" the giver in kind. Whereas the motive of gift-giving in circuitously structured societies is to strengthen communal bonds through ritual practice, the motive in reciprocating societies is to create personal dependencies of the kind that undergird a market economy. Hyde argues, however, that the ancient structure of the circuit lingers in the Western practice of artistic creation. The artist gives to an audience but cannot always expect to be repaid in kind; at best, the audience, by taking up the practice of art, may complete the circuit by participating in the sort of serially structured transmissions of language and influence hypothesized in Kenneth Price's study of literary tradition. And, of course, recognizing the truism that no one can make a living solely from writing, the literary artist has little hope that the creative product will repay the creative effort, at least not in money. Nevertheless, Hyde suggests, one who strives to write professionally is drawn into a tension-filled relationship with his or her art and audience, a relationship which alternates between the two conflicting patterns of gift-giving.

In Hyde's view, Whitman's writings reveal, at their center, just such a tension. The conflict is embedded in the twin artistic motives of "sympathy" and "prudence" mentioned in the 1855 preface (Hyde 170-84). The great artist, as depicted by Whitman, must give himself or herself sympathetically to the reader, but must also, through prudence (or "pride"), maintain a strongly distinct identity to be worthy of the reader's attention. The drive toward prudence is self-protective; the drive toward sympathy is self-releasing, tending always toward "the merge," the mystical experience of overcoming personal and social boundaries. Between the two poles of sympathy and prudence, the drama of Whitman's best poems plays out. This bipolarity corresponds neatly to a number of other diametrically matched pairs of social categories, as Hyde makes clear: "We have, on the one hand, imagination, synthetic thought, gift exchange, use value, and gift-increase, all of which are linked by a common element of eros, or relationship, bonding, 'shaping into one.' And we have, on the other hand, analytic or dialectical thought, self-reflection, logic, market exchange, exchange value, and interest on loans, all of which share a touch of logos, of differentiating into parts" (155). The tension between art as a gift (in the no-Western sense) and art as a product (in a market economy) thus goes beyond a mere adjustment to writing for pay. The cost is psychological and indeed spiritual.

Hyde's interpretation extends (or corrects) Bucke's reading in four crucial ways. It eliminates the elitist trend that sets Whitman up as a modern saint, it reveals more clearly the importance of physical life in Whitman's conception of spirituality, it treats the theme of comradeship in relation to the poet's apparent homosexuality, and it extends Bucke's treatment of comparative religion with a more sophisticated understanding of anthropology.

Even as he focuses on the spiritual aspects of the poet's accomplishment, Hyde keeps Whitman's democratic moral and political vision in sight. He shows that, for Whitman, the soul is identified with the blessed poor represented by the hungry creature that intrudes upon the vision recorded in the early notebook. Hyde argues that "The real substance of the [mystical] state Whitman has entered [in 'Song of Myself,' section 5] lies in the range of his attention and affections"— which extends now to include all creatures, plant and animal and human (and indeed the inorganic as well as the organic). This change affects both the form and the content of the poems, as Hyde demonstrates: "One of the effects of . . . Whitman's famous catalogs [for example] is to induce his own equanimity in the reader. . . . The poet's eye focuses with unqualified attention on such a wide range of creation that our sense of discrimination soon withdraws for lack of use, and that part of us which can see the underlying coherence comes forward. . . . Whitman puts hierarchy to sleep" (163). Hyde's own sense of hierarchy and propriety does not remain in a perpetual slumber, however. He understands that, because Whitman was driven by personal as well as social, moral, and political aims, some poems will be truer to his vision than others. He therefore argues (in the tradition of Allen) that Whitman's "frustrated yearning" for love "sometimes undercuts" the poems, leaving them "clammy," the work of a "pushy lover," who demands of the reader as much as he gives. By contrast, the "best poems," according to Hyde, are those in which "Whitman manages that poise, requisite to both art and love, which offers the gift without insisting" on a return upon the investment (192). The poet often resolves the dilemma of self-sacrifice and self-protection, Hyde suggests, through a "politics of inner light," his desire to respect and nurture "the idiosyncratic" until "democracy enfranchises every self—politically and spiritually" (196).

Hyde is also able to account more effectively for Whitman's poetry of the body. Though O'Connor and Bucke praise Whitman's courageous treatment of sexuality in a prudish age, they both assert vaguely that Whitman somehow "purified" the body. To be fair, we must allow that they may have picked this view up from Whitman. During the war years, when he first met O'Connor, the poet was constantly urging himself in his notebooks to keep "pure" and "clean" to prepare himself for service in the hospitals and to cultivate within himself a (ritualistically) appropriate response to the climate of war (Zweig 324). In the poems of the 1850s, however, Whitman had been more content to take the body as it was and indeed be guided by it in his spiritual adventures. In "Song of Myself," Hyde isolates three situations in which Whitman falls into a "gifted state" of inspiration and illumination: "Reckoning and dividing, talking and doubt, all leave him when his lover holds his hand, when the god-lover shares his bed and gives him the baskets of rising dough, and when the soul plunges its tongue into his breast" (166). In each of these situations, "Whitman's body is the instrument of conversion," introducing an "element of 'bodily knowing'" into the poet's "gifted state" (166, 169). Intense physical experience thus provides the means for both realizing and representing the transcendental experience—a view that, as Hyde notes, connects Whitman's seemingly eccentric spirituality with the tradition of religious "enthusiasm," which has always allowed for the perception of religious impulses through bodily effects. "Whitman was Emerson's enthusiast," Hyde remarks (echoing Floyd Stovall), "Emerson with a body" (169). In his commentary on enthusiasm, Hyde reveals Whitman's affinities not only with the prophets of the Old Testament, the apostles of the New Testament, and the "inner light" Quakers, but also with some of the more extraordinary manifestations of the religious impulse in nineteenth-century America—the Shakers and Pentecostal Christians, for example (166-68). Indeed, Hyde could also have noted the Oneida Perfectionists and the Mormons, two more products of revivalism in the "burned-over district" of New York state (see Kuebrich, chapter 3; Bloom, *American Religion*).

Hyde is equally willing to consider what made Whitman not only similar to, but also different from, his contemporaries. He looks unswervingly upon Whitman's homosexual tendencies, for example, which appear to have distracted the poet from his mission to speak for all men and women by confronting him with a crucial difference between himself and the culturally dominant heterosexual male. Drawing deeply on the work of Asselineau, Hyde suggests that "Whitman was a man disappointed in love," and that, despite an occasional tendency to impose his "neediness" upon the reader, he heroically brought forth from his disappointment not only effective materials for artistic development—"the figure of an inarticulate young man," for example, that appears again and again as the object of Whitman's concern and affection in art as well as in life (188-89)—but also a general attitude toward artistic practice that led him to spiritual enlightenment: "Every artist secretly hopes his art will make him attractive. Sometimes he or she imagines it is a lover, a child, a mentor, who will be drawn to the work. But alone in the workshop it is the soul itself the artist labors to delight . . . , and if it accepts our sacrifice we may be, as Whitman was, drawn into a gifted state" (191). Despite the power that Whitman conjured from frustrated emotion, though, Hyde also sees Whitman's struggle with his homosexual desires as lying behind the ultimate collapse of his body and his art in the years following the Civil War (210-11). "During the war," writes Hyde, "[Whitman] allowed himself to cease being the 'superb calm character' imagined in the journal, 'indifferent of whether his love and friendship are returned.' Instead, he took the risk and opened himself up. And the soldiers returned his love, but not on the terms he wanted. He was always 'Dear Father' to them, never 'My darling'" (211). From that point on, "he associated his failing [artistic and bodily] strength with his wartime illness" (211). Hyde thus follows Chase and other historicists in seeing the war years as a turning point in the poet's career.

Finally—and here he builds upon Bucke's work—Hyde provides the keys whereby, through comparative anthropology, we can grasp

Whitman's connection to religious phenomena outside the limited pale of Western mysticism. In addition to Bucke (as well as Emerson and Thoreau), a number of modern scholars have noted Whitman's relation to non-Western spirituality. V. K. Chari's book *Whitman in the Light of Vedantic Mysticism* (1964) deserves particular mention. With the same enthusiasm for Whitman's unbridled expression that Hyde calls forth, Chari demonstrates that Whitman shares with the Hindu mystics an unabashed acceptance of sexuality and indeed draws upon the body as a resource for ascension to the realm of the soulful. Chari and Hyde part company, however, on the issue of the dark tension in Whitman's poems, which Chari, stressing the epic and heroic qualities of the *Leaves*, tends to think Whitman resolved more successfully than Hyde suggests (see Chari 14-15). Hyde broadens the field of comparison beyond Asian lore, drawing upon the practices and metaphysics of American Indian and Polynesian shamanism as it affects social structure and political identity. By tying intersecting religious strands to the tradition of critical theory associated with historical materialism in the West (particularly Marx's theory of use-value and exchange-value), Hyde develops a secularized theory of the soul that ultimately implies a force capable of unifying and intensifying otherwise disconnected and contingent experiences of historical life. In the process, he reinscribes Whitman's notion (and Shelley's before him) that the poet is the priest of the New World—both the world of North American democracy broadly and radically interpreted and the world renewed by the soulful directions of the prophetic artist.

George Hutchinson picks up the thread from Hyde, adding a professionalism and scholarly tone to the thesis that Whitman aspired to be a modern American shaman. A number of critics have used the term "ecstatic" in describing Whitman's poems and have even called him a shaman. (Hutchinson cites Gelpi, Marki, Anderson, and Kaplan, for example.) But none goes quite so far as Hutchinson in showing how Whitman's prophetic ambitions reach beyond the merely literary to make claims upon religion and politics, and no one applies the anthropological literature quite so directly as Hutchinson. In providing readings of the poems that are both more extensive and more traditional than Hyde's, Hutchinson brings the discussion of shamanism back to the mainstream of Whitman studies, building his connections to the earlier criticism and to other work appearing in the 1980s.

The Ecstatic Whitman: Literary Shamanism and the Crisis of the Union (1986) is an interdisciplinary exploration of Whitman's "ecstatic utterances." At times it leans toward old-fashioned influence study, revealing, for example, Whitman's possible familiarity with the concept of shamanism, gained from his reading of Volney (35-36). But Hutchinson's strength lies elsewhere—in his readings of Whitman's poems and biography under the twin lights of political history and comparative religion. In an argument that foretells the concern of historicist scholars with Whitman's odd blend of radicalism and conservatism (see Wynn Thomas and Kerry Larson, for example), Hutchinson suggests that Whitman's response to the antebellum crisis "bore a civil-religious charge similar to that of the evangelism behind most of the reform movements" of his day, a charge "progressive in its millennial hopefulness," but "conservative and 'regressive' in the way it harked back to the days of the founding fathers" (11). He argues, "Behind the later revivalism, antebellum spiritualism and related movements" of the middle nineteenth century "is the fear of failing the promise of the Revolution . . . , a great anxiety that the nation is not turning out as it was supposed to and that the only answer is spiritual revitalization. For Whitman and his generation, the Civil War was the crisis toward which all of this anxiety tended, the historical substitute for the millennium that so many Americans were expecting in the middle of the century" (25).

Whereas the psychoanalytical critics see Whitman's prophetic utterances as a cover for personal crises, Hutchinson sees them as a somewhat more measured and deliberate response to cultural crises. He notes that moments of social crisis generally provide the "social conditions in which trance and possession phenomena associated with religious immediatism arise throughout the world" (24). Under such conditions, ecstatic utterances and revelations are not, according to the literature on religious sociology, "psychotic or neurotic in the normal sense"—that is, they are not simply the attempts of a frustrated individual to accomplish ends for which he or she has no means—but are rather representative of a large-scale attempt to bridge the gulf between cultural ends and institutional means (15, 24). The shaman or religious enthusiast plays out alternative roles that show others how it is possible to move toward new behavioral and cultural norms. The aim of the shaman is thus, in Whitman's words, to point out for people "the path between reality and their souls" (Leaves: 1855, 10).

Hutchinson does not idolize Whitman, however, nor does he absolutely deny the possibility of personal neuroses playing a part in Whitman's adoption of the prophet's mantle. He concedes that "Whitman's anxiety and acute sensitivity to sensual stimuli (exposed especially in 'Calamus') derived from the repression of his sexual desires" (28). However (in an argument that recalls Richard Chase's and James Miller's inversion of Esther Shephard's negative assessment of Whitman's "pose"), Hutchinson claims that Whitman's hypersensitivity and homosexual inclinations do not limit his prophetic power but, on the contrary, "reveal how well-suited he was to an ecstatic role" (28). Whitman's psychological make-up, in Hutchinson's reading, "calls to mind the frequency of shamanic transvestism and the large proportion of shamans who are homosexual in some cultures"; functionally, "the erotic component of ecstasy (not only in shamanism but in other religious complexes as well) answers the special contact difficulties of people whose desires for sensual fulfillment are frustrated in daily life" (28).

Whitman was thus a healer who had healed himself, a role he enacts in many of his best poems of the early period, from the 1855 "Sleepers" to "The Wound Dresser" of 1865. Hutchinson's readings of these great monodramas as shamanic exhibitions therefore account for psychological factors even as they embrace political significances and as they provide answers to a number of questions regarding form—such as, how do the different roles that Whitman takes in long poems like "Song of Myself" relate to the overall structure of the poem? Unlike the formalists, Hutchinson is able to justify the "poet's awareness of the audience," which distinguishes the shamanic trance from mysticism in the Christian and Vedantic traditions (70). Since the shaman's aim is to help others or to discover solutions to communal problems, ecstatic performances engage the audience directly in the experience of revelation and inspiration. The presence of the audience, the "you" of Whitman's poems, "complicates the 'phasal' progression" of the major poems, indicating an organic complexity beyond the stiff structural formulations of critics influenced by the New Criticism (for a summary, see Kuebrich 210-11, n. 3). "Song of Myself" and "The Sleepers" may not be closely unified according to central themes or structural principles, but they are, in Hutchinson's estimate, culturally unified by the concept of shamanic performance (séance or healing ceremony).

Hutchinson's thesis is thus that "Whitman repeatedly responded to crises in his life (usually connected with national crises from 1855 to 1865) by seeking symbolic mastery over them through ecstatic art, repeating the pattern of initiatory death and rebirth with results adapted to the situation giving rise to the performance" (162). Though he appears to have discovered a genetic principle by which Whitman's life work could be explained, however, Hutchinson concludes by molding his reading to the principles of cyclic organicism. In short, he agrees with most historical critics that Whitman's work was historically limited, declining quickly after the Civil War. "The tendency to minimize the importance of historical change in Whitman's aesthetic shift and decline," Hutchinson writes, "derives from the desire to separate the 'poet' from the 'prophet,' a reaction against the hagiography and single-minded historicism of earlier critics and biographers who hardly illuminated the aesthetic value of Whitman's accomplishment" (171). In an effort to renew interest in Whitman's prophetic content without neglecting the importance of aesthetic judgment and without arguing that Whitman's accomplishment was uniformly excellent or his development as a poet purely progressive, Hutchinson thus argues that, in Whitman's strongest poems, the poems in the early editions of *Leaves of Grass*, there is an effective blending of poet and prophet, but that "when the 'poet' and the 'prophet' separated they both became infirm" (171). The infirmity begins with "Passage to India," which, in

Hutchinson's reading, lacks "the sort of inspiration that went into Whitman's poems of 1855-67"; "Passage" fails to confront despair with the intensity of earlier poems and allows a bland optimism to take over; it views "transcendence as a progressive state of being rather than part of a rhythmic, alternating process of descent and emergence, death and rebirth, ebb and flow"; and thus "it indicates a degeneration of the ecstatic process itself, the loss of self-dissolution and radical self-questioning" (152).

Many of the key points in Hutchinson's argument are supported by the work of David Kuebrich. In *Minor Prophecy: Walt Whitman's New American Religion* (1989), Kuebrich follows Hyde and Hutchinson in attempting to revive a critical interest in Whitman's prophetic aspirations. He argues that Whitman wanted to establish a new American religion, a goal toward which *Leaves of Grass* contributed in a special way, complementing the slashing realism of Whitman's prose commentaries. Echoing Canby, Kuebrich explains the difference between Whitman's prose and poetry not as a simple difference of rhetorical and artistic writing, but as a difference between a world portrayed realistically and ideally. The poems, which depict an ideal world of soulful companions drawn together by spiritual love have, for Kuebrich, "two functions: to promote the spiritual development of his readers and to provide them with a coherent vision which would integrate their religious experience with the dominant modes of modern thought and action—science, technology, and democracy" (3). Like Hyde and Hutchinson, Kuebrich believes that Whitman's ambitions were consistent with the religious temper of his day, and he devotes a long chapter to delineating clear connections between Whitman's work and the work of other religious enthusiasts and millennialists of the middle nineteenth century. And, like his predecessors, Kuebrich places particular stress upon the political aspects of the spiritual dimension in Whitman's poems: "The most notable feature of Whitman's early use of [the] millennial tradition," he writes, "is that [the poet] extends the process of politicizing the millennium" (34).

Beyond these similarities, however, a gulf opens between Kuebrich's analysis and those of Hyde and Hutchinson. Kuebrich is more insistent than they are about what he sees as the systematic quality of Whitman's religious views and about the centrality of religion to the *Leaves*. Arguing primarily from the late poetry and prose works, Kuebrich maintains that Whitman's religious system is supported by a "fairly traditional . . . 'inner cosmology,'" a "process world view" that "cannot be understood apart from Whitman's conception of a divinity who is immanent and transcendent," so that Whitman's views are finally "theistic" and not "pantheistic" (13, 19-20). Drawing upon phenomenological hermeneutics, Kuebrich asserts that Whitman's poems are never merely literary or empty systems of self-referential signs; rather, they are informed by a "correspondential vision," with natural signs providing the vehicle for God's presence and manifestations (72). "Whitman's suggestive method," he claims, "requires ... spiritually active readers" open to "the dynamics of a particular, intense type of religious knowing: namely, religious symbolism" (66-67). In addition to espousing the concept of an immanent God, Kuebrich's Whitman is a champion of immortality, especially in his great poems on the theme of death, which begin to appear slowly in 1855 ("The Sleepers") and 1856 ("Crossing Brooklyn Ferry"), and then predominate in the later editions of the *Leaves*. "Song of Myself," Kuebrich implies, is not so successful as the late poems, because in it, "Whitman does not effectively exploit the resources of language to lure his readers into a mood that will move them to accept the intended but unstated meaning" but instead "he explicitly asserts the symbolic meaning and asks for the readers' tentative assent" (107).

Kuebrich is certainly aware that, in making such judgments, he swims against the tide of Whitman studies. He gives a long review of the critical thesis that Whitman's work declined after the war, only to assert that this view is mistaken in not seeing the superiority of the final edition, in which Whitman's spiritual work is refined and completed (194-95, n. 11). He mentions Allen's and Asselineau's treatment of spiritual matters, but finally judges their accounts "misleading" because they present spirituality "as a discrete part of [an] intellectual belief system ... rather seeing it as the fundamental dimension of [Whitman's] consciousness that informs his personality and unites all of his experience and poetic themes" (196). He inexplicably groups Hutchinson's work with that of Cowley, James Miller, and Thomas Crawley and then dismisses the lot for "speaking of religion as if it occurred in a historical vacuum" (6). And he takes issue with recent criticism that interprets "the 'Calamus' motif as a celebration of gayness" as an irresponsible treatment of Whitman's "alleged gayness as a separate theme that can be considered apart from his religious vision" (131).

In final analysis, Kuebrich shares more with Richard Maurice Bucke than he does with any critic writing in the 1980s (even though, despite his long footnotes, he barely mentions Bucke and does not cite the Bucke biography in his bibliography). Like Bucke (and O'Connor), he argues that Whitman spiritualized sexual matters rather than depending on the body for spiritual insights. The poet, he says, "blesses sexual intimacy by using it as a symbol of the soul's relationship with divinity" (83-84). Whitman celebrates nature, Kuebrich argues, not as some end in itself but because it reveals intimations of immortality. Again like Bucke, he argues that Whitman's most original contribution to nineteenth-century intellectual history was his appropriation of the doctrines of evolution and progressive development to matters of the spirit (14). Like Burroughs, he understands Whitman as a prophet with an overlay of modern science. But, more like Bucke, he claims that the growth of *Leaves of Grass* is architectonic rather than organic, that each new edition is an ever more stately mansion founded on the increasingly profound spiritual realizations of the poet-craftsman; not surprisingly, he reenacts the formalist enthusiasm for analyzing the complex structure of the long poems.

Thus, while Kuebrich shares with Hyde and Hutchinson an interest in nineteenth-century history, he lacks the attitude toward history evident in most other historicists in Whitman studies. He appears to have inherited almost intact a nineteenth-century outlook on the development of Whitman's poetic genius. In short, he keeps alive a deeply genetic and progressive organicism rather than submitting to the historicist penchant for cyclic and serial interpretations. Another difference is that, for Kuebrich, the term *spiritual* has a fairly narrow range. In his usage, spirituality implies a connection with God and immortality. Hyde and Hutchinson, on the other hand, imply a modernized definition. For them, the spiritual appears to involve whatever is deepest, most intense, and most universal in human experience. They want, it seems, to draw new boundaries for the realm of the sacred and the secular.

A similar semantic issue has worried other historicist scholars who consider Whitman's poetry not from the lofty perspective of Whitman's transcendental aspirations, but from the ground level of nineteenth-century politics. For them, the question becomes not what kind of religion Whitman had in mind when he sought to spiritualize politics (or politicize the spirit), but rather what kind of politics Whitman was thinking of. In the open society of which he dreamed, the boundaries of public and private—like the boundaries of body and soul—became ever more elastic and subject to reconfiguration.

The Body Politic and the Political Body

Any scholarly treatment of the poet's political significance requires the construction (or reconstruction) of a socio-historical context. The protomodern Whitman must yield to, or be reconciled with, the nineteenth-century Whitman. Reflecting the historical turn of literary criticism in the 1980s, recent scholars have scrutinized Whitman's claims that *Leaves of Grass* emerged "out of [his] life in Brooklyn from 1838 to 1853" and that the book continued to grow as he persisted in "absorbing a million people, for fifteen years, with an intimacy, an eagerness, an abandon, probably never equalled" (qtd. in Bucke, *Walt Whitman* 67). Exactly what it means to "absorb" a people becomes a major issue in the new studies, which blend literary criticism with analysis of the historical conditions of poetic production. Another issue, inherited from biographical and literary-historical research, is the question of diachronic change in Whitman's poetry, poetics, and politics. How did the periodic shifts in Whitman's compositional intensity and thematic interest correspond to historical and social changes? One approach is suggested in

Joseph Jay Rubin's *The Historic Whitman* (1973). In what seems an attempt to take literally Whitman's comment about the importance of the period of 1838 to 1853, Rubin gives a full account of Whitman's career as a journalist, politician, and worker, bringing the narrative to a close just at the time the 1855 *Leaves* appeared. By stopping at this crucial point, Rubin (perhaps unintentionally) reinforces the biographical and literary-historical implication that, in 1855, Whitman ceased to be "historical" and began to be "poetical."

Most historicists would balk at this implication. They see historical events and political currents as intervening in Whitman's poetic practice throughout his career. For them, political history leaves its mark upon *Leaves of Grass* as surely as climatic changes are recorded from year to year in the growth patterns of tree rings. With keen attention to how periodization, ideology, and cultural difference impinge upon poetic language, historicist criticism attempts to close the gap between rhetoric and poetics, between practical and aesthetic discourse.

Bearing out the contention of Edward P. J. Corbett that a resurgence of rhetorical studies occurs during "periods of violent social upheaval" (32), the historicist tradition in Whitman studies grew up between the world wars, a time of national and international turmoil. Patterns that persist in the work of current historicists were established as early as 1927 in Vernon Parrington's *Main Currents in American Thought*. Departing from the trend of critical biography and formalist analysis, Parrington presents Whitman not so much as a protomodern hero, but as a somewhat belated product of the late eighteenth- and early nineteenth-century revolutionary spirit. Indeed, he calls Whitman "the completest embodiment of the Enlightenment" left on the literary scene after the Civil War—"the poet and prophet that the America of the Gilded Age was daily betraying" (3.69). And yet, despite his continuing espousal of the old democratic values of Jefferson and Jackson, Whitman was himself subject to the winds of change throughout his career, in Parrington's view. With the "spirit of the radical [1840s]," the poet mixed influences from "the fervid emotionalism of the [1850s], the monistic idealisms of the transcendental school, and the emerging scientific movement" to produce the early editions of the *Leaves* (3.74-75). Parrington argues that Whitman remained a somewhat chastened "revolutionary" to the end of his life, ever committed to the values of the founding fathers and democratic reformers; however, "in his last years"—now under the influence of Herbert Spencer, who buttressed the Enlightenment theory of progress with new advances in scientific learning—Whitman "chose to call himself an evolutionist" (3.73). In suggesting that the poet's development was influenced deeply by intellectual and political contexts, Parrington appears skeptical about overstated claims of Whitman's originality or uniqueness. He argues, for example, that "the rude and ample liberalisms that so shocked his early readers were in no sense peculiar to Whitman, despite common opin-

ion, but the expression of the surging emotionalism of the times";
thus, "*Leaves of Grass* can best be understood by setting its frank paganism against the background of the lush fifties"—a period that also
brought forth figures as colorful as the perfectionist "free lover" John
Humphrey Noyes and Henry Ward Beecher, the "high priest of emotional liberalism" (3.74-75, 80).

Newton Arvin, in his 1938 study *Whitman*, follows Parrington in
noting Whitman's preservation of eighteenth-century revolutionary
doctrine, which the poet received through the heroes of his father's
generation, especially Thomas Paine, Frances Wright, and Robert Dale
Owen. Instead of Parrington's view that, in Whitman's generous nature, these ideas freely mixed with romanticism, however, Arvin suggests that Whitman was pulled in contrary directions by the two ideologies and that, as time passed, he shifted steadily toward romanticism
and the "flaccid irrationalism" of inner-light Quakerism. In Arvin's
reading, this spiritualism threatened to undermine the poet's claims
that his book was "pervaded by the conclusions of scientists" (174).
Unlike critics who see Whitman's spirituality as a support for his politics, then, Arvin—writing in the 1930s during the heyday of American
Marxism—understands Whitman's transcendental or mystical tendencies as a drag on his materialist leanings. For Arvin, the politics of the
body represent the core of Whitman's achievement as a poet-advocate
of free soil, the working class, and sexual liberation. When Whitman
drew most heavily upon his mystical individualism, Arvin argues, he
went astray, taking the wrong side on a number of issues, including
race and labor relations.

In a demonstration of the radical historicist's willingness to engage
texts ideologically, Arvin thus judges not only the literary success of
the poems, but also their claims upon political justice. For later writers,
this approach translates into the constellation of issues surrounding
"political correctness." In Sandra Gilbert and Susan Gubar's estimation,
for example, Whitman becomes the prototype of male assertiveness
and "phallic poetics," which compare unfavorably with the ironic re-
serve of Emily Dickinson (Gilbert and Gubar 556-57; compare
Killingsworth, *Poetry of the Body* 65). Far from dismissing Whitman's
overall achievement on such grounds, Arvin is more forgiving, more
willing to read Whitman as the victim as well as the champion of his
times. His conclusion seeks to balance the need to represent history as
it was with the desire to interpret it for the present: "Whatever his limitations as a person or poet," Arvin writes of Whitman, "his nature
was more sensitive, his sensibility more subtly responsive than those
of other writers to all that was freest, boldest, most popular, most com-
panionable in the contradictory life of his age: he had a magnificent
plastic power . . . in rendering it all with extraordinary life and originality in verse" (289). If Arvin is well off the mark in predicting that "what
is weakly transcendental or . . . waywardly personal in Whitman's book

will be . . . rapidly discarded and forgotten," he strikes home in anticipating the spirit of later ideological criticism: "Enough and more than enough remains to fortify the writers and men [and women] of our time in their struggles against a dark barbarian reaction, and to interest and animate the peoples of a near future in their work of building a just society" (289-90).

Arvin's conclusion was echoed by Richard Chase in 1955, but his hope for the transmittal of what was "freest" and "boldest" in *Leaves of Grass* could hardly have been realized by professional scholars working during the era of Joseph McCarthy and the Cold War, a time when the New Criticism, with its more conservative politics, prospered. Following the student rebellions and the "sexual revolution" of the 1960s and 1970s, however, critical interest in Whitman's socio-political significance revived in the American academy. Further impetus came from the fast-spreading organizations of the feminist and gay rights movements. Now politics could include not just matters of statehood and leadership, but could also deal with the publicizing of private life, a movement which had begun in earnest during Whitman's day and was carried forward into the twentieth-century by the middle-class institutions of psychoanalysis and "self-help." What the French theorist Jean-François Lyotard called the metanarrative of human liberation now stretched beyond its original application in liberal revisions of statecraft and reached into all fields of social life, social science, and the humanities. Demonstrating the fervor of the new social movements in her 1969 book *Sexual Politics*, the feminist Kate Millett writes, for example, "Sexual dominion obtains . . . as perhaps the most pervasive ideology of our culture and provides its most fundamental concepts of power" (45). From such extensions of the political platform, historical literary studies have generated a considerable intellectual energy (see also Foucault, *History of Sexuality*; Lyotard, *The Postmodern Condition*; Laclau and Mouffe, *Hegemony and Socialist Strategy*; and Killingsworth, *Whitman's Poetry of the Body* xiii-xix).

The expanded treatment of sexual politics has proven especially influential in Whitman studies, appearing first as a broadening and revision of literary-historical scholarship. One of the earliest experiments along these lines was Robert K. Martin's ground-breaking work on homosexuality in Whitman's poetry. In *The Homosexual Tradition in American Poetry* (1979), Martin's long chapter on Whitman places the poet at the start of a tradition, a tradition which overlaps with but also extends the standard canon of American literature (until recently the nearly exclusive haunt of white heterosexual male writers). The alternative tradition outlined by Martin does include canonical figures like Hart Crane and George Santayana, but also calls attention to writers all but forgotten by literary history, such as Whitman's contemporary (and rival) Bayard Taylor and the poet-critic Fitz-Greene Halleck, as well as recent poets not yet admitted to the canon, such as Thom Gunn, James

Merrill, and Edward Field. Grouping these poets by their willingness to place homosexual themes at the center of their poetry serves two functions—a literary function that makes clearer than ever before Whitman's line of descent in American literature and a political function that brings to light the need for homosexual men to have a history distinct from the history offered by the heterosexual culture of Western Europe and the United States. The ultimate effect of such studies is to collapse the distinction between the literary and the political.

Martin's chapter on Whitman was preceded by an important article in the *Partisan Review*, "Whitman's 'Song of Myself': Homosexual Dream and Vision" (1975), which sets the tone and establishes the method for his approach to *Leaves of Grass* as a whole. In the article, Martin argues that the prevailing "liberalism" of Whitman scholarship—"the tendency toward acceptance and tolerance" of Whitman's homosexuality, which suggests that homosexuals are not "really different" from heterosexuals—has done nearly as much as a more aggressive homophobia to cover over the radicalism of the *Leaves of Grass* (80). Martin contends that the homosexuality of Whitman's poetry cannot be contained in a discussion of the "Calamus" poems, a strategy which Whitman may have himself initiated as a defensive move in 1860 and which was certainly well established after the famous exchange with John Addington Symonds. For Martin, homosexuality is not merely an "aspect" of Whitman's overall achievement—the so-called "Calamus theme"; rather it is an abiding concern throughout *Leaves of Grass* and the poet's career (a literary claim later substantiated by the biographical studies of Charley Shively).

Martin thus avers that, from the first edition on, homosexuality drives the most ecstatic and politically radical utterances of the poet. For him, "Song of Myself" and "The Sleepers," for example, are inspired by homosexual emotion and derive their energy from the tropes of the homosexual imagination. Acts of fellatio, anal intercourse, mutual masturbation, and transvestism appear and disappear throughout the poems, thereby providing formal echoes of the "motifs of concealment and revelation" (*Homosexual Tradition* 10). These densely coded references, as Martin sees them, lie beneath obscure, but key passages, such as the infamous lines from "The Sleepers" beginning "The cloth laps a first sweet eating and drinking" (lines excluded when Whitman revised the *Leaves* after the Civil War) or the passage in section 28 of "Song of Myself" containing the lines "Blind loving wrestling touch, sheath'd hooded sharp-tooth'd touch!/ Did it make you ache so, leaving me?" (*Leaves: Norton* 627, 58). In Martin's reading, the two poems are revisions of the generic dream-vision lyric. In Whitman's version, "the sexual experience is revealed . . . to be the gateway to the visionary experience" so important to critics as different as Richard Maurice Bucke and James Miller. But Bucke evades the question of homosexuality, and Miller's concept of "inverted mysticism," according to

Martin, "diverts attention from the poetry's frankly and directly sexual nature" ("Whitman's 'Song'" 82). Worse yet, Martin says, psychoanalytical criticism, such as that of Edwin H. Miller, underestimates the political impetus of Whitman's poems by looking upon "homosexuality as an illness" (*Homosexual Tradition* 6). In the dream-vision poems, Martin argues to the contrary, it is the homosexual act itself, that allows the poet to break free of the "anchors and holds" of his society, to liberate himself from the close inside air of Victorian domesticity (institutionalized in Freudian psychoanalysis) in search of a new aesthetic and political freedom. It is, in other words, Whitman's acceptance of his homosexuality, not the sublimation of it that inspires the best poems of *Leaves of Grass*. In this reading, the release and free use of homosexual fantasy in the creative process not only allows the poet to value the company of men with a renewed fervor, but also frees him to identify with women and to avoid the tendency to "regard women as sexual objects even in his ostensibly heterosexual poems" (8; compare Aspiz, 211-36; Erkkila 135-38; and Killingsworth, "Whitman" and *Poetry of the Body* 62-87). Indeed, by Martin's lights, "Whitman makes no distinction between subject and object" at all; enabled by the fantasy of exchanging sexual roles, of being alternately passive and active, the poet diminishes the importance of such distinctions and opens himself to the sympathetic merging of opposites and the fluid spiritual motion of the mystic (8; compare Hutchinson; Moon).

In *The Homosexual Tradition*, Martin concedes that the dream-vision poems stop short of treating the homosexual activity as anything more than a means to an end. "What mattered to Whitman" in 1855, he writes, "was the role of sexuality in the establishment of a mystic sense of unity" (12). By the time of "Calamus," however, Whitman was beginning to turn his attention from homosexual acts to the development of homosexual consciousness. For the tradition of homosexual poetry (as well as the evolution of the gay rights movement), this shift was crucial because, as Martin suggests, "In the deepest sense, a person becomes a homosexual not when he or she has sexual relations with another person of the same sex but when he or she accepts homosexuality as an element of self-definition" (51). "Prior to Whitman," says Martin, "there were homosexual acts but no homosexuals. Whitman coincides with a radical change in historical consciousness: the self-conscious awareness of homosexuality as an identity." To stress the significance of this accomplishment, Martin appropriates a metaphor that shows him on the verge of a genetic organicism that would see *Leaves of Grass* as a homosexual book: "'Calamus' is the heart of *Leaves of Grass*, as well as its root; it is Whitman's book of self-proclamation and self-definition" (51-52).

Martin's work inaugurated a robust line of scholarship that reads Whitman by the lights of the gay liberation movement. In articles published in the middle 1980s, Joseph Cady, Alan Helms, and Michael

Lynch, in their different ways, analyzed the rhetoric of homosexual disclosure and concealment in *Leaves of Grass*. The key to understanding Whitman's sexual politics, according to these critics, is to recognize the degree to which the poet transformed literary themes, genres, and diction. His tropes upon the soldier-comrade motif in the elegiac *Drum-Taps*, the friendship tradition in lyric poetry, and the phrenological concept of "adhesiveness" represent an effort to create in (and through) his poems a political brotherhood based on an esoteric interchange between the "cruising" poet and the receptive reader (see also Harold Beaver's "Homosexual Signs" and Eve Sedgwick's *Between Men*). This approach to the poems is supported by the biographical revisions of Charley Shively, who hit upon the idea of reading not only Whitman's letters to his working-class and soldier comrades, but also their letters back to the poet. Shively uncovers a number of instances of apparently private language—including an odd and early use of the word *gay*—that may well point to a shared secret code among homosexual interlocutors.

A book that has been just as influential as Martin's, though in a very different way, is *Walt Whitman and the Body Beautiful* (1980) by Harold Aspiz. Aspiz considers the themes of health and the body in Whitman's poems, broadening the field of literature to include not only belles-lettres but also popular nonfiction writings from the middle nineteenth century on topics ranging from animal magnetism to sexology. He positions Whitman within a tradition of these now almost forgotten writings that focus on the power of the human body—a tradition wider than either the narrow field of literary history or historical stereotypes of "Victorianism" might suggest—and thereby provides the details of an intertextual network that both included and supported Whitman in his "language experiments." This mapping of the cultural context of *Leaves of Grass* demonstrates compellingly the need to account fully for the physical bases of Whitman's thought and writing and has supplied a strong underpinning for many new readings of the poems, not only in Aspiz's own work, but in that of other historicists as well (notably Hutchinson, Erkkila, Killingsworth, and Moon).

Aspiz argues that Whitman's "interest in the body and the physiological and medical lore of his day was an essential element in shaping *Leaves of Grass*, its themes, its metaphors, its vision of a splendid new race of men and women, and its portrayal of the Whitman persona" (x). In preparing to write the *Leaves*, Whitman came to believe, along with many of his contemporaries, that "genuine prophesy and poetry can originate only in the man of perfect body" (3). During his career, the poet constantly "retouched" his mythical self-portrait in the various editions—overlaying the "rough" of 1855 with "the magnetic folk-evangelist to the city masses" of 1856, the "softened and 'spiritualized' ... more distinctly Christ-like" hero of 1860, the "less proud and more respectable" figure behind the revisions of 1867, and the "backward-looking and wistful" poet in his last years (4-5). Aspiz demonstrates that, however much he changed, Whitman never entirely lost faith in his strange system of physiological idealism, which he drew directly from the medical, pseudoscientific, eugenic, and spiritualist literature of his times. Indeed, Aspiz's research reveals a need to reevaluate claims about the "spiritualization" of the later *Leaves* in light of the fact that nineteenth-century spiritualism was always a rather physical affair. Savants such as Andrew Jackson Davis freely introduced mechanical forces like electricity and magnetism into the weird world of popular metaphysics. At a time when physics was making major strides toward the understanding of natural phenomena and industry was being transformed by a second industrial revolution, Aspiz shows, Whitman and his contemporaries mixed the metaphors of science and spirituality to the point that the widening gap between positivistic science and religious practice seemed, magically, to disappear. They also tended, for the first time in history, to treat sex as a "problem" to be managed by scientific investigation and rational practice—a notion Whitman picked up from the phrenologists and authors of sex education manuals like Dr. Edward H. Dixon (whom the poet apparently visited while he was preparing the 1856 *Leaves*). Though Whitman's investigations into these nonliterary fields often inspired some of his most characteristic poses and tropes, the reactionary and ethno-centric sociology that informed much of the popular literature (especially that of the eugenicists), also made its way into his poems, so that what Richard Chase noticed—Whitman's "difference from us"—is underlined in Aspiz's work, though without the honorific implication of Chase's comparison. On the subject of race, for example, Aspiz must admit that "Whitman's attitudes toward non-Teutonic peoples were inconsistent or unfavorable" and that his "hoped-for superrace is Nordic." Like his contemporaries and despite his radically democratic views, Whitman "could not conceive of a society that was at once multiracial and egalitarian" (190-91).

Moreover, Aspiz reveals that, where they were not reactionary, Whitman's social views were often merely conventional, which is surprising in light of what seems his shocking intensity, his "determination to establish health and sexuality as cultural norms" (211). Nevertheless, at least in treating heterosexual themes, *Leaves of Grass* is not a free lover's manifesto (of which there were quite a few in Whitman's day), but instead the poet "idealizes lusty married lovers" (200) and grants his blessing to the "great chastity of paternity," the "great chastity of maternity," and the "well-married couple" (qtd. in Aspiz 200). Aspiz notes that "outside the bounds of marriage and motherhood, the poet reacts tepidly to feminine attraction" (228). Even in his advocacy of "physical fitness, sexual appetite, and a capacity for motherhood" as a program for women's liberation, Whitman "subscribed to a reformist trend which ran counter to the Victorian mainstream but was promoted by a forthright and important group of his contemporaries" (212). Although, in Aspiz's view, it would be "historically dishonest" to "judge [Whitman's] racial views [and sexual politics] by today's norms, as some critics have done" (190-91), the reader comfortable with an image of the poet as a social revolutionist must come away from this study with some disappointment.

Aspiz opened the way for further studies of Whitman's relation to noncanonical works, many of which have shed light on the problem of what Whitman shares with his contemporaries. In *Beneath the American Renaissance* (1988), for example, David Reynolds traces the connection between *Leaves of Grass* and the popular fiction and sensational nonfiction of Whitman's day. The tall tales and lurid samples of sexual fantasy that Reynolds rediscovers may well have influenced the poet more profoundly than the high-minded canonical figures he got used to invoking in his later letters and essays—the likes of Hegel, Carlyle, and Emerson. If Whitman borrowed as much of the spirit and indeed the letter of the popular writings as Reynolds suggests, we may well wonder what made him different. The obvious answer for Reynolds, writing in the tradition of formalist literary history, is style. Whitman transformed the raw material of popular culture into high art through the process the Russian formalists called defamiliarization, the "making new" that characterizes the work of all successful poets.

Aspiz hints at the same tendency with his emphasis on Whitman's poetics and his deemphasis of politics. In his preface, for instance, Aspiz hurries past the political implications of Whitman's debt to popular science: "Whitman certainly concurred with Emerson's statement that 'a good deal of our politics is physiological,' but he believed that a good deal of our poetics is physiological, too" (ix). In taking this emphasis, Aspiz cites the authority of Whitman himself, who at least on one occasion, when driven toward radical politics by his young disciple Horace Traubel, replied that the "whole business [of politics] comes back to the good body—not back to wealth, to poverty, but to the strong body" (qtd. in Aspiz 187). Unlike Martin and his followers in gay studies, Aspiz retains much of the older, narrower definition of politics, arguing, for example, that, for Whitman, "fathering healthy children is nobler than statesmanship . . . because only pure-bodied men and women can become the parents of the nation's greatest statesmen and poets" (189). Throughout Whitman's work, there does appear the rather conservative tendency, implied in Aspiz's interpretation, to defer real political change until a more suitable time in the future.

Given his findings on Whitman's racial views, Aspiz may well avoid or limit his treatment of political issues out of respect for the poet. But, like Reynolds, he also faces a limitation of his primarily empirical method. Both critics warrant mainly those interpretations that can be supported with evidence from the field of literature they survey. And, though this field is broader than that of conventional literary theory, it does have its gaps. On the question of homosexuality, for example, it is all but silent. The sensationalism of the popular literature surveyed by Reynolds stops short of homosexual fantasy, and "the very mention [of homosexuality] was shunned in the medical books" cited by Aspiz (208). To some extent, then, these books support Martin's contention that Whitman created a homosexual literary tradition to stand against the silence of the dominant culture, but they also point up the shortcomings of a strictly empirical literary-historical criticism and raise the question of the critic's freedom to interpret, which itself becomes an issue in historicist theory as it encounters reader-response criticism (in the work of Kerry Larson, for example). Such perceptions lead Robert Martin to proclaim (in a bold echo of the hermeneuticist's denial of liberal Christian historicism), "The historical Whitman is of no literary interest. He can vanish and leave behind the spiritual Whitman, the eternal lover, the risen god of male love" (*Homosexual Tradition* 89).

Martin thus joins Arvin in attempting to carry forward the revolutionary spirit of Whitman, while Aspiz and Reynolds sustain the empirical slant of Parrington's contention that "*Leaves of Grass* can best be understood by setting its frank paganism against the background of the lush fifties" (3.80). But none of these critics appear very interested in preserving the earlier historicists' adaptation of Marx's historical materialism to literary studies. As the revival of socially oriented criticism continued into the late 1980s, however, historical materialism was revived and significantly extended, nowhere more completely than in M. Wynn Thomas's already influential study *The Lunar Light of Whitman's Poetry* (1987).

Drawing upon the revisions of Raymond Williams and recent social histories of the American working class, and studiously avoiding the "claims to comprehensiveness" that turn many orthodox Marxist analyses toward an overweening historical geneticism (3), Thomas puts forward the thesis that *Leaves of Grass* grew out of, or was at least nurtured by, Whitman's commitment to the communitarian ethos of the artisanal culture in which he grew up. Recalling Parrington's and Arvin's implication of Whitman's belatedness, Thomas demonstrates how the poems of the 1850s struggle to preserve the face-to-face democracy of small town life against the insurgence of large-scale industrialism and what Alan Trachtenberg calls "the incorporation of America." According to Thomas, the "old artisanal dream of a free, egalitarian commonwealth," which Whitman celebrated in the "aggressive new form" invented by Thomas Paine and Frances Wright, "was already antiquated by the 1820s and totally out of step with the giant strides of capitalist development" (29). Indeed, "the very diversity of occupations valued by Whitman [in the 1850s] has in reality less to do with the multiplicity of traditional crafts and trades (with which he was surrounded when he was young) than with the divisions of labor created by the complex, impersonal demands of an extensive capitalist market" (16). More than belated, Thomas's Whitman is almost quaintly nostalgic. As his editorials from the late 1850s show, his attempts to "capture the business ethic for his own distinctive vision of democracy" ultimately failed, so that, by the end of the decade, the poet suspected "that the drift of the modern . . . was not toward, but away from, democracy as he conceived of it" (165-67). With the defeat of the South and the subsequent loss of regional diversity, Thomas argues, "the Civil War . . . rendered [Whitman's] poetry obsolete" (2). After the war, Whitman began more frequently to rely upon "the trick . . . of turning up the volume of his rhetoric in order to drown out the noise of his doubts" (266).

Like Arvin before him, then, Thomas sees Whitman's enterprise as deeply conflicted. Alluding to "Song of Joys," he writes, "Whitman's wish to use his tongue [the trope for both language and bardic poetry] to 'lead' America is well known, having been . . . vigorously proclaimed from the platform of his poetry. But the related inclination to 'quell America,' which arose from his obscure unease at the kind of society he saw developing all around him, was a violent impulse whose strength he, as a poet, could never comfortably admit" (6). In only one poem, "Respondez," did the poet give vent to "fierce disgust at his America," and the result was not among his highest aesthetic achievements (7). But the critical disposition displayed in "Respondez" and (with even less inhibition) in the prose works "gave both impetus and substance" to the best poems (6). In fact, the whole of the 1855 *Leaves* was, according to Thomas, "the direct result of a plunging economic crisis that severely hit the bastard artisan class to which Whitman then loosely belonged" (33). Finding himself, like many other Americans, out of work and on the verge of financial ruin, Whitman began to write exuberantly hopeful poems whose energy partly conceals social and political fears. Like the volcanic emotions of "Calamus," the driving political forces of the poems, as Thomas reads them, lie just beneath the surface, a source of aesthetically powerful tension.

Again like Arvin, Thomas looks skeptically upon Whitman's devotion to spiritual themes; unlike Arvin, however, he does not try to separate Whitman's ostensible spirituality from his political purposes and his poetic successes. Whitman's "prattlings about the soul," in Thomas's view, "bespeak his otherwise unspoken hope that in those 'workers' disqualified [or 'dispossessed'] . . . from participating fully in their society's opportunities, he would discover the tender growing points of an alternative consciousness" (13). In this hope, Whitman was "sadly mistaken," Thomas says, but adds that "it was nevertheless a conviction that served him well as a poet": "The nebulous word 'soul' is invoked to communicate to others [Whitman's] conviction that they have allowed themselves to be devalued, silently demoralized by accepting the current market prices for their lives and by relying

on the crude descriptive terms of social classification for their self-iden-
tity"; thus *soul* becomes "a term transparent in the historical rather
than the metaphysical sense of the word"—a "key critical term" for
Whitman, "nebulous" only because of "current society's false conception of what is real, substantial, and precise about human being" (12-
13).

The argument implied in Hyde and Hutchinson, then, is made
clear by Thomas: The Whitmanian soul is a political term of value
rather than a theological or metaphysical reality (Kuebrich to the contrary). Whitman's usage recalls the diction of his spiritual heir Kate
Chopin, who, in her novel *The Awakening*, provides her protagonist
Edna Pontellier with only the vaguest terms of dissatisfaction; her society gives her no discourse appropriate to articulate or understand the
wandering attention of her heart and mind. As Jorge Larrain explains
in his study of ideology, "the dominated . . . spontaneously formulate
their grievances in the language and logic of the dominant class" (157).
Thomas's analysis suggests that Whitman appropriated the language of
popular evangelical enthusiasm to breathe new life into a political
populism that was in danger of passing into oblivion. If both nature
and capitalist economics conspire to make men and women feel small,
then poetry becomes, in Whitman's theory, the antidote—an
"indispensable way of coping with the critical situation brought about
by change" (23-27, 39). "Song of Myself," for example, becomes a celebration of "the 'being' mode of existence" as distinguished from "the
'having' mode" (41). Like "soul," "Kosmos" is used in the poem as "the
antithesis of a prevailing state of affairs, deplored by Whitman, for
which he uses the term 'monopoly'" in the 1855 preface (73). Another
term from the preface, *prudence*, Thomas understands as signifying "a
militant reaction . . . against the new kind of economic thinking which
had come to prevail in America"—the historical forerunner, more or
less, of consumerism (58).

What emerges from Thomas's reading of the poems and the prose
works is that Whitman perceived very early the direction of American
government, science, business, and even literature toward the ultimate
mechanization and bureaucracy of early modernism. The poet's reaction against this cultural evolution was that of a steadfast opponent.
The problem was that, though the struggle was first rewarded by poetic
energy, the effort could not be sustained. The result was the inevitable
decline of power, the hallmark of a criticism based in cyclic organicism.
The historicist twist to the argument, so clearly managed in Thomas's
book, reveals the dependence of the poet's ethos upon historical conditions.

As Larry J. Reynolds points out in *European Revolutions and the
American Literary Renaissance* (1988), the historical conditions under
which Whitman produced *Leaves of Grass* included not only the passing of the artisanal culture and the onset of the Civil War, but also in-

ternational events like the French Revolution of 1848, which "profoundly stirred" Whitman. The international scene, Reynolds demonstrates, "shaped [Whitman's] poetic persona and inspired the major themes of *Leaves of Grass.*" Reynolds thus joins Thomas and the Soviet critic Maurice Mendelson in declaring "the importance of 'political passion' to Whitman's mature poetry" (125). Mendelson's term "political passion" hints at the historicist tendency to locate agency in historical conditions that influence, even if they do not utterly overwhelm the poetic agent. To borrow a trope from poststructuralism, we can say that history writes the poet insofar as events and contingencies create his "passion." But just as surely, the poet strives to "capture" the active role in responding to his passion. The action which presents itself is, of course, the act of writing. Whitman, in responding to the social changes Thomas and Reynolds document, tries to create poems that strip historical forces of their agency and make them merely part of the scene, the background of poetic action. The radical historicist reawakens the historical forces as a means of demarcating the poet's limits. Just as Walt Whitman and his *Leaves* "spring" from the ground of nineteenth-century history, to that dust they return. Thus his efforts to update and extend the "life" of his book beyond its "natural" limits could only result in frustration for Walt Whitman and a problematical editorial policy for the book.

While Thomas and Reynolds are, for the most part, content to hint at such theoretical issues and to follow fairly closely the harder materialist slant of earlier historicism, Kerry Larson pursues a more speculative path in *Whitman's Drama of Consensus* (1988). Larson carries historical analysis into the realm of language study, literary theory, and sexual politics, delivering in the process some dizzyingly close readings of the major poems. Building on the work of Donald Pease and Allen Grossman, and drawing deeply upon the rhetorically oriented critical theory of Kenneth Burke, Larson argues that "one regrettable legacy of the artificial division between the 'poet of the self' and the 'bard of democracy' has been to overlook or ignore the radical singularly of Whitman's conception of art," which comprises "neither a faithful transcription of the social world . . . nor a visionary attempt to take flight from its conditions." In Larson's view, *Leaves of Grass* rejects the standard metaphors for poetic vision—"the mirror and the lamp, both the familiar preference for art as a just representation of nature and a Romantic aesthetic of transcendence and transformation." Instead, "the central motive for [Whitman's] poetic . . . involves the evolution of a consensus framework which the poem does not recommend so much as embody." Thus, it is Larson's thesis that "the proper business of the poem," in Whitman's conception, "is not to sustain a drama, develop a cast of characters, mount an argument, explore a soul, plead a cause, or render a judgment; more fundamentally, its ideal aim is to gather together without artificially dichotomizing a host of 'opposite equals' in

what amounts to a convocation and tallying of their diverse energies"
(xiv). According to Larson, Whitman's verse engages these diverse energies in a "transactive process," so that "the achieving of consensus
can no longer be considered an external theme ... but an evolving
drama integral to the poet's design" (xv-xvi). In an interpretation that
suggests Hutchinson's idea of literary shamanism, Larson sees the poet
"as the connective link for the public discourse, one who does not bear
a message for his interlocutors but stands forth as the expressive site
and medium for its conveyance" (xvi). Quoting Arvin's conundrum
that "there [is] a great fund of conservatism in this radical [Whitman]
and unexpected practical conformities in this non-conformist" (Arvin
30-31), Larson argues that the "conservatism of [Whitman's] politics
and the radicalism of his verse" are "often compressed in one and the
same gesture"; and that, in the exposition of this "conservative radicalism," "the language of voluntarism edges irresistibly toward a language
of compulsion" until we feel that the poet "is bent upon persuading
himself of [his] faith no less than ourselves" (xx-xxi).

Thus Larson joins Arvin, Hyde, Hutchinson, and Thomas in the
historicist argument that Whitman is beset by deep conflicts that reca-
pitulate the social and political crises of the poet's age. But, though he
accepts to some degree the materialist concept that the greatest conflicts
arise between Whitman's ideal America and the historical reality,
Larson goes beyond this notion. Where he is most original is in his
demonstration that conflict is a poetical problem for Whitman, the
analysis of which discloses the poet's intense struggles with the limitations of language as an instrument of political reform. Larson tracks
this problem into three major areas of Whitman's poetical practice—
the treatment of the reader as "you" in the poems of direct address, the
development of the poet's organic theory of poetic form, and the thematic complex of sexuality and death in *Leaves of Grass.*

On the first topic, Larson argues, "By placing his auditors at the center stage of his verse, Whitman hopes to bring forward and actualize
the movement from isolated individuality ... to affirmed unanimity"
and thereby "to reconstitute the rules of communicative exchange that
govern the social world at large," leveling the distinction between
rhetoric and poetic and judging one by the highest standards of the
other (6). Instead of complaining about Whitman's "didacticism," as
the formalists are inclined to do, Larson lays bare "the thoroughly
volatile character of Whitman's undertaking" in his poems of direct
address (16). The poems are hardly "manipulative"—not nearly so
much so as the narrative intricacies of Hawthorne and Melville,
Larson argues; on the contrary, *Leaves of Grass* exhibits "a principled
aversion to such ironic control" (28). They do not presume, imply, or
create the reader so much as they court and make appeals to the reader.
At their best, they model an ideal political situation. "Crossing
Brooklyn Ferry," for example, "manifests itself to us not as a cunningly

deployed pattern of significances, a shrewdly arranged narrative, not even, in reality, as a 'field of action,'" but as "a gesture, summons, or petition," the goal of which is "not so much communication as communion" (10). At their worst, the poems embarrass the reader with their "overexertions" (27)—either in pursuing favor or in asserting a state of utter independence that fails to convince because of the frantic quality of the rhetoric it inspires. As Larson says of the poem "One Hour to Madness and Joy," for instance, "once a state of self-absorption is *asserted* it is no longer a state of self-absorption but becomes something else. In the hands of Whitman it becomes, particularly in his weaker moments, a fetish" (26).

A related theme is the "competition for meaning between listener and speaker." The tensions that result are "the product of a basic conflict . . . between the longing to abolish all mediations in the social discourse" and "the consternation that ensues over the withdrawal of such mediations" (28)—conservative radicalism again. Coming ever closer to the reader, the poet suddenly withdraws, withholding "the real me"; then, losing sight of the audience he so desires, he rushes forward again or offers himself sacrificially as a medium for social interchange. This dynamic, which drives the rhetoric of the early *Leaves*, in Larson's view, also reflects the constitutional crisis of the 1850s. Just as the poet alternates between communal sacrifice and defiant individualism, the states alternated between the commitment to union and the freedom of separate governments. The result, for Whitman as for the United States, is an "unnerving slippage of the autocratic and the democratic" (51). Ultimately Whitman is led to question rather than merely to assert his faith in the possibility of meaningful consensus, both on linguistic and social grounds. As Larson puts it, "Not a premise to rest upon but an arduous struggle to act out, the process of securing consent throughout his 'hymns of you,' as indeed throughout *Leaves of Grass*, repeatedly suggests that whatever is shareable in human experience has become attenuated to so extreme a degree that what is required can no longer be the mere *assumption* of a 'universal voice' but its lasting, unarguable confirmation" (73).

Turning to Whitman's efforts to enact an organic theory of poetry—and, for that matter, an organic theory of selfhood—Larson again meets conflict and self-contradictory impulses. "Song of Myself," for example, "feels itself to be simultaneously groping after an organic myth of 'free growth' even as it is oppressed by it" (81). The consequent "blend of aspiration and skepticism . . . energizes the manic buoyancy" of the poem (145). In this poem and in other writings, the poet matches his effort to engage the reader and thereby mediate coercion and consensus with a parallel attempt to confront language itself as yet "another interlocutor" (87). What he wants most in this transaction, according to Larson, "is not the certainty of meaning"—the aim of the positivist linguists whom Whitman rejected in his essays on language—"but its endless reproduction, as is reflected in his delight in likening linguistic energy to libidinal energy" (89). The trouble, as Larson sees it, is that, in an attempt of organicism to prove itself on its own terms, "the distinction between *legitimacy* (the source of value that renders power authoritative) and *legitimation* (the ongoing task of establishing, upholding, or defending that value" collapses, creating an impasse: the dynamic of "free growth" proves to be circular; every progression [is] also a regression . . . , each upward growth . . . also an inward growth, enriching the source even as it expands outward from it." Thus Larson arrives at "two central impulses: The emulation of that 'lawless germinal element' in language irreducible to the strictures of closure and a corresponding wish to foreclose the strictures of proof" (90-92). Thus Whitman's "fascination with the 'free growth' of 'perfect poems'" is tied inextricably to "the anxiety that his verse, like the Democracy it strives to voice, is at once prolific and barren." Noting how often *Leaves of Grass* alludes to the inexpressible, the secret, the meaning or referent that lies just beyond the reach of language or just beneath the surface of the poem, requiring the poet to depend upon "faint clews" and "indirections," Larson concludes that, for Whitman, "Voice itself is caught up in [a] frustrated dialectic, being invoked on the one hand as [a] supremely potent, ungovernable force and on the other as a buried, virtual seed hovering at the threshold of articulation" (97). Once again, Larson lays bare the connection between literary and political institutions, both of which "share the common plight of devising a vocabulary of justification which is not revealed to be inadequate or self-incriminating the moment it is asserted" (107).

Finally, Larson considers another troubled attempt "to appease the dissensions between the many and the one"—the thematic constellation of sex and death. He contends that, in the two groupings of poems first separated in the 1860 *Leaves* and finally titled "Children of Adam" and "Calamus," Whitman tries "to promulgate the gospel of social affection" but "falters on the question of what union of interests or larger generality might sustain this affection." Two possibilities emerge, neither of which is entirely successful. "Children of Adam" seeks "to totalize the notion of unanimity." Success completely eludes this effort, in Larson's view, and "Children of Adam' becomes "the first truly dismal stretch of writing that would make its way into *Leaves*," celebrating "a monolithic Oneness which, in binding all individuals to the 'irresistible gravitation' of sex, also enslaves them." Somewhat more satisfactory from the perspective of aesthetics, but no more politically successful, the "Calamus" poems, according to Larson, "alternately reach an extremity of their own in their implication that the value of comradeship largely consists in shunning any principle of integration." Both groups of poems—one "advocating the transcendence of union at the cost of individuality," the other "upholding the intimacy of private lives in silent disdain of a larger totality"—demonstrate "the growing strain in Whitman's attempt to join together the many and the one without neglecting either term." Eventually—in fact within five years of the poems' first publication as two separate groups within the 1860 *Leaves*—"the cluster of themes involving the body, sexuality, and comradeship would . . . recede before the lowest common denominator of all in Whitman's hymns to death." More cautious than other historicists (such as Thomas and Killingsworth), Larson stops short of arguing that "the unraveling of the country's social fabric parallels the unraveling of Whitman's vision of consensus," but he is willing to note that the years during which Whitman composed his poems of sex and death "bear witness to growing apprehensions on Whitman's part over the purpose and direction of his literary 'experiment'" (150-51). "The War," says Larson, "did not deliver a death blow to Whitman's mystic Unionism, as that idealism was already severely tempered by fears and reservations which concerned not simply the fate of the Union but the rationality of the policies guiding it. What the war did do was to heighten the divide between acknowledgment and meaning to particularly distended extremes, thereby draining it of any dramatic tension" (243).

Larson's language in this last passage reveals something of his own guiding metaphors. He tends to juxtapose against Whitman's organicism tropes that are spatial and inorganic and that ultimately point to a structuralist alternative to the organic tradition of Whitman studies. The metaphors, such as the reference to the "heightened divide" between the nominalized abstractions "acknowledgment" and "meaning," as well as the use of "draining," suggest the terminology of geology or archaeology (much in the manner of Levi-Strauss or the early Foucault—see the conclusion of *The Order of Things*, for example). In Larson's work, such language melds with the language of the courtroom, the legislature, and the stage—all sites where the give and take of discourse and human interchange prevail—as in this sentence: "Because 'Lilacs' does not develop by means of a sharply delineated narrative but through the accretion of hesitantly ventured analogies and juxtapositions, its opening stanzas provide more the scaffolding for the drama that ensues than a series of actions" (234). This description could apply to Larson's own organization, which, disdaining narrative, sets forth a key theme or observation that gradually builds through repetition and accretion. The method implied here appears to represent Larson's attempt to escape the organicism that Whitman imposes upon the critic. To do so, he must radically extend the concept of public conversation, or discourse, not as an event, but as an institution analogous to the writing of poetry. By treating politics, poetry, and sexuality as comparable forms of social discourse, Larson discovers an alternative to Whitman's alignment of the concepts within the general category of growth.

A fuller treatment of this alternative must wait until chapter 5, for it lies beyond the topic of historicist criticism. Essentially, Larson substitutes a synchronic criticism for a diachronic criticism of *Leaves of Grass* without abandoning the diachronic altogether. His chapters are arranged, for example, to allow him to deal last with the theme of decline in the poet's creative cycle after the Civil War. Thus the book retains the faint adumbration of the metanarrative that guides the dominant tradition of Whitman studies. Much as, in Larson's view, Whitman's dialectical energy gave out in the late 1860s, so we might say that Larson's resistance to the critical heritage also weakens as the book progresses. But not before he sets forth a strong alternative based upon the structuralist trope on discourse.

If Larson's critical energy derives from his use of discourse as a model for human action in general, Betsy Erkkila and other historicists in the late 1980s depend upon a comparable expansion of politics (which also recalls the newly secularized interpretation of *soul* offered by Hyde, Hutchinson, and Thomas). In *Whitman the Political Poet* (1989), Erkkila draws upon feminism and critical theory to argue that the political has implications beyond the art of government, encompassing the broader social field of power as it is transferred, displayed, exercised, and imposed in a variety of social settings and discourses. In an explanation of her title, Erkkila writes, "*Whitman the Political Poet* . . . is an attempt to restore a series of linkages—Whitman, political, poet—that have been torn asunder in the wake of Modernist, Formalist, and New Critical strategies." She defines *political* both "in the traditional Aristotelian sense as a specific concern with the governance of *polis*, or state" and in the "more recent—and still vigorously contested—sense as the network of power relations in which texts and authors are implicated." Thus, she treats the poet's "overtly political postures and designs" but also attends to "the more subtle and less conscious ways his poems engage on the level of language, symbol, and myth the particular power struggles of his time—power struggles that came to center on . . . issues of race, class, gender, capital, technology, western expansion, and war" (v).

Like Hutchinson and Thomas, Erkkila argues that "the signs of personal neurosis and crisis we find in his poems are linked with disruptions and dislocations in the political economy" (11); and, like Arvin, she sees the "'inner light' of religious spiritualism and the 'outer light' of the revolutionary enlightenment—the doctrines of the soul and the doctrines of the republic" as the "potentially self-contradictory poles of Whitman's thought" (16). Like Larson, Erkkila's aim is to reunite the political and the aesthetic as a dialectical pair "without neglecting either term" (to put the problem in the language Larson applied to Whitman's own task). But the results of her investigation are quite different from Larson's. At least in her discussion of the poet's gradual transformation from politician to political poet, she emphasizes

Whitman's successes rather than his inability to stay clear of the dialectical traps he set for himself. Unlike Larson, she stays with the dialectic of politics and poetry rather than adding the additional layer of give and take, sympathy and prudence. She thus argues that Whitman's "commitment to democratic ideology gave him the language, forms, rituals, and symbols through which to speak and act as an autonomous being with a significant relation to a rapidly transforming and potentially disruptive world." This commitment allowed the poet of the 1850s to "move away from the darkly brooding other of his early poems" to become first "the confident self-generating democrat of his journalism and prose," then to aspire to "equalize the traditional hierarchical relationship between writer and reader by presenting the author as a democratic presence, a common man who speaks as and for rather than apart from the people" (21, 3). Indeed, Erkkila contends, Whitman was interested in "transferring the ultimate power of creation of the reader" (91). Rather than an escape from politics, then, the 1855 *Leaves of Grass* was, according to Erkkila, "a continuation of politics by other means" (92). Erkkila's Whitman is a revolutionary; his great theme is empowerment. For him, "the turbulence of the people was a source of regenerative vitality" rather than a source of anxiety (103). If the poet of "Song of Myself" "dances on 'the very verge of the limit' of sexual appetite and hellish despair," he is, in Erkkila's view, "continually restored to an inward economy of equity and balance" (103).

But, for Erkkila, Whitman's success at resolving the conflicting elements of his world and his poems was short-lived. Already by the 1856 *Leaves*, the poet had begun to founder on the problem of man's relation to woman in poems that would eventually be collected in "Children of Adam." Erkkila argues that the poet's pairing of his ideal male and female in the 1856 version of "A Woman Waits for Me" "seems less the occasion for a dynamic pairing of equals and more the scene of a domestic rape" (138). Paired with the "strident nationalism" of the poem, this unfortunate couple points toward the ultimate decline of Whitman's tenuous faith in the democratic politics he celebrated with such apparent strength in 1855. In the 1860 *Leaves*, Erkkila detects a yet more noticeable and "disquieting undercurrent that registers the throes of personal and public dissolution" (155). From that point, the political force of the poet diminishes, and Whitman the prose-writer returns to center stage, completing the cycle of a life devoted to exploring the relation of the public and private.

Published in the same year as Erkkila's study, my *Whitman's Poetry of the Body: Sexuality, Politics, and the Text* (1989) also relies heavily on the metanarrative of cyclic organicism, even though it is less committed to biographical study than either Thomas's or Erkkila's. In many ways, my reading appears more inclined to replace Whitman as a poetical subject—the author—with Whitman as a historical personage driven this way and that by forces that he only dimly understood. It is somewhat ironic, then, that I see the poet's project in sexual politics as a more successful endeavor than Larson and even Erkkila can admit. Whereas Erkkila appears to argue that Whitman's revolutionary politics stumbles on the problem of sexual politics, I argue (more like Larson) that the very discourses that energize the finest poems of the first decade of *Leaves of Grass*—notably the heterogeneous blending of romantic ideology, scientific progressivism, and radical democracy—could also betray the poet. Romanticism could yield to a sentimental absorption in the self that precludes political participation. The appeal to science could drive the poet away from his faith in the sympathetic "merge" of self with others—which characterizes both the romantic imagination and the democratic polis—leading him instead toward a fascination with distance, analysis, extension, and division. His fascination with scientific knowledge (or his competition with science) could also inspire his encyclopedic and analytical transformation of *Leaves of Grass*—the separation of "Calamus" and "Children of Adam" in the 1860s, for example, which foreshadowed the medical "construction" of homo- and heterosexuality at the end of the century. Finally, the poet's democratic idealism, which provided the creative impetus for the greatest poems of 1855 and 1856, could also turn sour, leading the poet in the late poems and prose works to look upon the democratic experiment of American life with sardonic disdain and, with a weak gesture of despair, to defer into the future the hoped-for completion of democracy.

A key historical point in my argument involves the concept of the "merge" as Whitman developed it in 1855. The poems of that year's *Leaves* had no individual titles and were not grouped into sections; their lines seemed to flow beyond the limits established by a long tradition of practice in English poetry. There was no name on the title page, only a picture of the poet on the frontispiece wearing the costume of an ordinary workingman. The identity of the poet seems instead to emerge little by little, finally erupting in the middle of the long first poem, later "Song of Myself,' as the voice of the poem triumphantly proclaims himself "Walt Whitman, an American, one of the roughs, a kosmos,/ Disorderly fleshy and sensual"; from that point on, he strives not only to break the barriers of decorum but also to overwhelm the very limits of selfhood, becoming a medium for other "long dumb voices" (*Leaves* 1855, 50). The speaker "worships" his own body, offering it sympathetically and sacrificially to the reader, who becomes at once the lover and the alternate self of the poet (*Leaves* 1855, 51). Through the use of tropes, I argue, the poet of 1855 extends the meaning of words and phrases beyond their denotative significances—both (traditionally) as a method to set forth his themes and (more radically) as a formal adjunct to the themes of stretching, merging, and flowing. The same rhetorical effects and socio-political themes continue to pour forth in 1856 and 1860, but they do so with diminished force and in competition with the appearance of more traditional "poetic" language and themes that stress difference, prudence, distance, and caution. This shift corresponds to fairly specific historical changes—the waning of the hopeful spirit of 1848 and the increasing certainty of war. Indeed, some historians have suggested that the Civil War began in 1856 with the conflicts of free-soilers and slave-holders in "Bleeding Kansas" and the beating of the abolitionist Charles Sumner on the floor of the United States Senate (Potter 209-12). At this time, Whitman, busily "absorbing" the atmosphere of hostility, was preparing the second edition of the *Leaves*; little wonder, then, that the energetic optimism of 1855, already framed by anxious concern, makes way for attempts at structured management and "scientific" approaches to controlling human behavior in 1856 (when *Leaves of Grass* was issued by the phrenological firm of Fowler and Wells). Similarly, the enhanced spirituality and other-worldliness of 1860 eventually yields to resignation in 1865 and 1867. Thereafter, the "friendly and flowing savage" of 1855 becomes the "Good Gray Poet" of the later years.

In *Disseminating Whitman: Revision and Corporeality in Leaves of Grass* (1990), Michael Moon likewise concludes that the "Leaves of Grass project" died with the Civil War (220-21). He also locates the heart of the revolutionary Whitman in the 1855 *Leaves*, where images of fluidity and openness find expression as thematic and formal concerns in a text marked by the impulse to "'wash away' all boundaries between bodies" (77). While Moon does not ignore the inherent tensions of the 1855 text—the "asymmetrical 'arrangement' or disposition of bodies with respect to gender and race," for example (77)—he argues that what is an interchange of self-protection and self-release, of "solidity" and "fluidity" between self and others, drifts toward a more solidly fixed position of rigidity and defensiveness as early as 1856. Indeed, he writes, "the second (1856) edition of *Leaves of Grass* suggests that it was not designed to represent untroubled 'fluidity'—either of selves or texts—as the 1855 edition had been. The poems now have titles and other signs of authorially imposed division, and one may take these changes . . . as signs of the author's increased willingness to fulfill readers' expectations in the wake of the first edition's general failure to find an audience" (88). Further, Moon reads the signs as pointing toward Whitman's tacit admission of "the insuperable difficulty of simply overruling division and difference as he had attempted to do . . . in the 1855 *Leaves*" (89).

Moon's chief contribution is to restate these central problems of historicist criticism in the language of a psychoanalytical criticism revised under the influence of Lacan and deconstruction. Thus, he argues, "The aftermath of the publication of the 1855 *Leaves* represents the oedipal moment in Whitman's literary career, when the stream of largely undifferentiated ('fluid') and specular homotypes becomes riven by difference, when the recognition is forced on the subject that the actual achievement and enjoyment of the imaginary satisfactions of the 'fluid' realm have been and must be 'sternly deferred'" (89). Just as Kerry Larson, Betsy Erkkila, and I attempt to close the gap between the poetic and the political, Moon succeeds to some extent in bridging the psychological and the ideological—a gap represented perhaps most clearly by the distance between the interpretations of Edwin Miller and those of Robert Martin.

Moon also illuminates the difficulties inherent in Whitman's effort to overcome (or overwhelm) the epistemological problems on which deconstructionist and antifoundationalist philosophers and critics have focused in the last two decades—above all, the problem of how the constructed worlds of language (the haunt of the alienated human "subject") relates to the world beyond, outside, under, over, independent of, or in some way different from language-based worlds. Whitman struggled with the question of how the poetic world possibly interacts with the natural world, the social world, the world of objects, or more generally the world of others. Moon's reliance on psychoanalysis leads him to question how far Whitman was conscious of this struggle, however, and his deconstructionist bias leads him to present Whitman's dream of creating a poetry with instrumental or illocutionary power as doomed from the start (compare Bové; also Byers).

This provocative stance, which is quite similar to that of Larson, hints at the types of problems addressed by critics who have recently taken Whitman's "language experiment" as their topic. Their works will be considered more closely in the next chapter. The key point for now is that, even as it brings together the study of history and poetry, a criticism informed by structuralist or poststructuralist poetics begins with a theory that distinguishes diachronic and synchronic analysis and that tends to treat history and language as competitors, one ever trying to replace, absorb, or defeat the other. The result is usually a wavering between an organic and a mechanical or technological model of communicative relations. We have as yet no deep poetics of change—a model that can comprehend poetry like Whitman's, which challenges the critic to account at once for its own authority and its own organicism.

It is too soon, in all truth, to get a clear sense of how the problems raised by the recent historicist criticism of *Leaves of Grass* will be resolved (if they can be resolved). These studies have followed so closely on one another's heels in recent years that the authors have been unable as yet fully to assimilate and respond to one another's work. A few review essays have appeared that have taken the first steps, but the conclusions have been somewhat incomplete and contradictory so far. Gregory Jay, for example, enthusiastically welcomes the new historical emphasis on sexual politics, but neglects to assess Hyde's and Hutchinson's efforts to tie bodily politics to political spirituality

("Catching Up with Whitman: A Review Essay"). Jay evidently favors criticism built upon the foundations of historical materialism (more pronounced in the work of Martin, Thomas, Erkkila, Killingsworth, and, to a lesser extent, Moon). By contrast, David Reynolds—in an essay that groups Erkkila and Killingsworth with Price and Greenspan—complains that the historicist treatment of Whitman fails in comprehensiveness ("Review Essay: Walt Whitman Today"). In a conclusion somewhat reminiscent of Asselineau's charge that the New Criticism neglects content ("Walt Whitman" 264), Reynolds argues that, by focusing on the political, sexual, or historical Whitman, recent critics deal thoroughly with certain "aspects" or "themes" in the poet's work while overlooking or discarding others that may be of equal importance.

There are several defenses against Reynold's implied argument for a comprehensive viewpoint. We could say, for example, that the desire for comprehensiveness represents a somewhat regressive and imperialist "politics" of criticism, one that seeks to dominate and "close the book" on the poet, to standardize, overcome, and ultimately reduce the poet to manageable proportions, to suit the needs of the scholar. This argument, however, is not only needlessly aggressive (partaking of the very thing it would censure), but also inadequate. A less totalizing desire for comprehensiveness could well suggest that some readings of the poet's work are more complete than others and are therefore more suitable as a point of entry for students and nonprofessionals interested in criticism but overwhelmed by the profusion of studies on Whitman. By these lights, the works of Hyde and Hutchinson, for example, tend to be superior to other works discussed in this chapter, since the circle of their criticism more completely surrounds the political, aesthetic, and spiritual dimensions of Whitman's poems.

Setting aside comprehensiveness as the overriding concern, we may also apply other standards suggested by the work of the recent historicists. We may wonder which of the critics best opens the work of the historical Whitman to the understanding of the modern reader. This task involves a Janus-faced approach that at once brings to light historical materials that have slipped from modern memory and then reinterprets the concerns of the poet in the light of contemporary issues, such as class politics (Thomas), multiculturalism (Hutchinson), feminism (Erkkila), gay studies (Martin), and sexuality in general (Killingsworth). Given the current suspicion of unity (as dominion) and the emphasis on cultural difference (as both a positive diversity and a negative fragmentation), no one of these studies can claim a distinct advantage over the other, but must be content to have extended the poet's work along the lines of a single sociopolitical perspective, which, taken together, are complementary efforts to further the growth of *Leaves of Grass* into regions of concern that will involve various new readerships.

The critical issues of comprehensiveness and complementarity are, in fact, new iterations of the distinction in the organic tradition between the genetic approach, the quest for a single perspective that will comprehend the whole of Whitman, and the cyclic or serial version of organism, which fits the pieces of Whitman's accomplishment into a narrative of development. The difference between the two perspectives can also now be seen as a recapitulation of a major linguistic or rhetorical opposition—that between metaphor (since the genetic view understands Whitman's writing as revealed in or transformed by some key term or viewpoint) and metonymy (since serial organicism builds a narrative upon an implicit or explicit string of associations). Questions touching on these issues must, therefore, remain open as we enter the discussion, in the next chapter, of Whitman's language.

5: The Language

One of the most frequently quoted sayings from Whitman comes not from his poems or published prose, but from a conversation in old age, one of his many retrospective reflections on his poetic accomplishments. We get the sentence second-hand from Horace Traubel: "I sometimes think the *Leaves* is only a language experiment," Whitman is supposed to have told his young admirer, "an attempt to give the spirit, the body, the man, new words, new potentialities of speech" (*American Primer* viii-ix). Traubel gives the quotation in his introduction to the posthumous publication of Whitman's notes toward a study of language, *An American Primer*. It certainly seems to warrant an approach to the poems that allows an overriding concern with language to supersede or at least encompass interpretations centering on spirituality, sexuality, and history or politics—"the spirit, the body, the man."

But such an approach has been slow to develop in Whitman studies. This tardiness is understandable for the first generation of Whitman scholars, who, having actually known the poet, tended to take as literally as possible Whitman's (contradictory?) claim that his own person is somehow embodied in *Leaves of Grass*. But why did Whitman's reference to his "language experiment" fail to kindle scholarly interest well into the twentieth century? I suspect the reason is that, among literary scholars of the second and third generations in Whitman studies, linguistics and rhetoric were considered with indifference, if not outright contempt (see Riley). From an outsider's perspective, formal language study could only appear rather too analytical and mechanical in its orientation. How could the dryly technical models of behaviorism and structuralism possibly apply to a poet as "original" and "organic" as Whitman?

Not until the work of Jean Catel and F. O. Matthiessen were Whitman's many notes for lectures on language taken seriously. Matthiessen could surely say in 1941, "One aspect of Whitman's work that has not yet received its due attention is outlined in *An American Primer*" (517). Quoting Whitman's reference to his "language experiment," Matthiessen breaks the drought, opening his chapter on Whitman in *American Renaissance* with a discussion of the language of *Leaves of Grass*. Rather than bridging the gap between literary study and linguistics, though, Matthiessen actually widens it in an explication of Whitman's organicist notions about the poetry of "living speech"; he reveals, with some approval, views set forth by Whitman that today, in the wake of Derrida's critique of "presence," may seem naive. Matthiessen tells, for example, of the poet's notion of transparency, the idea that "a perfect user of words uses things" (qtd. on 517). Not surprisingly, Whitman had little use for positivist linguistics—the "linguists and contenders" of his age. As Matthiessen tells it, "He understood that language was not 'an abstract construction' made by the learned, but that it had arisen out of the work and needs, the joys and struggles and desires of long generations of humanity" and that, furthermore, "words were not arbitrary inventions, but the product of human events and customs, the progeny of folkways" (517). Portraying Whitman as an attentive student of language but an opponent of formal linguistic models, Matthiessen therefore reconciles the poet's organic model of language with a historical-materialist critique of academic elitism in language study. Whitman's "language experiment," Matthiessen argues, was intended above all to be a rival to the dry analysis of grammarians, a poetry built upon the speech of the streets, the political podium, the popular entertainments of opera and the theater, and indeed the sounds and rhythms of the body and nature at large.

Matthiessen accepts Whitman's organicism as a cogent theory of language use (including the creative uses of language in the "evolution" of poetic usage), but he goes beyond most critics of his day in his exposition of the theory and his questioning of it; as he promises in his introduction, he strives to determine how well the poet's practice bears out his theory [vii]. This method has proven valuable to the critics of Whitman's language who have followed Matthiessen. In some ways, it sets them apart from more purely biographical and historical critics. More conscious of theory, they must articulate the theoretical framework of *Leaves of Grass* before adopting it as their own. I say *before* rather than *instead of* adopting it because, as it turns out, these critics tend to apply their analyses to problems already defined by the dominant critical tradition and, in so doing, come back into the fold of the organic tradition. But a certain self-conscious or ironic disposition keeps them on the margins of the tradition, where they occupy an alternative position that has not yet been fully assimilated or exploited in Whitman studies.

I have already begun to sketch the dimensions of this alternative posture in my discussion of Larson and Moon in chapter 4 and to suggest that the 1980s witnessed an intensified interest in the language of *Leaves of Grass*. The pioneering work in this field was done by C. Carroll Hollis in his widely cited study *Language and Style in Leaves of Grass* (1983). This book has been followed by two full-length studies devoted to a linguistically oriented approach to Whitman's poetry— James Perrin Warren's book *Walt Whitman's Language Experiment*

(1990) and Mark Bauerlein's *Whitman and the American Idiom* (1991). Though very different, these works are, to some extent, a culmination, in that they attempt to keep alive the question of organic change— questions about the growth of *Leaves of Grass* raised by the biographical and historical critics—while at the same time reviving the analytical critics' thesis about the otherworldiness of the *Leaves*, the poetry's tendency to build up a world apart from the world of moral action even as it vigorously attempts to claim its place as a moral and political force— a tendency noted as early as 1953 by the analytical critic Charles Feidelson (to whom Richard Chase addressed a vigorous rejoinder). Yet I suspect that none of the recent critics of Whitman's language would claim to have squared these parallel lines of development—the architectonic conception of the poetic builder and the organic concept of the poetic medium. On the contrary, both Hollis and Warren (and to a lesser extent Bauerlein) claim to be opening rather than closing an investigation of Whitman's language experiment. Their own work is thus, like the poet's, experimental.

The Linguistic Turn

Hollis takes as his point of departure a dual mission. His first goal is to bring into Whitman scholarship the "many new discoveries, approaches, and analytic tools for examining poetry," the instruments of analysis developed in linguistics, semiotics, and structuralist criticism. Hollis notes that these "tools" have not been applied to *Leaves of Grass*, but he sees no good reason for this neglect. Having educated himself in the new terminology and methods, he finds their usefulness undeniable in describing what is going on in the poems. Hollis's success in introducing the new theories and methods is indicated by his significant influence upon critics like Larson, Warren, and Bauerlein. No doubt, given the direction of current scholarship, someone would have taken Whitman studies around the "linguistic turn" had Hollis not done so himself. But anyone else might have had considerably more trouble than Hollis, who, at the time he wrote, already had behind him a long career and a distinguished reputation as a professor of American literature. The fact that no major study before his had ventured to apply the new techniques to *Leaves of Grass* suggests a rather strong resistance to this approach; 1983 is a late date for such a study, so late indeed that the book, with its teacherly tendency to summarize the theories and findings of what ought to be well known in the field (the basic texts of speech act theory, for example), may already seem dated to a reader in the 1990s. Given the likelihood that his readers entertained a willful ignorance of such matters, however, Hollis's approach seemed entirely appropriate in the early 1980s. Having earned the right to lecture through decades of service in the field, Hollis opened a door that had remained too long shut and ushered in an expanded study of Whitman's rhetoric and language use.

But Hollis does not stop with a mere introduction of new methods. His second, more substantive goal is to shed light on the differences between "Whitman's early poetry" and "that written after the Civil War" (ix). Before Hollis, this difference had been assumed, noted, or analyzed in a fairly cursory way by biographical and historical criticism; and it had been ignored or explained away by critics inclined to formalism. Hollis sets out to analyze the shift rigorously, but his results, as he hints himself, are mixed. Certainly, his methods allow him to describe changes in tone and style more thoroughly and more compellingly than anyone before him. However, while he can effectively describe what changed in the poems, his methods do not allow him to explain the changes. On the limits of his study, Hollis writes, "I have not wanted to depart from a study of the text to the quite different task of hypothesizing the person who created that text" (ix). The purpose of this studied avoidance of genetic criticism is to maintain the focus upon questions involving the hard surface of rhetorical and stylistic features among the different poems and editions of the *Leaves*. But the reader, faced not only with the changes but also with the biographical and critical framework mentioned by Hollis, can only wonder why the changes occurred; and Hollis's structuralist commitment keeps him from addressing this question head-on. He does offer "occasional guesses as to why [Whitman] did this or that," but he cautions that these "guesses" should not "be considered with the same seriousness . . . given to the stylistic examination of the poetry" (ix).

Nevertheless, the nagging problems of critical biography—how Whitman became the poet of *Leaves of Grass*, why Whitman changed directions after the Civil War—continue to haunt Hollis. His frustration at being unable to answer these questions is evident in his account of the shortcomings of critical biography: "The trouble is that we still do not know enough about the man to be certain how the style was achieved" (xi). Attempts to reconcile the descriptive power of anti-genetic rhetorical and linguistic studies with the explanatory power of biographical and historical criticism, while beyond Hollis's intended scope, ultimately inform many of his "guesses," which (despite his plea that they lack "seriousness") represent some of the most noteworthy efforts in Whitman studies to link genetic criticism with technical analysis. A similar effort drives the work of Hollis's descendents (especially Larson and Bauerlein, but also Hutchinson, Killingsworth, Greenspan, Moon, and Warren).

Thus, even as he plies the "tools" of a more technical approach to the poems, Hollis is driven to solve the problems dictated by the organic tradition in Whitman studies. He begins by locating an area of general agreement that yet leaves a gap to be filled by further work. Scholars agree, he points out, that "there is an oratorical element in

Whitman's poetry"; but, he adds, few critics have made much of this element, probably because "the role of the orator has so diminished in our day that most of us would find it hard to give credence to the notion that a genius of Whitman's rank should be tempted by the podium" (4-5). He goes on to present a genetic thesis carefully crafted to allow him to support it with evidence derived from his linguistic methods: "The reason *Leaves of Grass* did appear in 1855 was that Whitman found a way to overcome or to circumvent his inability to carry out a prophetic mission in the public and oral manner of traditional orators, bards, public speakers, lyceum lecturers, by finding a way of transmitting his message in print without losing the efficacy of its presumed public presentation" (18). Citing the earlier research of Clifton Furness, Jean Catel, and F. O. Matthiessen (and arguing against Asselineau, who dismisses the connection between oral performance and Whitman's verse), Hollis writes, "What Whitman did was to rewrite, reshape, revamp his never-given speeches to gain and maintain the immediacy, the urgency, the audience involvement, the excitement, the emotional uplift of the public performance that might have been" (18). These qualities, in Hollis's estimation, were precisely those the poet lost in his late poems, in which "he covered up his lack of prophetic inspiration by pretentious, over-'poeticalized' language" (26). Why did he succeed early on and fail later? Hollis "guesses" that he was led, then misled, by an "inordinate craving for the regard of the audience, which he never did find (enough to satisfy the craving, anyway)" (27). In his first chapter, we therefore see, along with a willingness to broach these genetic issues, Hollis's willingness to introduce aesthetic judgment as an additional complement to his linguistic analysis. Like the analytical critics of the 1950s, though with far different methods, he is interested not only in what changed in the poems but also the effect of these changes upon the quality of the verse. To the thesis that the poems written before the Civil War were different from those written after (a point he can establish by linguistic analysis) he thus adds that the early poems were better (a point which must be made on other grounds and which throws him back into the old debate about which edition of the poems is the best, a dispute usually associated with Malcolm Cowley and his interlocutors in the 1950s).

After the first chapter, however, such matters are presented mainly in brief asides, as Hollis focuses on the instrumental question of how—"the one question this book . . . professedly tries to answer by an explanation of Whitman's poetic language" (27). He demonstrates how Whitman (only half-consciously—that is, with both conscious craftsmanship and a good measure of "instinct" for oral effects) employed oratorical devices like the *cursus* to revise English prosody to suit his own rhetorical needs (chapter 2); how the poet used negation to signify his own confidence and to emphasize the positive qualities that he brought forward (chapter 4); and how he involved the audience with a skillful use of metonymy, which tends to create an "open text" in contrast to metaphor, which completes identities and leaves little for the creative reader to do (chapter 5). Hollis makes these claims only for the early poems. Surveying the shift in the various editions of *Leaves of Grass*, he argues that the poet—increasingly anxious after the war about "how to alert . . . readers to the experiment he was engaged in" (51)— "turned away from the oral foundation of his art," writing and revising so that his lines became more regularly metrical and more attuned (he must have imagined) to the appetites of an audience conditioned by the culture of literacy (52). And the shift involved much more than verse form, Hollis claims. The revisions of "Song of Myself," for example, indicate a "pulling back from the prophetic stance in order to enhance the lyrical aspect of the poem" and a similar distancing of himself from the "roughs" (with whom he had identified in 1855) indicated by the reduction in the number of street expressions and slang terms (like "foosfoos") (56-57). Shifting into the historicist mode, Hollis argues that Whitman "backs away from [an] identification with . . . working people," seeking in his later years "to catch the sympathetic attention of the educated, somewhat disaffected members of . . . society" (58). In such arguments, Hollis mingles rhetorical criticism with sociolinguistics and discourse analysis. He contends that the poet's conception of his audience continued to shift throughout his career until, finally, "the awareness of an audience in front of him no longer held his imagination"; in the late poems, "he no longer spoke with and for the people, his presumed audience, but for himself" (64).

Perhaps the most illuminating demonstration of this thesis occurs when Hollis applies the premises of speech-act theory to a reading of *Leaves of Grass* before and after the war. Hollis explains that, in discourse, the illocutionary act involves the making of "promises, bequests, bets, and bids" in a grammar that renders the first-person subject as an authority worthy of such binding acts and the second-person recipient as the beneficiary of such acts ("I bequeath upon you . . .") (76). In the imaginative world of literature, however, the actual authority and benefits of these acts are, of course, null and void, but (despite the somewhat literal-minded objections of Austin and Searle, the founders of speech-act theory) the effects of an illocutionary grammar in literature are similar to the effects of the speech acts in "real life." The difference involves the insertion of a persona and implied audience between the poet and the actual audience. Within this second-order semiotic system, readers may either accept or reject the role of the implied reader, much as (at least in a democracy) the recipient of a promise or bet may accept or reject the terms of the disclosure. Thus, as Hollis suggests, "Illocutionary acts, whether in life or in literature, add such a burden of personal involvement and intensity (for both speaker and listener, poet and reader) that they can be destructive of perlocutionary effects"—effects related to the reader's response (74). According to

Hollis, Whitman "strained this illocutionary tension so far that he can never be successfully imitated but can be easily parodied"—so much depends upon the peculiar relation of "I" and "you" that he set up (74-75). If the "you" replaces the "I," the structure of authority is reversed; and (as Larson shows) Whitman experimented with just such reversals in transmission, though never altogether successfully. Hollis notes, "Perhaps Whitman never realized the dangerous similarity of the serious and the comic, the sublime and the ridiculous, profundity and prolixity, prophesying and posturing" that adheres to his illocutionary advances in the poetic medium (75).

What the illocutionary grammar of the early poems did allow Whitman to do, according to Hollis, was to create an impressive "prophetic style"; for this result Whitman had to settle, for style alone does not make a prophet (81). Thus, in Hollis's view, "though Whitman was really no prophet, or shaman, he certainly did want to sound like one" (104). And he was able at least to satisfy this desire in literary (if not political, social, or religious) practice. This judgment turns upon Hollis's acceptance of Richard Ohmann's contention that in literature illocutionary speech acts are, at best, mimetic (Hollis 76). From this observation, it is an easy step back to the thesis of critical biography and analytical criticism: Whitman was not a prophet or even a very significant political figure, but he was an "extraordinary poet" (81). If speech acts in literature can perform no action outside of the literary context (as J. Hillis Miller points out in his now famous essay "The Critic as Host"), the poet can only be a poet.

Having verged on removing the line of demarcation between rhetoric and poetry, speech and writing, action and language, Hollis therefore retreats to the conclusion that Whitman used rhetorical devices 'for poetic (that is, nonrhetorical) ends" (234). Throughout the book, Hollis points to the worked-over notebooks to insist that conscious artistry gave rise to *Leaves of Grass*, but he also betrays some doubt about whether Whitman knew exactly what he was doing at any given point. The problem here is one of theory and practice. Whitman was no theorist, Hollis suggests, but a practitioner with a good enough sense of what he was about. This qualified view of Whitman's intentionality serves two functions (which, I suspect, the critic, like the poet before him, perceives half-consciously). First, it allows Hollis to praise the poet's craftsmanship (even if it is only partly driven by sound theory). Second, it opens the way for the critic to complete the poet's work, adding a theoretician's finish to the poetic project.

Into this same opening have come James Perrin Warren and Mark Bauerlein, each seeking his own way of producing a complementary text to *Leaves of Grass*. In *Walt Whitman's Language Experiment* (1990), Warren takes up the old role of Whitman's defender, mounting a campaign to demonstrate that Whitman was more than just a good craftsman. In Warren's view, he was a fully conscious and impressive theorist of language as well.

Warren begins by clearing away a number of premises that have driven Whitman studies (and modern criticism in general). "Rather than accept the distinction between a *Person* and *literature* as absolute," he says, "I would argue that the two are by no means mutually exclusive" (2). In an era that allows the mind and the text to be equal partners in constructing one another, this contention seems reasonable. But then Warren moves on to the "distinction between theory and practice" so important to Matthiessen and, in a different way, to Hollis. Instead of enabling, Warren finds this concept crippling: "Whitman's vision of language is so fundamental to his vision of his own poetry, and vice versa, that the poems are as 'theoretical' as they are 'practical,' just as Whitman's pronouncements concerning language are as performative and rhetorical as the poems" (3-4). For similar reasons, he attacks yet another distinction, that between "extrinsic, contextual criticism and intrinsic, formalist criticism" (4). For Whitman, Warren writes, "the language of literature [is] a distillation of the language at large, and both of these are the verbal embodiments of American culture" (4).

In these methodological statements, Warren reveals both a generosity toward the poet, a willingness to take Whitman on his own terms, and a clear, though qualified Whiggish attitude toward the growth of Whitman criticism. He accepts the professionalist premise "that Whitman scholarship has gradually moved [away] from a naive form of hagiographical criticism," but he also implies that the crowning achievement of this scholarship is not to transcend or better the poet, but to meet him on equal ground, to be worthy of him. The key to such worthiness lies not in any particular critical method, Warren suggests, but rather in "an eclectic blending of approaches" (3). Such a blend he offers himself, combining "rhetorical or formalist" readings with an awareness of the culture "embodied" in language and the shifting purposes of the poet. Warren wants above all "to pay attention to the language of Whitman's poetry and prose" and "to allow the language to shape [the critical] argument" (3). According to Warren (Borges to the contrary), this attentiveness and willingness to conform to the poet's language—considered as a "fundamental" concern in all of the poet's activities—make criticism open enough and large enough to overwhelm the distinctions he has dismissed, distinctions which define a number of important but restrictive critical categories. Reaching beyond these categories, criticism as Warren conceives it is able, at last, to comprehend the whole of Whitman's vision. However, to defeat the limitations of the categories, Warren must keep other implicit distinctions active—namely the distinction between conscious and unconscious artistry and the competing images of Whitman as hero (the master builder of an impressive poetic artifice) and Whitman as victim (driven in contradictory directions by psychological, historical, or linguistic forces that he only dimly comprehended).

Warren hints in his introduction that, in addition to the "rhetorical or formalist" element in his critical method, he adds a "poststructuralist" or "deconstructive" dimension, though he leaves vague exactly how he employs these diverse elements, which are usually considered contradictory. Eventually, a clear dialectical pattern develops, however. Warren presents an aspect or theme from Whitman's theory-practice of language, then challenges it with a deconstructive thrust, charging that the self-contradictory elements of Whitman's concepts threaten their undoing—much in the manner of Larson and Moon. Ultimately, however, he disarms his own deconstruction, not on rational, but on rhetorical grounds, usually by claiming that Whitman was perfectly aware of the problems his assertions generated and that his management of contradictions within a framing purpose is an essential component of the power of his rhetoric. In other words, rhetoric transcends logic in the hands of the poetic theorist-craftsman. The figure of the poet emerges heroically, and Warren joins Bucke and James Miller in a vindication of the poet as a conscious artisan of language, now (with the help of his appreciative critic) able to defend himself not only against the old formalist attack on his status as a literary artist but also against the psychoanalytical-deconstructionist update of the old naiveté thesis—the argument that Whitman did not know what he was doing.

An example of Warren's method appears in his treatment of the knotty problem of the relation of words and things and the related question of the simultaneously diachronic and synchronic nature of language. Warren first shows that Whitman frequently "leaps the gap between the silent past and the 'lispings of the future' just as [he] bridges the gulf between things and words" (37). The difficulty of this Herculean historicism and poetic engineering (time-leaping and gulf-bridging) arouses the deconstructionist in Warren: "The problem with this double leap is, of course, that the poet cannot escape the confines of metaphor itself. There is no direct, unmediated relation between words and things, since language is itself the mediator"; thus "Whitman attempts to evade the mediating influence of language by proclaiming the things of the earth to be the words of a cosmic language" (37). And yet, though "the rhetoric is self-contradictory, to be sure, . . . it is also powerful, for Whitman's strategy is to employ figuration in order to deny the basically figural, formal quality of all language" (37-38). By pushing these figural relations as hard as he can, Whitman ultimately reveals what words and things share. They are at once static and dynamic; they exist at the same time they change; they combine being and doing.

Building upon the concept of transcendental unity inherited from Hegel and Humboldt, Warren's Whitman adds evolution into the mixture, dissolving the metaphysical qualities of unity into the organic concept of unity-within-change. As in his theory, so in his practice, Warren argues: "By mingling . . . more dynamic, temporary agential nouns with . . . more stative, permanent agential nouns, [for example,] Whitman blurs the distinction between flowing activity and stable identity. The direct result of the innovative ways in which he exploits the products and possibilities of English word formation, Whitman's dynamic deverbal style becomes a formal equivalent of his theory of linguistic and spiritual evolution. . . . Although the poet continually nominalizes a verbal base, the 'naturally' stative character of the noun tends to assume the dynamic character of the verb" and likewise "personal identity tends to assume the temporal, flowing character normally associated with actions and activities" (58).

Thus, Warren's linguistic analysis brings him more or less back to the formalist position of Howard Waskow on Whitman's "bipolar unity." In extended readings of "The Sleepers" and "Crossing Brooklyn Ferry," Warren discovers some heroic bipolar resolutions, but here they occur at the syntactical and organizational levels rather than the morphological level. Whitman's mastery of the free verse form is revealed in his complex, but closely ordered use of parallel structure. In "The Sleepers," Warren argues, "the catalogue functions as an ultimate expansion beyond the rhythmical frame, where the expansion paradoxically effects the closure of the poem" (93). Likewise, in "Brooklyn Ferry," he asserts, "the catalogue and rhythmical frame function together in a clear formal structure" (94). Warren sees the clear marks of intentionality in Whitman's structural "strategy" in "Brooklyn Ferry," the aim of which is "to create a series of three orderly expansions. The nine sections of the poem divide neatly into three movements, where each movement begins with a short section, expands to a somewhat longer section, and culminates in a catalogue" (94). The parallel structure turns at once on two critical axes roughly equivalent to a syntagmatic aspect (the movement indicated by the chronological unfolding of the sections from 1 to 9) and a paradigmatic aspect (indicated by the parallel structural relation of sections 1, 4, and 7, sections 2, 5, and 8, and sections 3, 6, and 9). Repetitions and thematic links support the formal relations and vice versa in what can only seem, in light of Warren's reading, as a virtuoso performance.

Warren's treatment of the "twin dialectic" in Whitman's poetry and writings on language (136) leads him, like other critics with a formalist bent, toward a tolerance of Whitman's later poems and revisions that is missing in historical, psychoanalytical, and biographical research. He sees no frantic search for an audience, no belatedness, no sublimation, no failure of inspiration. His Whitman remains, for the most part, in control of himself and his materials; like a classical rhetor, the poet weighs his effects and arranges for them in advance. Without denying the difference revealed in any linguistic analysis of the poems written before the war and those written after the war, Warren is inclined to grant Whitman his right to alter his poems according to a changing view of the function of literature. Thus, he argues that "Whitman changes the focus of his theory of language between 1856 and 1892" and that the "diction, syntax, and organization of the poetry" in the last four editions of *Leaves of Grass* reflect Whitman's changing theoretical concerns" (3). Despite such changes, Warren claims that there is "a fundamental continuity" in his ideas on language, "a continuity based on his persistent vision of linguistic and spiritual evolution in America" (137). What variations do occur, according to Warren, are "variations in emphasis . . . rather than absolute differences in conception or principle" (137). While it is true that after the Civil War Whitman resorts to a more traditional poetic diction and rhythm, these shifts in practice are "explained," Warren says, by a corresponding shift in theory: "Whitman begins to stress the cumulative, retrospective qualities of . . . American English" (138). Of course, if the shift in theory "explains" the shift in practice, then on this change a number of resolutions have come undone. Above all, the distinction in theory and practice reappears in the critic's reasoning, and the pressing fact of the possible influence of the Civil War intrudes. *Why* did the poet change precisely at this moment in history?

Warren declines to answer such questions, for though his method is "eclectic," it returns to a treatment of poetry that is fairly closely confined to the world of language and letters. He does not, however, take the usual formalist route in resisting the critical trend toward a cyclic organicism. Indeed, he agrees with "the foremost critics" that "Whitman suffers . . . a significant falling off of poetic power" in his later years. But his agreement is carefully qualified; it applies primarily to the production of individual poems. Though he accepts that all the great poems were written by 1871, Warren suggests in an original revision of traditional criticism that "poetic power is not therefore absent [in the late editions of the *Leaves*]; rather it makes itself felt on a new formal level." Warren identifies two specific manifestations of this formal power in the last four editions. First, Whitman's "cluster arrangements" demonstrate anew "the play of continuity and succession" that accounts for the technical excellence of many of the early poems. Second, Whitman's use of clusters and annexes brings him back to the "spatialization of form," an effect with which he had experimented in "Lilacs" at the pinnacle of his poetic career (195). This spatialization does not indicate, in Warren's view, a lack of growth; instead it signifies a different kind of growth—architectonic accumulation and arrangement or perhaps inorganic growth, crystallization. If the late editions of the book no longer exhibit syntagmatic growth corresponding to the advance of the biographical subject toward maturity, they at least demonstrate the poet's artistry through paradigmatic growth. Structuralist poetics will accept either kind of growth as a sign of progress, as Warren suggests. But the fact remains that, in the early poems, the poems developed in both directions under the powerful guidance of Whitman's twin dialectic. The late Whitman, as Warren must concede, leaves the reader with an image of diminished power.

While Warren thus defends the conscious artistry of *Leaves of Grass* and the intellectual gains of the poet throughout his career, Mark Bauerlein gives an entirely different impression, one influenced by the very deconstructions that Warren has challenged. Instead of a skilled theorist-craftsman whose work transcends the distinction of theory and practice, Bauerlein's Whitman does battle with theory, thereby betraying a "genuinely American antiintellectualism" that "sets against the depleted formulae, remote vocabularies, and frigid arguments of critics and academics an organic poetic idiom rife with passionate intensity and grounded in felt existences, purified of poetic diction and heedless of 'literary' detail" (4-5). This anti-poet "realizes and contends with the unflagging threat that theory poses to naturality and all the mystifications naturality founds and supports" (6). Bauerlein takes up the challenge not as Whitman's defender but as an exponent of theory, which represents the ultimate end of much recent criticism. He argues that, though "Whitman wishes to regard representation . . . as a solution, as an answer to the personal call he awakens to in the early 1850s and as a seminal catalyst in America's ongoing 'evolution,'" in the end "theory intervenes in this progressive or expressive linguistic design and instead converts representation per se into a 'problem,' a precarious activity necessitating interrogation before action" (6). In Bauerlein's view, Whitman himself experienced a growing awareness that he could not continue to "look at language representationally, that is, as a group of signs bound to nature"; hardly naive, then, the poet clearly perceived but only gradually accepted the need to "regard language semiotically, that is, as a system of reference made up of signs bound to each other" (7). Consequentially, over several editions *Leaves of Grass* left the world of things and actions it once proclaimed as the real poems of America and went to live in a world of language and literature.

It makes a good story, even though it is "one of decline": "although Whitman's guiding intention is to overcome language, to fend off the possibility that words bear properties that cannot be reduced to human experience, the individual poems and pieces of criticism springing from the Orphic intention nevertheless register its dismemberment" (9). While "testifying to their natural origins and workings, Whitman's writings also declare themselves as instances of failing resistance to linguistic play" (9-10). Ironically, "the more Whitman insists upon his language's organic basis, the more a semiotic vocabulary creeps into his poems" (10). The fears that he will be misunderstood, misread, misinterpreted drive the poems toward constant self-accountings, beginning as early as 1860 with poems like "Out of the Cradle," that speak in the same breath about the genesis of poetic inspiration and the realization of death. On the one hand, "Whitman aggrandizes language" (22). On the other, he "condemns language for its wanton artificiality" (23). Ultimately, "the social and technical pitfalls of being a published poet" defeat Whitman. The broken text, showing the traces and signs of battle, falls open before the critic, who claims *Leaves of Grass* as his own and takes it on his own terms: "Whitman's poetry and poetics is an investigation into the theory and practice of criticism" (16).

In many ways, Bauerlein reiterates much of Larson's reading of *Leaves of Grass*. He shares especially Larson's (and Moon's) view of the impossibility of Whitman's project to overcome language through language. Thus deconstruction forms a continuity with the radical formalist regime that understands the chief topic of poetry to be poetry itself. For Bauerlein, "Song of Myself," for example, is "a poem about writing and composition" (55). But, unlike the formalists, Bauerlein contends that Whitman's goal to create "another nature" lies beyond the production of either "a golden world to lift us imaginatively out of this brazen world" or a mere replication of the "real" nature; rather, he "intends to create a 'Nature without check with original energy'" (59-60). This aim motivates his most impressive poetic exertions but ultimately founders on the problem of how to achieve "original energy" (which Bauerlein reads as the energy of the original experience of worldliness) in an experience mediated by language. Language becomes, in the terminology of deconstruction, a supplement, a residue that defies Whitman's (metaphysical) effort to purify his alternative nature. Thus, his inevitable "textualizing of nature reverses the usual thrust of Whitman's poetics—to naturalize the text" (63). Language, on which the poet depends, is finally "the poem's counterinspiration," giving rise to "the inscribed problematics that haunt the poet's desire for auto-insemination" (60). The metaphorical connection of writing to masturbation in "Song of Myself" and many other poems (notably "Spontaneous Me") raises the stakes yet higher, for now the poet must defeat not only language but also nature itself; in Bauerlein's view, "both references—to writing and to masturbation—lead to the same conclusion: for Whitman to succeed as man and poet, his poetic genius-masculine potency must rival nature's fecund creativity" (64).

Against such odds, it is little wonder that, as early as 1856, the poet begins to doubt the power of productivity (composition) and turns his attention to consumption (reading): "Now grimly conscious of the pitfalls of being read, Whitman loses confidence in words' power to bring about an unmediated experience" and thus begins to explain himself and indeed to defend himself against the onslaught of the reader, his next enemy. The final stage of this development witnesses the poet's abandonment of his embattled texts, his retreat from the forceful assertion of his own presence. In Bauerlein's words, "Poems appearing in editions following the Civil War seem to emerge from a more static and controlled aesthetic. Specifically, one finds that Whitman more and more often opts for a style and a subject matter in which the 'I' in linguistic process—reading and writing, translating and interpreting—has all but vanished" (152). The persona drops his heroic pretensions and becomes "a watchful but anonymous and somewhat uninvolved observer carefully recording the impressions of life. The problematics of observing and recording are suppressed, and the poems are scaled down into brief reports of an image or feeling or insight the poet immediately intuits" (152). Thus Bauerlein concludes that "Whitman's 'language experiment' ended in 1860, that he recognized the impracticality of his poetic project and adopted a different attitude toward his role as a poet and toward the nature of poetic language. That recognition comes when he is faced with the fatal consequences of semiosis" (153).

Unlike Larson and Moon, however, who present Whitman primarily as a victim of these "fatal consequences of semiosis," Bauerlein strives to retain much of the heroic image of Whitman that we find in writers like Richard Chase, James Miller, and James Warren. Bauerlein's Whitman is a fighter who, though he did not always perfectly estimate the odds against him, certainly "understood his nostalgias better than he is usually given credit for" (46). "For those living in the wake of the 'linguistic turn,'" says Bauerlein (with characteristic hyperbole), "the possibility of a transparent language is not simply doubtful, but unthinkable"; but, while he finds it easy enough to "point out the contradictions and fallacies in Whitman's poetics by invoking one of several convincing arguments against transparency (for example, Derrida's logic of the supplement, de Man's deconstruction of the Romantic symbol, or Austin's category of the performative)," Bauerlein demurs in the end. Such arguments "would not explain Whitman's struggle with the sign," nor would they show, as Bauerlein contends, that "Whitman knew well the contradictions his theory led him into." As Bauerlein reads him, Whitman "welcomed those contradictions as the material of great poetry" (52). Whitman's "failure," then, was a heroic one, not the response of a passive victim, but the inevitable fall of one who aims too high.

Bauerlein's and Warren's treatments of Whitman differ in many ways, but they have in common a tendency to treat language as the fundamental problem of *Leaves of Grass*. In one sense, they go well beyond their predecessor Hollis, who tends to treat language primarily as a tool, a medium, a means to an end. Bauerlein is quite conscious that some readers will see his medium-is-the-message approach as a reduction and will ask, what about the radical democrat, the American shaman, the wound-dresser, the crusading homosexual? "To be sure," Bauerlein admits, "there are other important conflicts in *Leaves of Grass* than expressive, compositional, and interpretive clashes—namely political, sexual, and religious ones—but take away the linguistic dilemmas framing those thematic conflicts and Whitman's poetry becomes notoriously dull" (160). In making this point, Bauerlein goes farther than Warren, who takes a more integrated approach, arguing, for example, that sexual issues are tied to questions of grammatical gender and that spiritual issues crystallize with linguistic topics around the poet's concern with evolution. Warren, that is to say, refuses to reduce extralinguistic matters to mere themes or even to countenance the idea of "extralinguistic" matters. By suggesting that *Leaves of Grass* is primarily an allegory of the poet's struggle with language, however, Bauerlein does reduce the poems. In addition, he bridges the gap between deconstruction and the earlier formalism of the New Critics. While he adopts the narrative mode and the cyclic progression preferred by historical and biographical critics, he tightens the circle of referentiality, cutting off the poem from wider contexts and leaving open only the more limited possibilities of a closed, self-referential text.

Upon Closing: Two Reflections

As I suggested in the conclusion to chapter 4, the recent profusion of criticism makes it difficult to gain a metacritical perspective on Whitman studies. Since questions involving the historicity and language of *Leaves of Grass* appear to remain unanswered, a more satisfying conclusion—in the sense of something that draws things tidily together—is impossible. I would like to close, instead, with two reflections upon the critical tradition that have occurred to me in this survey of what has been from the start and what remains a diverse field of practice. The first takes the form of a historical allegory; the second is a pragmatic and rhetorical extension of my theme of organicism in Whitman studies. Both suggest that, in criticism, there are motives beyond the interpretation and preservation of the texts studied. The critics have agendas as urgent for themselves as the appreciation of literary art.

There are, first of all, social or cultural motives. It was important for the first generation of Whitman studies to create an image of human knowledge as robust, far-reaching, and pressing toward completion. Scientists of the day dreamed of an encyclopedic knowledge in which nature would be reduced to a compendium of factual information. Everything would be explained. As hope in this vision waned at the end of the progressive age, and as the order of the world collapsed into the chaos of world war, the irony and skepticism of twentieth-century modernism took hold. The second generation of Whitman studies, while yet admiring their subject insofar as he could rise above his age, could only feel distance from his "naiveté" and indulgence in Victorian enthusiasms for phrenology, spiritualism, and the like. A similar reception has greeted Whitman in the more recent works of some feminist critics and will likely be repeated by third-world critics, who may align the poet with masculinist, patriarchal, or imperialist

ideologies—the product of his age and a continued threat for many potential readers. The "international Whitman," a topic on which I have
barely touched, remains ripe for critical attention, as the forthcoming
works of scholars like Ed Folsom and Walter Grunzweig are likely to
show. I suspect a deeper analysis of the response to Whitman from
readers around the world will reveal a layered development of critical
views. Whether the emphasis falls upon Whitman the man, the poet,
the prophet, the ideologue, or the language experimenter (or upon
some yet undetermined Whitman) will depend largely upon the historical conditions under which he has been received.

Certainly, it seems clear that history has conditioned the response
of the critics I have surveyed in this monograph, though space limitations prohibit me from exploring historical currents in depth. I have
suggested that the dominant Anglo-American trend in criticism between World War II and the 1970s was devoted to keeping creative literature alive as an alternative to the perceived wasteland wrought by
the culture of science and technology. Since the 1970s, the aim of criticism has been directed more to preserving the act of critical reading itself, which now may seem threatened by the mass media's inspiration
of a new orality that competes with the culture of literacy enshrined in
the academic institution of literary scholarship. Critics provide
"readings" as a seemingly crucial cultural complement to the writing of
the poet. Beginning with the work of Matthiessen and the analytical
critics, Whitman was viewed as a kind of ur-critic, a writer fumbling
after theory. By the time of Bauerlein, we hear that "Song of Myself,"
rather than being an epic representation of personality in nineteenth-
century America, is above all "a poem about writing and composition"
(Bauerlein 55). The theoretical and critical work of the poet can only
seem incomplete in the eye of a reader committed professionally to the
single focus of criticism in the service of literacy. The task of completing the poet's initial efforts at self-interpretation and literary theory lies
tantalizingly before the reader empowered by the sophisticated new inventions of literary theory—an aspiring equal and a technical competitor with technocratic institutions. Though recent criticism tends to
recoil from the conservative or escapist trend of studies that arose in
the 1950s and 1960s under the sign of the New Criticism, both the revival of ideological historicism and the introduction of linguistic and
poststructuralist criticism continue therefore to suggest the otherworldliness of Whitman's poems. The other world of the contemporary critic
is ever more frequently the world of reading and writing. If Whitman,
after becoming frustrated in the worlds of business and politics, saved
himself by taking up the profession of writing, perhaps we critics can
hope for the same.

The notion that criticism can at once begin with the poet and complete the work of poetry leads me to the second, related reflection. In an
insightful comment, Kerry Larson notes that the "chief nemesis" of

Whitman's organicism is "an extreme form of prolepsis that closes off the prospect for development before it can be elaborated" (93). Both Larson and Bauerlein interpret the poet's work as an anxious struggle to resist any force that would restrict the growth of his own poems while yet, especially in his later poetry and prose, he labors to authorize certain views of *Leaves of Grass* that would severely restrict the growth of an unauthorized critical tradition. But, with respect to the development of that tradition, the same argument applies. If, as Larson says, "both literary and political institutions share the common plight of devising a vocabulary of justification which is not revealed to be inadequate or self-incriminating the moment it is asserted" (107), the same can be said of critical discourse. The reader with which, in Bauerlein's view, Whitman struggles is precisely the critical reader, who hopes the tradition will remain open to receive his or her contribution.

We critics must thus find a point of entry and an appropriate language to hold commerce with the poet and with our own readers. Just as the concept of a poet misunderstood or underappreciated in his own time provided such an opening for the first generation of amateur critics (and still, to some extent, supports the work of gay and feminist studies), the concept of a poet beautiful yet flawed (by naiveté, a lack of self-knowledge, historical belatedness, or theoretical inadequacy) provides the opening for the special competence of professional critics. For such critics, it becomes difficult to accept a successfully organic poet, if, as Bauerlein says (with some anxiety, it seems), "The conception of Whitman's poetry as unmediated emotion . . . leaves the critic with little else to say" (18).

As critics of America's great organic poet, we view our own task as organic so that we can discover something to say, to add our voices to the century-old conversation on Whitman's poems, to put ourselves forward—whether humbly or arrogantly—as worthy interlocutors with the poet and our predecessors in Whitman studies. The danger, of course, is that, in contemplating the openness of *Leaves of Grass*, we will fall into what Eric Havelock calls the "method of reduction" that, in his view, has dominated studies of Plato—a method which "consists in pruning his tall trees till they are fit to be transplanted into a trim garden of our own making" (Havelock 7). Like the other problems identified in this study, therefore—such questions as how the person Walt Whitman relates to Walt Whitman the hero of *Leaves of Grass*, how the world of poetry relates to the seemingly separate worlds of nature and human action, how the synchronic forces of stability and the diachronic forces of change interact within the composition and reading of poetry—we must add to the agenda of future critical studies the problem of how to preserve the authority of the poet (or the poetic text) even as we assert our own authority as critics.

Works Cited

Abrams, Meyer H. *The Mirror and the Lamp*. New York: Oxford UP, 1953.

Allen, Gay Wilson. *The New Walt Whitman Handbook*. New York: New York UP, 1975.

_____. *The Solitary Singer*. New York: Macmillan, 1955.

_____. *Walt Whitman As Man, Poet, and Legend*. Carbondale: Southern Illinois UP, 1961.

_____. *Walt Whitman Handbook*. Chicago: Packard, 1946.

Anderson, Quentin. *The Imperial Self*. New York: Knopf, 1971.

Arvin, Newton. *Whitman*. New York: Macmillan, 1938.

Aspiz, Harold. *Walt Whitman and the Body Beautiful*. Urbana: U of Illinois P, 1980.

Asselineau, Roger. *The Evolution of Walt Whitman: The Creation of a Personality*. 2 vols. Cambridge, MA: Harvard UP, 1960.

_____. "Walt Whitman." *Eight American Authors: A Review of Research and Criticism*. Revised Edition. Ed. James Woodress. New York: Norton, 1971. 225-72.

Bazalgette, Léon. *Walt Whitman L'Homme et son Oeuvre*. Paris: Mercure de France, 1908.

Barrus, Clara. *Whitman and Burroughs, Comrades*. Boston: Houghton Mifflin, 1931.

Bauerlein, Mark. *Whitman and the American Idiom*. Baton Rouge: Louisiana State UP, 1991.

Beaver, Harold. "Homosexual Signs." *Critical Inquiry* 8 (1981): 99-119.

Beaver, Joseph. *Walt Whitman: Poet of Science*. New York: King's Crown, 1951.

Bercovitch, Sacvan. *The American Jeremiad*. Madison: U of Wisconsin P, 1978.

Berman, Morris. *Coming to Our Senses: Body and Spirit in the Hidden History of the West*. New York: Bantam, 1989.

Bertz, Eduard. *Der Yankee-Heiland: Ein Beitrag zur Modernen Religionsgeschichte*. Dresden: Reissner, 1906.

Binns, Henry Bryan. *A Life of Walt Whitman*. 1905; rpt. New York: Haskell House, 1969.

Black, Stephen A. *Whitman's Journey into Chaos: A Psychoanalytical Study of the Poetic Process*. Princeton: Princeton UP, 1975.

Blasing, Mutlu Konuk. *American Poetry: The Rhetoric of Its Forms.* New Haven: Yale UP, 1987.

Blodgett, Harold W. *Walt Whitman in England.* London: Oxford UP, 1934.

Bloom, Harold. *The American Religion: The Emergence of the Post-Christian Nation.* New York: Simon & Schuster, 1992.

_____. *The Anxiety of Influence: A Theory of Poetry.* Oxford UP, 1973.

Borges, Jorge Luis. "Note on Walt Whitman." Rpt. in Perlman, Folsom, and Campion 143-48.

Botkin, Daniel B. *Discordant Harmonies: A New Ecology for the Twenty-First Century.* New York: Oxford UP, 1990.

Bové, Paul. *Destructive Poetics: Heidegger and Modern American Poetry.* New York:, 1980.

Bucke, Richard Maurice. *Cosmic Consciousness.* 1901; rpt. New York: Dutton, 1969.

_____. *Walt Whitman.* 1883; rpt. New York: Johnson Reprint, 1970.

Burke, Kenneth. *A Rhetoric of Motives.* Berkeley: U of California P, 1969.

Burroughs, John. *Notes on Walt Whitman as Poet and Person.* 1867; rpt. New York: Haskell House, 1971.

_____. *Whitman: A Study.* Boston: Houghton, Mifflin, 1896.

Bychowski, Gustav. "Walt Whitman: A Study in Sublimation." *Homosexuality and Creative Genius.* Ed. Hendrick Ruitenbeck. New York: Astor-Honor, 1967. 140-80.

Byers, Thomas B. *What I Cannot Say: Self, Word, and World in Whitman, Stevens, and Merwin.* Urbana: University of Illinois Press, 1989.

Cady, Joseph. "Drum-Taps and Nineteenth-Century Male Homosexual Literature." *Walt Whitman: Here and Now.* Ed. Joann P. Krieg. Westport, CT: Greenwood, 1985: 49-59.

Campbell, Jeremy. *The Improbable Machine: What New Discoveries in Artificial Intelligence Reveal about the Mind.* New York: Simon and Schuster, 1989.

Canby, Henry Seidel. *Walt Whitman: An American.* Boston: Houghton Mifflin, 1943.

Carpenter, Edward. *Some Friends of Walt Whitman: A Study in Sex Psychology.* London: Francis, 1924.

_____. *An Unknown People.* London: Bonner, 1897.

Catel, Jean. *Walt Whitman: La naissance du poète.* 1929; rpt. St. Clair Shores, MI: Scholarly Press, 1972.

Chari, V. K. *Whitman in the Light of Vedantic Mysticism.* Lincoln: U of Nebraska P, 1964.

Chase, Richard. *Walt Whitman Reconsidered.* New York: Sloane, 1955.

Corbett, Edward P. J. *Classical Rhetoric for the Modern Student.* 2nd ed. New York: Oxford UP, 1971.

Cowley, Malcolm. "Introduction." *Walt Whitman's Leaves of Grass: The First (1855) Edition.* New York: Viking, 1959.

_____. "Walt Whitman: The Miracle." *New Republic* 114 (1946): 355-88.

_____. "Walt Whitman: The Secret." *New Republic* 114 (1946): 481-84.

Crawley, Thomas Edward. *The Structure of Leaves of Grass.* Austin: U of Texas P, 1970.

Derrida, Jacques. *Of Grammatology.* Trans. Gayatri C. Spivak. Baltimore: Johns Hopkins UP, 1976.

De Selincourt, Basil. *Walt Whitman: A Critical Study.* London: Secker, 1914.

Dewey, John. *The Quest for Certainty.* New York: G. P. Putnam's Sons, 1929.

Donaldson, Thomas. *Walt Whitman, the Man.* New York: Harper, 1896.

Elliott, Robert C. *The Literary Persona.* Chicago: U of Chicago P, 1982.

Ellis, Havelock, and John Addington Symonds. *Sexual Inversion.* 1897; rpt. New York: Arno, 1975.

Erkkila, Betsy. *Walt Whitman among the French.* Princeton: Princeton UP, 1980.

_____. *Whitman The Political Poet.* New York: Oxford UP, 1989.

Faner, Robert D. *Walt Whitman and Opera.* Carbondale: Southern Illinois UP, 1951.

Feidelson, Charles. *Symbolism and American Literature.* Chicago: U of Chicago P, 1953.

Folsom, Ed. "Approaches and Removals: W. S. Merwin's Encounter with Whitman's America." *Shenandoah* 29.3 (1978): 57-73.

Foucault, Michel. *The History of Sexuality: Volume 1, an Introduction.* Trans. Robert Hurley. New York: Pantheon, 1978.

_____. *The Order of Things: An Archaeology of the Human Sciences.* New York: Random House, 1970.

Freedman, Florence Bernstein. *William Douglas O'Connor: Walt Whitman's Chosen Knight.* Athens: Ohio UP, 1985.

Gelpi, Albert. *The Tenth Muse.* Cambridge: Harvard UP, 1975.

Giantvalley, Scott. *Walt Whitman, 1838-1939. A Reference Guide.* Boston: G. K. Hall, 1981.

Gilbert, Sandra M., and Susan Gubar. *The Madwoman in the Attic: The Woman Writer and the Nineteenth-Century Literary Imagination.* New Haven: Yale UP, 1979.

Goffman, Erving. *The Presentation of the Self in Everyday Life.* Garden City, NJ: Doubleday, 1959.

Greenspan, Ezra. *Walt Whitman and the American Reader.* Cambridge: Cambridge UP, 1990.

Griffith, Clark. "Sex and Death: The Significance of Whitman's Calamus Themes." *Philological Quarterly* 39 (1960): 18-38.

Grossmen, Allen. "The Poetics of Union in Lincoln and Whitman: An Inquiry toward the Relationship of Art and Policy." *The American Renaissance Reconsidered.* Ed. Donald S. Pease and Walter Benn Michaels. Baltimore: Johns Hopkins UP, 1985: 183-208.

Havelock, Eric A. *Preface to Plato.* Cambridge: Harvard UP, 1963.

Helms, Alan. "'Hints . . . Faint Clews and Indirections': Whitman's Homosexual Disguises." *Walt Whitman: Here and Now.* Ed. Joann P. Krieg. Westport, CT: Greenwood, 1985: 61-67.

_____. "Whitman Revised." *Études Anglaises* 37 (1984): 257-71.

Hier, H. P., Jr. "The End of a Literary Mystery." *American Mercury* 1 (1924): 471-78.

Hindus, Milton, ed. *Walt Whitman: The Critical Heritage.* New York: Barnes and Noble, 1971.

Hollis, C. Carroll. *Language and Style in Leaves of Grass.* Baton Rouge: Louisiana State UP, 1983.

Holloway, Emory. *Free and Lonesome Heart: The Secret of Walt Whitman.* New York: Vantage, 1960.

_____. *Whitman: An Interpretation in Narrative.* New York: Knopf, 1926.

Hungerford, Edward. "Walt Whitman and His Chart of Bumps." *American Literature* 2 (1931): 350-84.

Hyde, Lewis. *The Gift: Imagination and the Erotic Life of Property.* New York: Vintage, 1979.

Jay, Gregory. *America the Scrivener: Deconstruction and the Subject of Literary History.* Ithaca: Cornell UP, 1990.

_____. "Catching Up with Whitman: A Review Essay." *South Atlantic Review* 57.1 (1992): 89-102.

Kaplan, Justin. *Walt Whitman: A Life.* New York: Simon & Schuster, 1980.

Kennedy, William Sloane. *The Fight of a Book for the World: A Companion Volume to Leaves of Grass.* West Yarmouth, MA: Stonecroft, 1926.

Killingsworth, M. Jimmie. "Whitman and Motherhood: A Historical View." *American Literature* 54 (1983): 28-43.

_____. *Whitman's Poetry of the Body: Sexuality, Politics, and the Text.* Chapel Hill: U of North Carolina P, 1989.

Kuebrich, David. *Minor Prophesy: Walt Whitman's New American Religion.* Bloomington: Indiana UP, 1989.

Kummings, Donald D. *Walt Whitman, 1940-1975. A Reference Guide.* Boston: G. K. Hall, 1982.

Laclau, Ernesto, and Chantal Mouffe. *Hegemony and Socialist Strategy: Toward a Radical Democratic Politics*. London: Verso, 1985.

Larrain, Jorge. *The Concept of Ideology*. Athens: U of Georgia P, 1979.

Larson, Kerry C. *Whitman's Drama of Consensus*. Chicago: U of Chicago P, 1988.

Lawrence, D. H. *Studies in Classic American Literature*. New York: Doubleday, 1953.

Leitch, Vincent B. *American Literary Criticism from the Thirties to the Eighties*. New York: Columbia UP, 1988.

Lewis, R. W. B. *The American Adam: Innocence, Tragedy, and Tradition in the Nineteenth Century*. Chicago: U of Chicago P, 1955.

_____, ed. *The Presence of Walt Whitman: Selected Papers from the English Institute*. New York: Columbia UP, 1962.

Loving, Jerome. *Emerson, Whitman, and the American Muse*. Chapel Hill: U of North Carolina P, 1982.

_____. *Walt Whitman's Champion: William Douglas O'Connor*. College Station, TX: Texas A&M UP, 1978.

Lynch, Michael. "'Here Is Adhesiveness': From Friendship to Homosexuality." *Victorian Studies* 29 (1985): 67-96.

Lyotard, Jean-François. *The Postmodern Condition: A Report on Knowledge*. Trans. Geoff Bennington and Brian Massumi. Foreword by Fredric Jameson. Minneapolis: U of Minnesota P, 1984.

Marki, Ivan. *The Trial of the Poet: An Interpretation of the First Edition of Leaves of Grass*. New York: Columbia UP, 1976.

Martin, Robert K. *The Homosexual Tradition in American Poetry*. Austin: U of Texas P, 1979.

_____. "Whitman's 'Song of Myself': Homosexual Dream and Vision." *Partison Review* 42 (1975): 80-96.

_____, ed. *The Continuing Presence of Walt Whitman: The Life after the Life*. Iowa City: University of Iowa Press, 1992.

Matthiessen, F. O. *American Renaissance: Art and Expression in the Age of Emerson and Whitman*. London: Oxford UP, 1941.

McGann, Jerome. *The Romantic Ideology: A Critical Investigation*. Chicago: U of Chicago P, 1983.

Mendelson, Maurice. *Life and Work of Walt Whitman: A Soviet View*. Trans. Andrew Bromfield. Moscow: Progress Publishers, 1976.

Merchant, Carolyn. *The Death of Nature: Women, Ecology, and the Scientific Revolution*. San Francisco: Harper and Row, 1980.

_____. *Ecological Revolutions: Nature, Gender, and Science in New England*. Chapel Hill: U of North Carolina P, 1989.

Miller, Edwin Haviland. *Walt Whitman's Poetry: A Psychological Journey*. New York: New York UP, 1968.

_____. *Walt Whitman's "Song of Myself": A Mosaic of Interpretations*. Iowa City: U of Iowa P, 1989.

Miller, F. DeWolfe. "Before *The Good Gray Poet*." *Tennessee Studies in Literature* 3 (1958): 89-98.

Miller, James E., Jr. *The American Quest for a Supreme Fiction: Whitman's Legacy in the Presonal Epic*. Chicago: U of Chicago P, 1979.

_____. *A Critical Guide to Leaves of Grass*. Chicago: U of Chicago P, 1957.

_____. *Walt Whitman*. New York: Twayne, 1962.

_____. "Whitman's Omnisexual Vision." *The Chief Glory of Every People: Essays on Classic American Writers*. Ed. Matthew J. Bruccoli. Carbondale: Southern Illinois UP, 1973. 253-59.

Miller, J. Hillis. "The Critic as Host." *Deconstruction and Criticism*. New York: Seabury, 1979: 217-53.

Millett, Kate. *Sexual Politics*. New York: Avon, 1969.

Moon, Michael. *Disseminating Whitman: Revision and Corporeality in Leaves of Grass*. Cambridge: Harvard UP, 1991.

Myerson, Joel. *Walt Whitman: A Descriptive Bibliography*. Pittsburgh: U of Pittsburgh P, forthcoming.

Nash, Roderick. *Wilderness and the American Mind*. 3rd ed. New Haven: Yale UP, 1982.

Nicolson, Marjorie H. *Mountain Gloom and Mountain Glory: The Development of the Aesthetics of the Infinite*. Ithaca: Cornell UP, 1959.

O'Connor, William Douglas. *The Good Gray Poet*. New York: Bunce & Huntington, 1866. Rpt. in Loving 157-203.

Parrington, Vernon Louis. *Main Currents in American Thought: An Interpretation of American Literature from the Beginnings to 1920*. 3 vols. New York: Harcourt, 1927.

Pease, Donald E. *Visionary Compacts: American Renaissance Writings in Cultural Context*. Madison: U of Wisconsin P, 1987.

Perlman, Jim, Ed Folsom, Don Campion. *Walt Whitman: The Measure of His Song*. Minneapolis: Holy Cow! Press, 1981.

Perry, Bliss. *Walt Whitman*. Boston: Houghton Mifflin, 1906.

Piasecki, Bruce, and Peter Asmus. *In Search of Environmental Excellence: Moving Beyond Blame*. New York: Touchstone, 1990.

Popper, Karl R. *The Open Society and Its Enemies*. 2 vols. Princeton: Princeton UP, 1966.

Potter, David M. *The Impending Crisis 1848-1861*. Ed. Don E. Fehrenbacher. New York: Harper and Row, 1976.

Price, Kenneth M. *Whitman and Tradition: The Poet in His Century*. New Haven: Yale UP, 1990.

Reynolds, David S. *Beneath the American Renaissance: The Subversive Imagination in the Age of Emerson and Melville*. New York: Knopf, 1988.

_____. "Review Essay: Walt Whitman Today." *ESQ* 36 (1990): 255-65.

Reynolds, Larry J. *European Revolutions and the American Literary Renaissance.* New Haven: Yale UP, 1988.

Ricoeur, Paul. *Time and Narrative.* 3 vols. Chicago: U of Chicago P, 1984-88.

Riley, William Parker. "Where Do English Departments Come From?" *College English* 28 (1967): 339-51.

Rivers, W. C. *Walt Whitman's Anomaly.* London: G. Allen, 1913.

Rorty, Richard. *Consequences of Pragmatism.* Minneapolis: U of Minnesota P, 1982.

Rubin, Joseph Jay. *The Historic Whitman.* University Park: Penn State UP, 1973.

Schyberg, Frederick. *Walt Whitman.* Trans. Evie Allison Allen. Intro. by Gay Wilson Allen. New York: Columbia UP, 1951.

Sedgwick, Eve Kosofsky. *Between Men: English Literature and Male Homosocial Desire.* New York: Columbia UP, 1985.

Shephard, Esther. *Walt Whitman's Pose.* New York: Harcourt, Brace, 1938.

Shively, Charley. *Calamus Lovers: Whitman's Working Class Camerados.* San Francisco: Gay Sunshine Press, 1987.

Stern, Madeleine B. *Heads and Headlines: The Phrenological Fowlers.* Norman: Oklahoma UP, 1971.

Stovall, Floyd. *The Foreground of Leaves of Grass.* Charlottesville: U of Virginia P, 1974.

Symonds, John Addington. *Walt Whitman: A Study.* 1893; rpt. New York: Blom, 1967.

Thomas, Brook. *The New Historicism and Other Old-Fashioned Topics.* Princeton: Princeton UP, 1991.

Thomas, M. Wynn. *The Lunar Light of Whitman's Poetry.* Cambridge, MA: Harvard UP, 1987.

Tichi, Cecelia. *New World, New Earth: Environmental Reform in American Literature from the Puritans through Whitman.* New Haven: Yale UP, 1979.

Trachtenberg, Alan. *The Incorporation of America: Culture and Society in the Gilded Age.* New York: Hill and Wang, 1982.

Triggs, Oscar. "The Growth of 'Leaves of Grass.'" *The Complete Writings of Walt Whitman.* New York: Putnam's, 1902.

Warren, James Perrin. *Walt Whitman's Language Experiment.* University Park: Pennsylvania State UP, 1990.

Waskow, Howard J. *Whitman: Explorations in Form.* Chicago: U of Chicago P, 1966.

Whitman, Walt. *An American Primer.* Ed. Horace Traubel. 1904. Stevens Point, WI: Holy Cow!, 1987.

_____. *The Correspondence of Walt Whitman.* 6 Vols. Ed. Edwin Haviland Miller. New York: New York UP, 1961-77.

_____. *Drum-Taps and Sequel, 1865-66.* Ed. F. DeWolfe Miller. Gainesville, FL: Scholars' Facsimiles and Reprints, 1959.

_____. *The Illustrated Leaves of Grass.* Intro. William Carlos Williams. Ed. Howard Chapwick. New York: Grosset & Dunlap, 1971.

_____. *Leaves of Grass* (1855). *Complete Poetry and Collected Prose.* Washington, DC: Library of America, 1982. 1-145.

_____. *Leaves of Grass: A Norton Critical Edition.* Eds. Sculley Bradley and Harold W. Blodgett. New York: Norton, 1973.

_____. *Leaves of Grass: A Textual Variorum of the Printed Poems.* Ed. Sculley Bradley, Harold W. Blodgett, Arthur Golden, and William White. 3 Vols. New York: New York UP, 1980.

_____. *Prose Writings of Walt Whitman.* Ed. Floyd Stovall. 2 vols. New York: New York UP, 1964.

_____. *Uncollected Poetry and Prose of Walt Whitman.* 2 vols. Ed. Emory Holloway. Garden City, NJ: Doubleday, 1921.

Wilson, Christopher P. *The Labor of Words: Literary Professionalism in the Progressive Era.* Athens: U of Georgia P, 1985.

Zweig, Paul. *Walt Whitman: The Making of a Poet.* New York: Basic, 1984.

Index

Abrams, M. H., 71, 82
Allen, Evie, 52
Allen, Gay Wilson, ix, x, xi, 18-19, 20, 22, 23, 24-34, 36, 39, 40, 46, 49-50, 52, 58-59, 63, 74, 91-92, 100
Analytical criticism, 49-74
Architectonic model of poetic composition, 16-17, 62-68, 100-1, 132-35
Arvin, Newton, 103-4, 110, 111, 114
Asmus, Peter, 17
Aspiz, Harold, 36, 87, 107-10
Asselineau, Roger, ix, x, xi, 18, 32-37, 39, 40, 46, 58-59, 66, 74, 79, 100, 129
Austin, John L., 130, 138

Bauerlein, Mark, 57, 127, 131, 136-41
Bazalgette, Léon, 20
Beaver, Joseph, 74-75
Beecher, Henry Ward, 103
Bercovitch, Sacvan, 85
Berman, Morris, 75
Bertz, Eduard, 38, 52
Binns, Henry Bryan, 19, 20-21, 25
Black, Stephen A., 39, 43-44, 46, 60
Blasing, Mutlu Konuk, 2
Blodgett, Harold W., 58, 80
Bloom, Harold, 9, 56
Borges, Jorge Luis, 46, 132
Bowers, Fredson, 65-66
Brooks, Cleanth, 26
Bryant, William Cullen, 80
Bucke, Richard Maurice, 6, 9, 10, 14-18, 19, 33, 45, 54, 84, 87-89, 91, 92, 93, 95-96, 100-1, 105, 133
Burke, Kenneth, 113
Burroughs, John, x, xi, 6, 9, 11-18, 19, 22, 25, 41, 45, 51, 63, 78, 90, 91, 100
Bychowski, Gustav, 39
Byron, George Gordon, Lord, 3

Cady, Joseph, 106-7

"Calamus," 2, 21, 23, 30, 31, 35, 38, 42, 44, 45, 47, 54, 65-66, 78-79, 105, 106, 111, 120
Campbell, Jeremy, 74
Canby, Henry Seidel, 87, 90-91, 99
Canonization, 55, 57-58
Carlyle, Thomas, 33, 54, 80
Carpenter, Edward, 15, 19, 35, 38-39
Catel, Jean, 39, 40, 43, 58, 125, 129
Cavitch, David, 44
Chari, V. K., 96
Chase, Richard, xi, 59-63, 70, 79, 86, 95, 96, 104, 108, 127, 138
"Children of Adam," 11, 120
Chopin, Kate, 81, 112
Civil War, x, 31, 37, 44, 59, 60, 83, 95, 97, 105, 111, 112-13, 116-17, 120, 128, 129, 137-38
Clapp, Henry, 25
Coleridge, Samuel Taylor, 40
Corbett, Edward P. J., 102
Cowley, Malcolm, 14, 37-38, 41, 73, 100, 129
Crane, Hart, 104
Crawley, Thomas Edward, 69-71, 79, 100
Critical biography, 18-37
"Crossing Brooklyn Ferry," 30, 110, 114-15, 134

Dana, Charles A., 51
Davis, Andrew Jackson, 108
De Man, Paul, 138
Derrida, Jacques, 34, 138
De Selincourt, Basil, 20, 52
Dewey, John, 28, 84
Dickinson, Emily, 44, 103
Dixon, Edward H., 108
Donaldson, Thomas, 18
Drum-Taps, 6, 13, 31, 50, 54, 60

Eliot, T. S., 28
Elliott, Robert C., 47-48
Ellis, Havelock, 38, 39

Emerson, Ralph Waldo, 13-14, 28-29, 33, 34, 51-52, 54, 55, 58, 71, 73, 75-79, 82, 84, 95, 96
Erkkila, Betsy, 80, 87, 118-19, 120, 122

Faner, Robert D., 74
Feidelson, Charles, 127
Fern, Fanny, 58
Field, Edward, 105
Folsom, Ed, 140
Forester, E. M., 81
Foucault, Michel, 34, 117
Furness, Clifford, 129

Garland, Hamlin, 81
Giantvalley, Scott, ix
Gilbert, Sandra, 103
Gilchrist, Anne, 15, 18, 46-47, 76
Golden, Arthur, 66
Greenspan, Ezra, 50, 79, 81-84, 86
Griffith, Clark, 30-31
Grossman, Allen, 113
Grunzweig, Walter, 140
Gubar, Susan 103
Gunn, Thom, 104-5

Habermas, Jürgen, 34
Harlan Incident, 11, 12
Harned, Thomas, 19, 91
Harvard Poets, 81
Havelock, Eric, 141
Hawthorne, Nathaniel, 55, 58
Helms, Alan, 106-7
Hicks, Elias, 54
Historicism ("New" and otherwise), 85-124
Hollis, C. Carroll, 7, 57, 82, 126-31, 138
Holloway, Emory, 20, 22, 23-24, 25, 27, 31, 58, 67
Hungerford, Edward, 33
Hutchinson, George, 86, 87, 90, 96-99, 101, 112, 114, 118, 122-23
Hyde, Lewis, 86, 87, 90, 92-96, 99, 101, 112, 114, 122-23

Ideology, 2-3, 85-124
"I Saw in Louisiana a Live Oak Growing," 83
"I Sing the Body Electric," 86

Jackson, Andrew, 102
James, Henry, 50
James, William, 64, 84
Jay, Gregory, 87, 122-23

Jefferson, Thomas, 102

Kaplan, Justin, 36
Keats, John, 3
Kennedy, William Sloane, 18, 52
Kuebrich, David, 66, 87, 99-101, 112
Kummings, Donald D., ix

Lacan, Jacques, 21
Larrain, Jorge, 112
Larson, Kerry, 57, 87, 110, 113-18, 120, 126, 137, 140-41
Lawrence, D. H., 91, 92
Leaves of Grass: different editions of, ix, 4-9, 16, 17, 29-32, 34, 54-55, 67, 69-70, 71, 73, 79, 82, 85-86, 87-88, 107-8, 116-17, 119, 120-21, 130, 135, 136-38; preface to 1855 edition, 10, 28-29, 30, 73, 85-86, 93
Leitch, Vincent, 26, 28
Lewis, R.W.B., 62
Literary-historical criticism, 49-50, 52, 54, 74-84
Loving, Jerome, 50, 77-79, 86
Lynch, Michael, 106-7

Marki, Ivan, 73-74, 79, 83
Marx, Karl, and Marxism, 3, 84, 110, 103
Martin, Robert K., 31, 80, 87, 104-7, 109-10, 122, 123
Matthiessen, F. O., 6, 55-58, 77, 125-26, 129, 132, 140
McGann, Jerome, 2-4, 82
Melville, Herman, 55, 58
Mendelson, Maurice, 113
Merrill, James, 104-5
Miller, Edwin Haviland, 39-43, 68-69, 79, 106, 122
Miller, James E., Jr., x, xi, 37, 44, 87, 121-23, 126, 137
Millett, Kate, 104
Muir, John, 17
Myerson, Joel, ix

New Criticism, 6, 26-28, 31, 36, 41, 48, 49, 50, 59, 60, 62, 63, 65, 69, 70, 72-73, 104, 139, 140
Norton, Charles Eliot, 51
Noyes, John Humphrey, 103

O'Connor, Ellen, 15
O'Connor, William Douglas, 6, 8, 11, 12, 15, 19, 44, 45, 52, 87, 89-90, 91, 92

Ohmann, Richard, 131
"Once I Pass'd through a Populous
    City," 20, 23
"One Hour to Madness and Joy," 115
Organic theory of art, ix, x, 1-8, 21-22,
    27-28, 46-47, 62, 67-70, 113-17, 125,
    139-41; cyclic organicism, 1, 2-8, 29-
    32, 36, 54-55, 59-62, 77-79, 83, 98-99,
    111, 124; genetic organicism, 1, 2-8,
    15-16, 57, 72-73, 124; progressive
    organicism, 1, 2-8, 24, 67-68, 98-99,
    132-33
"Out of the Cradle Endlessly Rocking,"
    63, 71-72, 76, 136-37
Owen, Robert Dale, 103

Paine, Thomas, 103, 110
Parrington, Vernon, 55, 102-3, 110
"Passage to India," 63-64, 65, 79, 98-99
Pease, Donald, 113
Perry, Bliss, 21-23, 25, 34, 91
Piasecki, Bruce, 17
Plato, 141
Poe, Edgar Allan, 80
"Poem of the Many in One," 30
Pound, Ezra, 48
Price, Kenneth, 50, 79-81, 83-84, 86, 93
Psychoanalytical criticism, 20, 22, 25,
    36, 37-45, 60, 121-22

Quakerism 21, 54, 103

"Respondez," 111
Reynolds, David S., 36, 60, 109, 122-23
Reynolds, Larry J., 112-13
Ricoeur, Paul, 84
Rivers, W. C., 38
Romanticism, 2-8, 14, 21-22
Rossetti, William Michael, 12
Rousseau, Jean-Jacques, 21
Rubin, Joseph Jay

"Salut au Monde," 30
Santayana, George, 81, 104
Schyberg, Frederik, 37, 53-55, 58, 74
Searle, John, 130
Sexual politics, 101-110, 118-23
Shakespeare, William, 80
Shelley, Percy Bysshe, 28
Shephard, Esther, 19, 52-53, 60, 63, 96
Shively, Charley, 31, 36, 105, 107
"Sleepers, The," 2, 63, 64, 72, 98, 100,
    105, 134
Smuts, Jan Christian, 18

"So Long," 48
"Song of the Broad-Axe," 17
"Song of the Exposition," 17
"Song of Joys," 111
"Song of Myself," 2, 26, 40, 41, 42, 43, 59,
    60, 63, 64, 69, 73, 76, 88-89, 93-94, 98,
    100, 105, 112, 115, 119, 120, 130, 137,
    140
"Song of the Redwood Tree," 17
Specimen Days, 80
Spencer, Herbert, 102
"Spontaneous Me," 137
Stovall, Floyd, 13, 50, 75-77, 80, 95
Sumner, Charles, 121
Symonds, John Addington, 20, 23, 24, 38,
    39, 52, 105

Taylor, Bayard, 104-5
Thomas, Brook, 87
Thomas, M. Wynn, 60, 87, 110-13, 114,
    123
Thoreau, Henry David, 14, 51052, 55,
    58, 96
Tichi, Cecilia, 17
Trachtenberg, Alan, 10, 110
Traubel, Horace, 14-15, 18, 19, 77, 81, 87,
    91, 125
Triggs, Oscar, x, xi
Trowbridge, John Townsend, 19, 33
Twain, Mark, 60

Warren, James Perrin, 57, 60, 126-27,
    131-36, 138
Waskow, Howard J., 49, 70-73, 79, 83,
    134
"When Lilacs Last in the Dooryard
    Bloom'd," 59, 60, 64-65, 72, 76, 135
Whitman, Walt: as poetic craftsman,
    46-85, 136; as critic, ix-x, 10-11, 46-
    48, 85-86, 101, 125; as prophet, 85-
    124; biography of, 6, 8-45, 54-55, 77-
    79, 82-83, 87-91; defenses of, 50-58;
    fiction of, 43; homosexuality of, 20-
    21, 23-24, 30-31, 34-36, 38-39, 43-44,
    65-66, 96-97, 104-7; journalism of, 14,
    23, 32, 82-83; political views of, 85-
    124
Williams, Raymond, 110
Williams, William Carlos, 20-21
"Woman Waits for Me, A," 17, 119
Wordsworth, William, 22
"Wound-Dresser, The," 98
Wright, Frances, 103, 110

"Year of Meteors," 83

Zweig, Paul, 37

DATE DUE

PRINTED IN U.S.A.